Becoming a Self-Differentiated Leader

Becoming a Self-Differentiated Leader offers a transformative framework to understand why ruptures in communication happen and equips readers with the tools to overcome them.

Authentic leadership potential hinges on bridging the gap between the sway of external pressures and your own internal compass. Drawing from decades of experience in psychology, executive leadership, and coaching, the authors provide a psychological and theoretical understanding of secure and insecure attachments, relational systems, and how they feed into our everyday motivations, behaviors, and decisions. This book uncovers the hidden dynamics of Loyalty Contracts – the spoken and unspoken agreements we make with ourselves and others that can quietly erode leadership, fuel burnout, and diminish impact. Each chapter equips readers with practical tools as well as case studies to seamlessly elevate your leadership effectiveness, breaking free from self-sabotaging tendencies that can lead to relational and organizational dysfunction, stagnation, and breakdown.

Whether you are a business leader, executive coach, manager, mentor, HR professional, organizational psychologist, or pursuing your own journey of self-differentiation, this book delivers the tools, insights, and practices required to lead and thrive in the age of artificial intelligence.

Patricia Gianotti, Psy.D., is a licensed psychologist, coach, and educator. She has over 30 years of experience working with individuals, couples, and groups, specializing in attachment, executive coaching, conflict management, and sexual/workplace harassment. She is also the Academic Director of The Institute for Advanced Psychotherapy at Loyola University Chicago and managing partner of Woodland Psychological Services.

Stephen Gianotti, M.S., B.Ed., is founder of The Woodland Group, a local, regional, and global organizational development firm. He has been a practitioner of individual, group, and organizational effectiveness for over 30 years on 5 continents with a specific focus on thinking and acting from a systems perspective.

Hoh Kim, Ph.D., founder of THE LAB h, is an executive sounding board for global leaders. Combining his experience as former MD of Edelman Korea with INFLUENCE AT WORK and Team Management Systems, he helps the C-suite ask future-defining questions. A woodcraft artist and author of 9 books, he views communication as a craft.

Becoming a Self-Differentiated Leader

Harnessing the Power of Loyalty and Motivation in the Workplace and in Life

Patricia Gianotti, Stephen Gianotti, and Hoh Kim

Routledge
Taylor & Francis Group
NEW YORK AND LONDON

Designed cover image: Getty Images

First published 2027
by Routledge
605 Third Avenue, New York, NY 10158

and by Routledge
4 Park Square, Milton Park, Abingdon, Oxon, OX14 4RN

Routledge is an imprint of the Taylor & Francis Group, an informa business

Library of Congress Cataloging-in-Publication Data
Names: Gianotti, Patricia, 1949– author | Gianotti, Stephen C. author | Kim, Hoh author
Title: Becoming a self-differentiated leader : harnessing the power of loyalty and motivation in the workplace and in life / Patricia Gianotti, Stephen Gianotti and Hoh Kim.
Description: New York, NY : Routledge, 2027. |
Includes bibliographical references and index. |
Identifiers: LCCN 2026020225 (print) | LCCN 2026020226 (ebook) |
ISBN 9781041029090 paperback | ISBN 9781041029137 hardback |
ISBN 9781003621393 ebook
Subjects: LCSH: Leadership–Psychological aspects | Interpersonal relations
Classification: LCC BF637.L4 G495 2027 (print) | LCC BF637.L4 (ebook)
LC record available at https://lccn.loc.gov/2026020225
LC ebook record available at https://lccn.loc.gov/2026020226

ISBN: 9781041029137 (hbk)
ISBN: 9781041029090 (pbk)
ISBN: 9781003621393 (ebk)

DOI: 10.4324/9781003621393

Typeset in Sabon
by Newgen Publishing UK

Contents

Acknowledgments

The journey of crafting *Becoming a Self-Differentiated Leader: Harnessing the Power of Loyalty and Motivation in the Workplace and in Life* has been, for each of us, not just an intellectual endeavor, but a profoundly personal voyage. Spanning 13 time zones, 2 vastly different cultures, 3 unique heritages, 3 totally different family backgrounds, we authors found a garden of inspiration. For over 18 months we have tended to this garden with genuine curiosity, healthy debate, a global search for feedback, unleashed creativity, and an ever-present joy to be able to experience this venture together.

First and foremost, no book comes into existence without an editor whose hand is steady and whose commitment matches that of the authors. To Julia Giordano, our editor at Routledge, of the Taylor Francis Publishing Group, we give our deep gratitude. Julia, your keen sense of readership, editorial acumen, and unwavering belief that this book was one worth writing have been an immense source of encouragement from inception to completion. You have steered us through the complexities of the publishing process with patience and much welcomed insight. We are forever grateful to you.

Our deepest appreciation goes to our endorsers:

- Daniel H. Kim, Ph.D., Former Research Director, MIT Center for Organizational Learning, Founding Trustee of the Society for Organizational Learning
- Paul Laudicina, Chairman Emeritus, Kearney and Korn Ferry CEO Coach, leadership columnist for Forbes
- The Rt. Rev. A. Robert Hirschfeld, D.D., Episcopal Bishop of New Hampshire
- Patricia Findley, Dean, School of Social Work, Loyola University Chicago

- Jeffrey Hull, Executive Director, Institute of Coaching, Harvard Medical School Affiliate, Co-author of *Thinkers50* award winning book, *The Science of Leadership*.
- Mark Alan Rittenberg, Founder and Chief Creative Officer Berkeley Executive Coaching Institute; Senior Lecturer and Leadership Communications Professor Haas school of Business, University of California – Berkeley
- Margaret Wheatley, Ph.D., consultant, teacher, trainer, Harvard University, author of numerous books on organizational behavior, from *Leadership and the New Science* (1992) to *Restoring Sanity* (2024).

We are both honored and grateful for your time, your support, and your generous votes of confidence in the relevance and importance of this book.

We also want to thank Sara Demos for providing the design for all of the Tables and for doing the formatting and layout for the manuscript. Thanks also goes to Trevor Barlett for his patience in designing and redesigning all of the graphic images for this text. To you both, your expertise, creativity, humor, and patience was invaluable support.

Next, we must express our heartfelt appreciation to the 34 extraordinary readers whose generosity of time, curiosity, constructive candor, and wisdom have left an indelible mark throughout this book. Spanning all seven of the world's continents, your voices have reached across oceans and time zones, bringing with them nuanced feedback and cultural awareness that flowed from your innate wisdom and each of your own immense perspectives and experiences:

Your willingness to devote time, energy, and intellect to the formative stages of this manuscript has immeasurably shaped our thinking, sharpened our writing, and enriched the book's substance and spirit.

Additionally, each of the authors has our own circle of acknowledgments.

Stephen

Much of my writing was done overlooking a river, an ocean or sitting outside under our tent, beneath a tree or on a breezy porch where Mother Nature's fresh air of imagination and possibilities infused me with inspiration that guided my keystrokes. I would be remiss to not mention her name.

My deepest respect goes to my many lifelong mentors, teachers, friends, and colleagues who have generously shared their wisdom, offered guidance, and provided encouragement on my own journey towards psychological adulthood and professional competency. Each of you, in your own way, has helped me to find my voice as a writer and to practice, study, fall down and get back up, and articulate the craft of leadership with courage and humility.

Name	*Title/Company organization*	*Country*
Natasha Ilijeva Acevska	Founder and CEO, Intuitive Horizon, CEF Associate Fellow	North Macedonia
Anamaria Aristizabal	Master Certified Coach, Author, Founder of Re-Vision Academy, Culture Transformation Consultant	Colombia
L. R. Berger	M.A., Private Practice Psychotherapist, Poet, Author	United States
Cindy Charlton	MA, PCC, Executive Leadership Coach	United States
Nayla Choueiter	Managing Partner – Bluestorm Consulting, Professional Coach	Morocco
Isabel Jeha B. de Azevedo	Post Graduate Student of Biological Sciences, Universidade Anhembi Morumbi	Brazil
Guy duPlesis	Director-South African Logic-Based Therapy & Consulting Institute and Researcher	South Africa
Sylvie Faisandier	Coaching Professional and Facilitator	France
Patricia Findley	DrPH, MSW, LCSW. Dean, School of Social Work Loyola University Chicago	United States
Julia Giordano	Editor, Mental Health, Routledge Publishing, Taylor Francis Group	United States
Hugo Andres Gutierrez	Vice President Quality Assurance, The Clorox Company	Colombia
Jen Hess	Professional copyeditor, National Geographic, Little Brown Book Group and The Hired Pens	United States
Toby Hone	Senior Learning and Development Consultant and Master Trainer, Team Management Systems APAC	Australia
Jeffrey Hull	Ph.D. BCC, Executive Director, Institute of Coaching, Harvard Medical School Affiliate	United States
Sabine Kaben	Interior Design, Investor/developer in International Real Estate	Germany
Adam Kahane	Co-Founder of Reos Partners, Global facilitator of complex and conflictual problem-solving processes. Best-selling author	Canada and S. Africa
Maninder Khalsa	Ph.D., Executive Coach, Mentor, Facilitator and Educator	India
Anubha Khanna	Director – Coaching and Development, Threefish Consulting	India
Euy-Ryoung Kim	Ex-Vice President and Content Head, Design House	Korea

(Continued)

Figure A.1 (Continued)

Name	*Title/Company organization*	*Country*
Eun-Young Kim	MD, Ph.D., Associate Professor, Department of Human Systems Medicine, Seoul National University College of Medicine	Korea
Donna Knudsen	Psy.D., Clinical Psychologist, Faculty – Institute for Advanced Psychotherapy, Loyola University Chicago	United States
Theresa MacDowell	Columbia University student, Masters of Science – Sustainability	United States
Terry Northcut	Ph.D., Chair, Doctoral Program, School of Social Work, Loyola University Chicago	United States
Pradnya Parasher	Ph.D., Managing Director – Threefish Consulting	India
Jason Parker	Owner, Centrix Work Disability Solutions	Canada
Mark Rittenberg	Ed.D., Sr. Lecturer and Leadership Communications Professor Haas School of Business, Univ. of California-Berkeley	United States
Shahrzad Saderi	Organizational Development Expert	Middle East
Evita Salles	Ed.D., SPHR, Assistant Professor at National Defense University, Human Resources, US Navy	United States
Marcelo Salina Santos	Antarctic logistics expert/ consultant and trainer. Iaato Antarctic Ambassador	Antarctica
Shin Chze Tang	Principal Trainer and Co-Founder, Level 99 Consultancy	Malaysia
Hope Tian	Professional Artist and Gallery Collaborator, MBA – Rensselaer Polytechnic Institute	China
Tzu-Wen Wang	Senior Coordinator – Character Education Department, Buddhist Tzu Chi Education Foundation	Taiwan
Jim Wayne	M.S.W, M.F.A., Former Member of the Kentucky House of Representatives	United States
Margaret Wheatley	Ph.D., Harvard University; Consultant, teacher, trainer, and author of 13 books on organizational behavior	United States

Figure A.1 List of readers

My decades long and dear colleagues at the Global Association for the Society of Organizational Learning have exponentially broadened my perspective. Dr. Daniel H. Kim, your influence upon me has been profound. Dr. Peter Senge, your impact informs just about everything I do. My early teachers Ken Bowlen, Rick Gremlitz, and Carol Lucha Burns gave me some of the healthiest loyalty contracts I could imagine. Dr. Jane Kilcoyne, little did I know decades ago your powerful, yet humble self-differentiated leadership planted seeds for this book. My deep gratitude also goes to Elephant Havens in Botswana for being a living example of creating new relational loyalty contracts that bond and benefit local communities to help save the African Elephant. Your work is living proof of this book.

To my co-authors, Hoh Kim and the chance meeting that led us here and to Patricia, my wife of 38 years, the ballast for my boat and the wind that fills my sails, thank you both for the joy and the honor of this once-in-a-lifetime experience.

Hoh

This book is the culmination of a journey that began long before the first words were written and I am filled with gratitude for those who have walked it with me. To my client leaders across six continents, workshop participants and book club members in Seoul – your experiences brought these concepts to life. In sharing your challenges, you allowed me to witness firsthand the power of unspoken loyalty contracts and the courageous process of navigating rupture and repair. I am deeply humbled by the trust you placed in our work together, and your courage has been a constant inspiration.

To Patricia and Stephen, what a remarkable journey. Our partnership has been a model of the differentiated, respectful collaboration we write about. To Dr. Michael Gold, who taught me that life, like jazz, is best played with improvisation. To Dr. Robert Cialdini, our collaboration has been a masterclass in influence and integrity. I am grateful for your profound impact on my journey. To David Chard, for the conversation at Changi Airport that inspired my shift from consultant to coach.

To my lovely wife, Eunryoung, my bedrock. You have rewritten my understanding of connection, providing a healthy loyalty contract of love, support and understanding – the true foundation from which all great life can grow.

Finally, this work is deeply personal, born from a profound empathy for anyone who has struggled with the weight of an unhealthy loyalty contract forged in childhood. Because I know this is a lifelong practice, I share these ideas with humility. Even as an author, I continue to walk the path of becoming a self-differentiated leader and I look forward to being on that journey with you, our reader. May this faithful companion offer clarity and compassion as you write your leadership story.

Patricia

For some time now, I have wanted to find a way to translate the wisdom and the richness of psychological theory into language that would ignite excitement and hope in the hearts and minds of the general public. As a psychologist, author, and educator, I've had a growing sense that my sphere of influence was too small to reach those who had the power to influence real change.

Leadership is where true cultural transformation happens. And although there have been numerous books written on leadership, there seemed to be a missing element that had yet to be addressed. That element had to do with how to interrupt beliefs and behaviors that get in the way of fully harnessing our collective potential.

To ensure this book resonated globally, I relied on my co-authors, Stephen and Hoh whose brilliant minds and candid feedback helped me find the right blend of academic rigor, making my contributions more accessible and relatable. Your diverse perspectives, humility, and decades of experience in organizational facilitation added immeasurable depth and richness to our book.

My deepest appreciation goes to my long-time colleagues Jim Wayne, Donna Knudsen, Terry Northcut, LR Berger, and Cindy Charlton for your feedback, encouragement, and love. Special thanks to Patricia Findley for believing in this work, and to Adam Kahane for gently encouraging us in the early stages of writing to go back to the drawing board because "we hadn't hit bedrock quite yet". And Stephen, for your loving support. It is the only bedrock I truly need.

Finally, gratitude goes to my grandmother, Anna Romanow. Sacrificing your own dream of becoming an educator in exchange for caring for others is what has given me the focus and fortitude to try to reach that dream for us both.

And now to our clients – we give you a huge shout out for entrusting your individual leadership, your team's effectiveness, your organization's success, and your professional and personal aspirations with us as coaching partners. Your level of vulnerability and willingness to learn was nothing short of profound.

To protect the privacy and confidentiality of our clients, the names, identifying details, and specific circumstances in our book's case studies have been altered as needed. In some cases, we have combined elements from more than one real-life situation to create scenarios reflecting nagging challenges, common experiences and the foundational elements of our book. While each of our stories are grounded in real events and reflect common experiences, any resemblance to a specific individual or company is coincidental.

We are deeply grateful to our families, who have stood beside us through the long months of research, writing, and revision. Your forbearance with our distractions, your belief in our work, and your readiness to celebrate both milestones and setbacks have made the completion of this book possible. The late-night brainstorming sessions, the weekends spent at computers and not at family gatherings, the patience with our absences, and the willingness to listen to ideas when they, often unexpectedly, showed up and as they took shape, these are contributions that have silently made this book possible.

Finally, to the many people who have crossed our paths, some briefly, many for a lifetime, thank you. Each of you has contributed to the substance and heart of this work. Your collective healthy loyalty contract with us is the true DNA from which this book was born.

As we send this book out into the world, we do so with gratitude for the interconnectedness of our lives and the unimagined possibilities that arise when we strive, together, toward greater understanding and purposeful leadership.

In gratitude,
Hoh
Patricia
Stephen

Introduction

Imagine This …

The mood in the room was a familiar mix of urgency and uncertainty. The CFO presented large screen AI generated graphs and charts showing the economic forecast for the company. With oversized red ink behind him, he removed his glasses and looked directly at the leadership team and said, *"Ladies and gentlemen, our company is staring into the abyss of bankruptcy."*

The audience gasped and then fell silent staring at the larger-than-life red numbers in front of them. As the palpable panic began to spread throughout the room, the leadership team began to splinter. Some were demanding severe cuts, others challenged the data or blamed marketing and sales and still others said it was time to sell the company. Emotions were ricocheting off the walls as people grasped for some kind of quick fix amongst the chaos.

Unscripted, the COO, Janis, got up from her seat, walked over to the podium and with intentional emphasis said: "Please shut off the projection!" Charts and graphs with red numbers now gone, all eyes were on Janis. "This data is useful," she said firmly, "but it can't tell us who we need to be right now." Instead of reacting to the urgency of the numbers or absorbing the panic around her, she asked a different question: *"What fear is driving our instinct to self-protect rather than collaborate?"* Silence fell again as everyone took in Janis' question and the reactivity began to subside.

People began naming what was actually happening inside the room, not just what was happening on the screen. They moved from panic to curiosity, from reactivity to responsibility, from defending turf to turf building. The solution they eventually built was informed by AI projections but no longer dictated by it.

In this moment of crisis, Janis embodied today's imperative of leadership. When information is cheap and infinite, the rarest form of

> intelligence is the ability to remain grounded, connected, and deeply human. That is the power *and* the necessity of self-differentiation in the 21st Century of AI.

Why is this quality so rare? Because Artificial Intelligence is now the smartest one in the room in terms of knowledge and information. Given this, what does it mean to be a Self-Differentiated Leader in the age of AI?

This question is no longer a distant, philosophical puzzle. It is an immediate, practical challenge knocking on the door of every leader, every professional, every parent. For generations, we have built our definition of value on the currency of knowledge. The one who knew the most – about the market, the process, the strategy – held the power and was seen as the leader. We have built our educational systems and corporate ladders around the acquisition and demonstration of this knowledge. But as AI becomes a ubiquitous utility, that paradigm is collapsing. The competitive advantage of being a walking encyclopedia is vanishing.

This book proposes that the "Human Algorithm" (Coleman, 2020) – our unique ability to build trust, navigate emotional friction, and repair fractured loyalty – is the necessary counterbalance to the thinking machine. The future of leadership will not be defined by what we know, but by "relationship smartness." This is no longer just a soft skill; it is the core competency of the 21st century. An AI can draft a strategic plan, but it cannot sense the subtle tension in a team. It cannot intervene to transform a conflict into a creative breakthrough. And here is why.

Our Two Fundamental Needs

We all have two fundamental needs that must be met in order to survive and thrive (see Figure I.1).

- The first is our need to safely feel a **sense of belonging.**
- The second is our need to be **valued as a unique human being.**

It really is that simple. And yet we still can't seem to get the balance quite right. As individuals, families, corporations, and cultures, we tend to over-emphasize the value of one and minimize the importance of the other. As an example, in Western societies autonomy and independence tend to be over-valued rather than seeing the importance of the interconnectivity of us all. In many Eastern societies, honor and obedience to family and authority create a sense of belonging. However, this often comes at the expense of sacrificing one's individual voice and personal vision (Triandis & Gelfand, 2012).

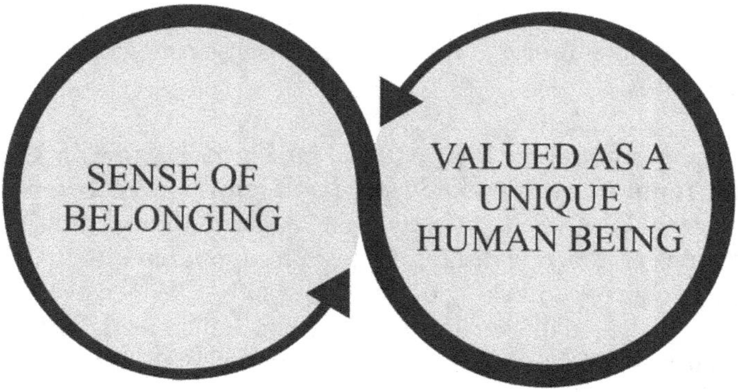

Figure I.1 Our two basic needs.

In either scenario there is a cost. And that cost means that some important part of our whole being gets diminished or even lost, creating a collective imbalance that has now become too costly to ignore. As individuals and as leaders of institutions, families, and governments, we must change this trajectory...because we're running out of time. And on some level, most of us know it.

In the past several decades leaders and educators that represent a variety of disciplines have been calling for a shift in how our ideologies drive our behaviors. Some have framed this as a call to shift from "me to we", where every voice is important, not just one's own (Siegel, 2022). Some have drawn our attention to the unsustainability of continuous consumption driven by a belief that the earth's resources are limitless. Rather, they draw our attention to the reality that we are all living on an increasingly fragile planet that is crying out for our greater collective care.

This book is a call to action to change our shared trajectory. We can only do that if leaders at every level of influence begin to shift the priorities within their own spheres of responsibility and control. We believe that if we are shown *how* to lead with emotional smartness, (supporting our two fundamental needs simultaneously) the larger system at play will begin to naturally correct itself. To underestimate the urgency of all of this is the great denial. And it's time that we name it as such.

The Danger of "Yesterday's Logic"

The urgency and complexity of the global issues we are facing are only compounded by the fragmentation of institutions that used to provide us with support and stability. This confluence of collapsing systems – both institutional and planetary – threatens to send us on a collision course with no solution in sight.

We are facing leadership challenges like no other time in history, and the on-going imperative is to learn how to collaborate in ways that we have yet to demonstrate. This is not a soft notion that calls for everyone to get along. It is a call to find new ways of listening and interacting with each other that will reduce ever-growing polarization and paralysis. The challenges we face will not be solved by using yesterday's logic, where the ideology of competition has been the predominant beat that orchestrated our dance steps. The rhythm of this dance only leaves us with winners and losers and, eventually, no one left on the dance floor.

Today's logic requires purposeful intention, where we are guided and grounded by the systemic reality of interconnection. As leaders, the ability to show up with intention is predicated on freeing ourselves from our past. Peter Drucker (1980) offers a stark warning that resonates perfectly with the central thesis of this book: acting with yesterday's logic is the *real* danger. In a rapidly changing world, clinging to old business models or outdated strategies is a recipe for failure. But the most dangerous form of yesterday's logic is not in a business plan; it is etched into our nervous systems.

Otto Scharmer (2016) states that leadership in its essence requires the capacity to make shifts in the "inner place" from which we operate. Often leaders overlook the importance of understanding their inner operating systems, which Scharmer says creates a blind spot in understanding what shapes a leader's actions and decisions. These blind spots often stem from learned assumptions that remain unchallenged. This compromises the leader's ability to operate with full clarity and intentionality.

This book is, in large part, an instruction manual that approaches the problem of using yesterday's logic by focusing on our blind spots as well as providing more effective capacities that set us on a path of personal mastery. We provide a framework that shows the clarity required to lead from a place that enables us to envision an emerging future rather than operating from and being unwittingly controlled by outdated logic.

The Emerging Imperative

The ability to create a healthy workplace environment in today's climate requires that leaders possess a thorough knowledge of the conditions that enable people to maximize their full potential. This means we have to become more adept at the "soft skills" – which are actually "hard skills" because they are difficult to master. We must learn to listen to each other and start conversations with curiosity rather than certainty. We must engage with people who do not see the world as we do. It requires that we recognize that we operate in deeply interconnected systems, where one person's failure becomes everyone's risk. We simply cannot solve today's systemic problems without a higher quality of collaboration.

We are not implying that leaders need to act as psychologists or social workers. The minimum price of admission for an effective self-differentiated leader is understanding the quality of each and every relationship. This is where the heart of true collaboration resides.

Robert Greenleaf in his seminal work on servant leadership wrote about the importance of foresight.

> *The failure (or refusal) of a leader to foresee may be viewed as an ethical failure; because a serious ethical compromise today (when the usual judgement on ethical inadequacy is made) is sometimes the result of a failure to make the effort at an earlier date to foresee today's events and take the right actions when there was freedom for initiative to act. The action which society labels "unethical" in the present moment is often really one of no choice. By this standard, a lot of guilty people are walking around with an air of innocence that they would not have if society were able always to pin a label "unethical" on the failure to foresee and the conscious failure to act constructively when there was freedom to act.*
>
> (1970, p. 13)

The above quote, written nearly 50 years ago, is as relevant today as it was then. It reminds us that foresight is fundamental to effective leadership. But foresight is the by-product of Self-Differentiation. Without it, non-Self-Differentiated Leaders often lack the ability or the initiative to make the difficult choices that require acting with ethical imperative. This book is about having that freedom to act, no matter how unpopular or uncomfortable that action is. Climate change, the challenges of AI, world hunger, warring aggression and human migration are but a few of the global disruptions and instabilities begging for Greenleaf's foresight and our individual and collective willingness to act.

Turning a blind eye, or minimizing the importance of taking action does not excuse not stepping up to the ethical responsibility of true leadership. A leader's understanding, that is anticipating, and preparing for workforce, global, environmental, and societal changes, is and always has been at the center of effective leadership.

Most of us are aware of the challenges before us. But how do we prepare leaders to create more productive, healthier, safer, workplace environments? How do we encourage employees to harness their creativity to meet, head on, our clear and present dangers?

Figure I.2 Four essential leadership and life masteries.

The Solution: The Four Cornerstones of Effective Leadership

Within the chapters of this book, we provide four cornerstones of leadership that outline how to fully realize your personal and professional potential (see Figure I.2). You will also gain a better understanding of what motivates productivity, initiative, creativity, and loyalty in your employees. These cornerstones are the key to uncovering personal and systemic blind spots that fuel uncertainty, reactivity and negativity that get in the way of personal mastery.

The four cornerstones are:

- The **Loyalty Contracts** that govern your life.
- How well you **Self-Differentiate** from other people in your life.
- The degree you operate from a place of **Psychological Adulthood.**
- How well you **Integrate** your full authentic self in all aspects of your life.

Figure I.2 illustrates the interconnectivity between these four cornerstones. Let's look at each of them separately.

Figure I.3 Healthy Loyalty Contracts.

Loyalty Contracts

The first cornerstone is the concept of Loyalty Contracts (Gianotti, 2022) (see Figure I.3). It is rooted in the foundational science of attachment theory (Bowlby, 1988). Think of Loyalty Contracts not as legal documents, but as the invisible, internalized rules of engagement we learned in childhood to secure connection and safety. Our Loyalty Contracts become the bedrock that guides our decision-making, our expectations of self and others, our fears and fragility as well as our resilience.

If I am a loyal friend, for example, my expectation is that I will have your back, I will keep your confidences, I will show up when you need me. I will be your friend forever. The dictionary definition of loyalty, after all, implies faithfulness that is steadfast. Loyalty renounces the temptation to desert, abandon, or betray.

But what if your definition of a loyal friend isn't the same as mine? What if being a loyal friend means that I must always agree with you and never challenge you? What if I must listen to your complaints even if you never take the time to listen to mine? And then, what happens if we experience hurt or disappointment? Will you feel betrayed by me if I disagree with

Figure I.4 Self-Differentiation.

you? Will we be able to talk about our disagreements, or will the fracture feel so great that the loyalty bond between us is broken?

For most people, when disappointment erupts, it is often difficult to repair the hurt because many of the expectations we hold remain somewhat fuzzy or way too rigid. And, sadly, we often don't even talk about them. However, once we understand the binds of our Loyalty Contracts, we are then able to open a pathway to a more focused and effective way of operating in the world and a greater degree of self-differentiation.

Self-Differentiation

The second cornerstone is Self-Differentiation (see Figure I.4). The concept of self-differentiation is not new. Therapist and author, Murray Bowen (1978), introduced the concept to describe family dynamics in the 1950's. Edwin Friedman used the term to discuss how rabbis and priests can use the concept in their work with their parishioners (Friedman, 1985). The field of psychology has used the term individuation and self-differentiation interchangeably. In short, Self-Differentiation refers to the ability to distinguish between your own thoughts and feelings and the thoughts and feelings of others.

So, what is a Self-Differentiated Leader? A person with a well-differentiated "self" has learned how to establish a realistic and appropriate inter-dependence with others. They know how to stay calm and clear headed in the face of conflict, criticism, and rejection. They remain able to rely upon thinking rooted in a careful assessment of the facts.

In so doing, thinking is less likely to be clouded, controlled, influenced or even hijacked by the emotional state of others. This does not mean we ignore the inherent emotions in every human interchange. In fact, it means just the opposite. Self-differentiated leaders know exactly what is going on emotionally AND they become skilled at not letting those emotions take control.

The reason this all matters is that the art of effective leadership and mutuality-based personal relationships demands mature clear-headed decision-making. Building upon our understanding of the power of Loyalty Contracts and Self-Differentiation, we next introduce the third key concept of Psychological Adulthood.

Becoming a Psychological Adult

The third cornerstone is becoming a Psychological Adult (see Figure I.5). In many if not most cultures, age often determines what we consider to be maturity. In some countries, turning 16 you can drive, 18 you become a legal adult and at 21 you are legally old enough to drink alcohol. We call this becoming a "chronological adult" often based on laws and traditions. Regardless of our culture and how old we are, becoming a chronological adult does not automatically make us what we call a "psychological adult."

A **psychological adult** is someone who can regulate their emotions, take responsibility for their choices, and act in alignment with their values rather than being driven by impulses or the expectations of others. They are both aware of and intentional about how they treat others, how they react to disappointments, how they communicate expectations, and how they handle the often-complex choices they make that comprise the rhythm of daily living. Psychological adults seek and offer relational mutuality, a sense of fairness, personal recognition, and an ever-growing sense of connection and purpose throughout the lifespan.

Finally, Psychological Adulthood is the lived expression of Self-Differentiation. The more differentiated we are, the more consistently we can show up as an adult in relationships, balancing our rightful autonomy while remaining connected as the given situation requires. And the practice and patience needed for the first three cornerstone concepts of this book leads us to our fourth and equally important concept – Integration.

Figure I.5 Psychological Adulthood.

Living an Integrated Life

The fourth cornerstone is Living an Integrated Life (see Figure I.6). This is when our actions, based on our beliefs, values, and emotions, are aligned and not fragmented or in conflict with each other. While often not obvious, how we behave in the various arenas of life are interconnected and mutually reinforcing, whether that be in the workplace or at home. This is particularly relevant in our modern work from anywhere reality, where the physical boundaries that once separated our professional and personal personas have largely evaporated. We can no longer easily leave our work self at the office door when the office is the kitchen table.

Furthermore, the rise of AI-driven productivity tools creates a relentless 24/7 digital pace that challenges our ability to disconnect. In a world where our machines never sleep, the human discipline of integration – consciously aligning our internal values with our external boundaries – becomes the ultimate act of self-preservation. Moving fully into psychological adulthood means living with the intention of combining the various aspects of our lives not separating them.

Why is that? Because when we separate parts of our lives from each other, we in effect are "splitting off" a part of who we are. This results in

Figure I.6 Integrated Life.

inner turmoil that always evidences itself. An example could be at play in a work situation where something said in a meeting is still bothering me, but I choose to bury it or "split it away" from discussion. This creates a separation – the opposite of integration – in the working relationship.

The issue that caused the separation or fracture continues to exist. Not addressing the issue doesn't make the problem disappear. It only goes underground causing rupture, creating further division or disconnection over time. For individuals to continue to grow throughout their lives, splitting stagnates our growth.

From the Therapy Room to Our Daily Lives: A New Responsibility

It is our belief that key psychological concepts with regard to understanding behavioral patterns can have a direct impact on improving overall leadership effectiveness, productivity, and interpersonal communication. Sadly, these concepts have been largely kept behind the closed doors of psychotherapy. Here we have translated them into relevant and realistic tools for leadership, and coaching practices.

Although we realize that there is a very real distinction between the coaching and mental health professionals, the line between the two has always been unclear. The concepts of self-differentiation and loyalty contracts provide powerful bedrock upon which both professions can rely. Helping an individual become more conscious, conscientious, and intentional about how to become a psychological adult, leading a more fully self-differentiated and integrated life, does not only belong to the domain of the psychological community.

Quite interestingly, you, the readers, have an opportunity to use the information provided in this book in a way that could have an exponentially far greater reach than the mental health professions have had to date. Effective leadership within our organizations has the power to create leverage that can harness cultural change, increase efficiencies, and even heal wounds and disappointments that interfere with forward movement.

However, the line in the sand between coaching practices and psychotherapy must also be clear and well delineated. When it comes to slipping into the more delicate and serious waters of personal trauma, risk assessment, and symptom reduction, this is and must remain the domain of mental health professionals.

A Note About Word Choice: Grounding Our Work in Mutuality

At various times we struggled with choice of language while writing this book. One of our major challenges had to do with how to honor cultural differences, while at the same time finding common language that applied cross-culturally to the human condition. One of the measures we took to guard against our own unconscious cultural biases was to solicit feedback from across the globe, hearing from voices of experts from all seven continents. And yet, in spite of their helpful feedback, we still faced challenges with language choice and descriptive terms that were subject to interpretation or confusion.

This was especially true when it came to describing the concepts of Loyalty Contracts and the power of Self-Differentiated leadership. In terms of loyalty contracts, we decided on the descriptive terms of "healthy and unhealthy", although we understood we ran the risk of sounding pejorative or judgmental. After all, we thought, who gets the final say as to what is healthy or unhealthy? We realized that what might be considered "normal or healthy" in places such as Asia or Africa might run counter to standards used by Western cultures to measure health, success, and well-being.

Each of us viscerally understands how cultural norms influence our beliefs, values, and sense of self. But does a culture's definition of what is normal equate to what is healthy and mutually fair for all of its members? This begs the question,

If something is seen as normal, does that make it fair?

This book speaks to the idea of mutuality and fairness as a grounding principle for any level of effective leadership as well as our own health and well-being. This is the proverbial unspoken elephant in the room in any leadership situation. Turning a blind eye to the question of mutuality and fairness is what allows for "power over vs. power with" systems to exist (Follett, 1942; Joy, 2019).

Connecting the idea of mutuality and fairness as a way of measuring health vs non-health became one of the fundamental grounding principles for this book. Whether we made references through the lens of psychology, neurobiology, or attachment theory, or whether we focused on statistics that measured life satisfaction (Helliwell et al., 2024), personal safety (Institute for Economics & Peace, 2025), or rates of depression and suicidality (World Health Organization, 2023), the one common denominator boiled down to whether relational conditions (Loyalty Contracts) were mutually beneficial to all parties.

Why This Book Matters to Your Life

Being able to perform at work and being satisfied at home with intentional positive reactivity is in fact possible. What you need is **a curiosity mindset, specific skills, and commitment.**

Curiosity will allow you to be open to something different. The skills we offer in this book will provide you the tools you need to expand your thinking and calm reflexive reactivity. Commitment will keep you on track to make the kinds of changes that can transform your life. Having the ability to change how you understand your reactions, values, and assumptions is the bedrock upon which this book is written.

Becoming a Self-Differentiated Leader (someone who is not controlled by the fear of how others might react or what they might think) provides a compelling rationale for how and why this book is important for several audiences (see Figure I.7).

- **Organizational Leaders:** Whether in the C-suite or leading a project/remote team, this book is for those responsible for driving results and managing complex tasks and relationships. We define leadership by

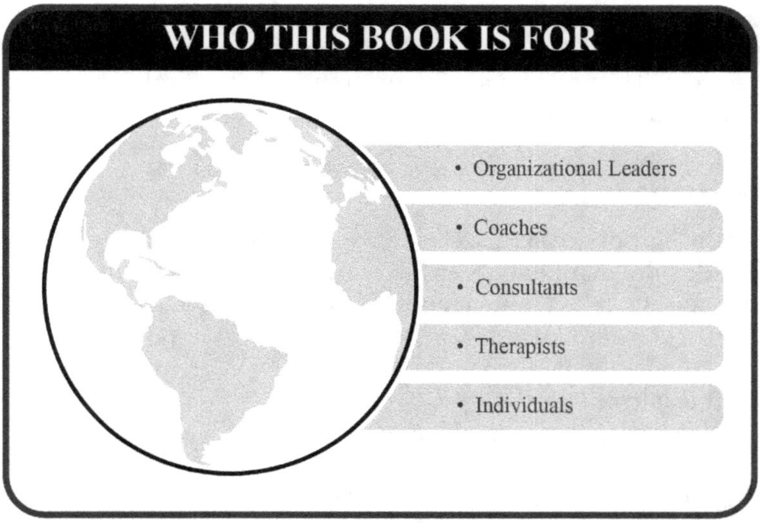

Figure I.7 Who this book is for.

influence and responsibility, not title, offering tools to navigate the inherent friction of the modern workplace.

- **Coaches:** For navigators of human potential, this framework deepens your practice. It provides specific tools to help clients move beyond surface-level behavioral fixes, addressing the root causes of stagnation to unlock their capacity to lead across diverse cultures and systems.
- **Consultants:** For change agents and strategic advisors, this book offers a lens to diagnose the hidden psychological dynamics stalling your clients. It provides a framework to move beyond structural fixes and address the root causes of organizational resistance and culture clashes.
- **Therapists:** This book serves as a bridge between clinical concepts and daily life. It translates attachment theory into practical language, offering a roadmap to help patients calm reactivity and understand how early injuries continue to exert influence in their present professional lives.
- **Individuals:** Perhaps our largest audience is the individual reader seeking personal growth and the courage to shed toxic relationships. While you might not hold a formal management title, we view you as the ultimate leader of your own life's decisions.

Regardless of our professional title or our role at home, we must all lead ourselves first. We are intentionally reaching out to this wide scope of leadership because the challenges of our time – from the rise of AI to the complexity of global interconnectedness – require more than just technical management. They require a collective future that is healthier, safer, and more productive for us all.

The Invitation

You might be wondering: How is it possible for me to change my ways over the decades that I have been alive? All too often, many if not most of us automatically take our assumptions and beliefs as a given. We tend to say to ourselves and others:

> *This is just who I am.*
> *This is just the way the world works.*
> *It is too much work to change.*
> *I really want to change, but I don't know how.*

This type of self-talk is a set of learned responses that attempt to mitigate disappointment, avoid risk, and regain a sense of control. However, it also has the unintended consequence of creating a shutdown in our growth potential, and it can also affect our offspring and the generations that follow. This type of self-talk is a form of abdication of our responsibility, for doing the work it takes to master our personal interactions with other human beings.

The idea of Personal Mastery was introduced as a formal concept by Peter Senge in his book *The Fifth Discipline* (1990, p. 7). In it he writes:

> *Personal mastery is the discipline of continually clarifying and deepening our personal vision, of focusing our energies, of developing patience, and of seeing reality objectively.*

Building upon Senge's monumental work, our book begins to deepen the practice of personal mastery by clarifying what it is we truly want, how to understand what is truly going on inside of ourselves, and providing a specific process to master our personal Self-Differentiation. It is important to note that Senge uses the term mastery not as "gaining dominance over people or things" but as having "a special level of proficiency" (1990, p. 7).

Highly successful leaders viscerally sense potential in themselves and find ways to harness, reshape, and then release that potential. They capitalize on long dormant emergent properties within themselves that pave a new and exciting future for themselves and others. While this is not always an easy task, and it can even be a bit unsettling, these feelings of uncertainty are normal.

While holding whatever uncertainty you might feel in one hand, your other hand extends to you a set of keys to open many doorways of greater understanding of what holds you back, robbing you of your true self and what will catapult you forward.

We are offering you this set of keys within the pages of this book.

Chapter 1

Understanding Healthy and Unhealthy Loyalty Contracts

We begin Chapter 1 by examining the first of our leadership skill sets – *Loyalty Contracts*. We are defining the term Loyalty Contracts as the internalized set of rules learned in childhood that continue to shape our beliefs, expectations, fears, and behaviors well into adulthood.

On the surface, most people would agree that loyalty is a positive attribute, a sign of honor, duty, dedication and even an expression of love. And yet, loyalty can be a "hot button," one that often leads to misunderstood expectations, ruptures in communication, fractured relationships both at home and in the workplace. In its most extreme form, unexamined loyalty can allow these fractures to cause polarization, targeted incivility, all or nothing thinking, abuse, even fanaticism.

If left unexamined, early Loyalty Contracts continue to govern our behaviors often in ways that limit our ability to act with intention. By exploring the power of these early internalized beliefs and assumptions, we create a bridge of understanding that can be used to better answer the question,

Why do people behave the way they do?

How we were treated in childhood creates the foundational set of "rules we live by." Our early experiences create a sense of who we are, how we view the world, and the other people in it. If we are better able to understand the early conditions and drivers that motivate people, we unlock one of the most important doors to becoming a more effective, agile leader in the 21st century.

Loyalty Contracts can be recognized by the behavioral patterns that propel us as well as limit us from achieving life satisfaction and life balance. Being able to identify and eventually change ingrained patterns and assumptions that operate on autopilot is a critical first step in becoming a psychological adult and a more fully Self-Differentiated Leader.

DOI: 10.4324/9781003621393-1

Like the proverbial horse that must be placed *before* the cart, understanding how the rules and relationships we experienced in childhood shaped us provides a jumping off point where we can choose to develop new strategies and behaviors that better allow us to reach our full potential.

As we dive deeper into styles of leadership, we begin this chapter with a series of questions with the goal of exploring how you can become a more effective business leader, family member, partner, and friend.

1 *Do you ever wonder what motivates you and where the expectations that drive your motivations come from?*
2 *Have you ever thought about the relationship between your management style in the workplace and how you were treated in childhood?*
3 *Are there areas of your life that you tend to avoid because you're afraid of what you might uncover?*
4 *Have you ever received feedback about a behavior that you needed to change, but you chose to ignore it?*
5 *Do you ever wonder why certain strategies you attempt often end up in the same type of frustration or disappointment?*

Bringing curiosity to these questions is a way of beginning a self-reflective process that we believe will lead you to greater clarity about where your values and motivations come from, and how you can make changes in your life that will enable you to gain a greater sense of purpose, control, and personal mastery. So, we begin this book by looking backward, not to dwell on the past, but to generate the momentum required for exponential forward progress.

Childhood and the Person You Are Today

Almost everything that happens to us in our early years of development will be influenced and shaped by the quality of our first relationships with the people who were our caregivers. Therefore, we begin this chapter by explaining the foundational touchstones of connection – how our expectations, fears, and relational patterns are shaped by early relational experiences that leave a lasting imprint on our brains, our emotions, and our sense of self.

Let's face it. Nobody gets a free pass from working on unfinished business from the past, especially if you are a leader who wants to grow and remain at the top of your game. People in the helping professions, coaches, psychologists, those working with executive teams, and even parents know that leading is largely dependent on how successful you are in understanding and managing relationships.

Psychological and neuropsychological infant research (Beebe & Lachmann, 1988; Beebe et al., 2005, 2010; Bowlby, 1951, 1958, 1990; Bretherton, 1992; Fuchs & Flügge, 2014; Stern, 1985, 1989; Tronick, 2007; Tronick & Gold, 2020) show that our values, assumptions, and expectations, how people handle conflict, disappointment, and creative visioning all have their roots in what we learn through our experiences in childhood.

Evidence from the medical community supports the impact of early childhood upbringing across the lifespan. The Adverse Childhood Experiences (ACE) Study, conducted by Kaiser Permanente and the Centers for Disease Control (1995–1997), shows that certain experiences, such as physical, sexual, and emotional abuse or neglect, witnessing domestic violence, sudden separation from a loved one, poverty, racism, and discrimination, or violence in the community are major risk factors for illness, poor quality of life, and earlier morbidity rates (Felitti, 2002). Findings include increased incidents of cancer, heart disease, diabetes, substance abuse, unwanted pregnancies, depression, anxiety, and suicide.

Figure 1.1 illustrates the ways that adverse childhood experiences have throughout the lifespan.

For the purposes of this book, the point of this study definitively shows that adverse childhood experiences are carried with us throughout the life span. This is true whether individuals believe that early attachment patterns have a lasting effect or not. While the original ACE study focused on physical health outcomes, for leaders, the implications extend far beyond medical charts. They could show up in a tense meeting, stalled negotiation, awkward performance review, and ultimately bleed into the balance sheet.

The good news is that the brain can change itself (Solomon & Siegel, 2017; Peckham, 2023; Doidge, 2007). We now know the brain has a lifelong capacity called neuroplasticity. Simply stated, the brain is designed to be adaptive structurally, and able to change and rewire itself in response to new learning and experience. This allows for the creation of new opportunities to expand our thinking, calm our reactivity, and hold greater degrees of complexity.

How is this done? By understanding our old patterns and giving our brains the new information necessary to change our wiring thereby creating healthy and mutually fair emotional experiences in the present that will promote emotional health. This is called creating new neuropathways, which can support healthier, more productive behaviors.

Neuroscientific evidence shows that human beings are hard-wired for attachment (Schore, 2012, 2016, 2019; Siegel, 2003, 2007; Siegel & Solomon, 2003) which means that human beings seek relational connection to feel safe, secure and loved. Insecure bonding in infancy and

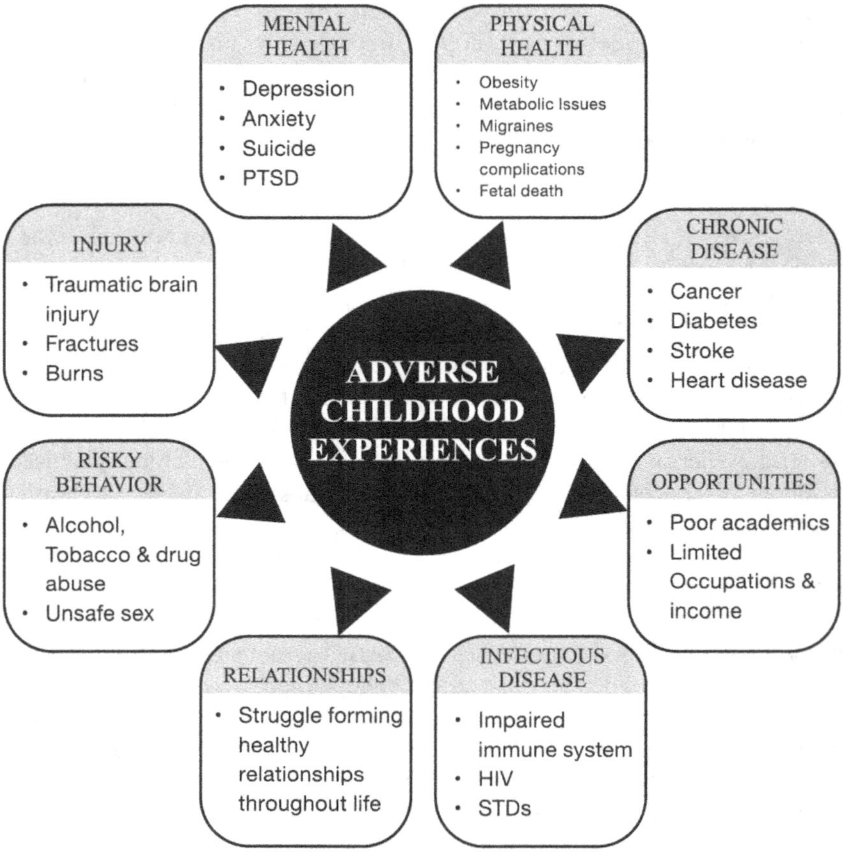

Figure 1.1 The effects of adverse childhood experiences.

childhood can have a lasting impact on neurological development, impulse control, cognition, and the quality of relational connections throughout a lifetime.

Therefore, many of the principles and suggested techniques provided in this book are grounded in our understanding of human behavior from these scientific perspectives. Our ability as leaders to fully comprehend these scientific findings will determine, almost entirely, how effective we are as leaders and as healthy human beings.

Families are our earliest teachers. This is where we learn how we must behave in order to receive love, remain safe, and develop a sense of personal worthiness. Our families also teach us how to treat others, and we watch our parents (as well as messages from the culture) in terms of learning how to handle differences of opinion, express anger, resolve conflicts, and weather the storms of disappointment.

We are calling these rules of engagement ***Loyalty Contracts***, and we will use this as a framework for understanding how we make decisions, develop our values, our beliefs, and our assumptions. In that regard this chapter creates the foundation upon which the remainder of the book rests.

What Are Loyalty Contracts

Loyalty – the word commands a powerful resonance, one that taps into our emotions at the most primitive level of our being. Loyalty is dependent upon and connected to our desire to be recognized as a valued member of society. Although the term loyalty is generally seen as positive attribute, our reactions to what it means to be *disloyal* evokes fear and/or the need to punish those who dare to question the idea of being anything other than loyal. It is as if curiosity is automatically shut down by people's emotional reactivity to loyalty, without much examination as to why.

Loyalty always commands a price, a price that actually becomes an informal contract. Sometimes the conditions of that contract are fair and equitable; sometimes the contract demands a level of obedience that requires sacrificing something that is very precious and costly to ourselves in the long run.

Most relationships are influenced by contractual parameters or agreements. Marriage is a contractual agreement. A person's job description or salary compensation is a form of a contractual agreement, even a handshake can be a contractual agreement. Most legal systems around the world are based upon contractual agreements.

Organizational consultant, Denise Rousseau (1995), expanded our conventional understanding of contracts, where she moved from an exclusively legal vantage point to suggesting that most contracts have a psychological component that is rarely or explicitly discussed. She explains that all contracts contain written as well as unwritten agreements or assumptions that operate as aspects of a working relationship, and she states that it is important for an employer to understand that much of what comprises the unwritten aspects of contractual agreements has to do with the desire to be valued by both parties. This implies that both parties enter into the contract with good intentions and a clear understanding of expectations.

In this chapter we have expanded upon Rousseau's viewpoint to include *the concept of loyalty as a driving factor* that is often contained within the psychological component of contractual agreements. What we mean by this is that most of us remain "loyal" to the messages we received in childhood. How we were raised does matter in so far as the conditions we experienced when we were most vulnerable and dependent on others continues to have lingering effects in the present moment. And those lingering effects play out in the form of unspoken expectations we bring into the conscious agreements we make with one another.

Organizational consultant Robert Fritz (1989) had a similar observation in terms of how the past informs the present, drawing our attention to the fact that many of us have a "dominant belief that we are not able to fulfill our desires." He states that limiting self-beliefs are almost always a by-product of messages that we heard growing up, and if we are continually told as children that we can't have or do certain things, those messages will be carried with us into adulthood.

Like Fritz, we have observed certain individuals that displayed patterns of behavior that continually got in their way. Despite receiving feedback to correct the situation, or despite the repeated experience of negative consequence, their behaviors or their mindsets didn't seem to change. It almost felt as if we had encountered some form of impenetrability, where the person was incapable of or disinterested in listening to feedback that would help correct a situation. It seemed as though the individual was abiding by an invisible set of beliefs (contract) that was difficult to understand or penetrate. Hence, the term Loyalty Contract came into being.

The term Loyalty Contract is actually grounded in a psychological understanding of development explained through the lens of early relational experience known as attachment theory (Bowlby, 1983, 1988). Loyalty Contracts can be conceptualized as:

> *learned behavioral assumptions that were created and deeply rooted in early parent-child interactions, as well as the experience of the particular environment or culture that a person grew up in.*
>
> (Gianotti, 2022)

Loyalty Contracts reflect the spoken as well as unspoken rules that one must obey in order to remain safe, preserve connection with others, as well as developing a sense of personal value in relation to the world and others. The framework of Loyalty Contracts illustrates the effects that healthy as well as unhealthy contracts have on the individual as well as the collective.

The Internal Operating System: How Contracts Are Installed

Attachment theory teaches us that our sense of self and our expectations of others are installed early. As children, we learn the "rules of engagement" from our caregivers. We learn that if we follow these rules, we are safe; if we break them, we are vulnerable. Over time, these external rules become internalized self-talk. They become the silent script of our Loyalty Contracts.

- If the environment was safe: "I believe there is good in the world."
- If the environment was critical: "You can't trust anyone who's not family."
- If the environment was performance-based: "I need to be the smartest in the room to be valued."

Because these scripts are installed before we have the language or self-reflective capacities to question them, they become our default "Operating System." We rarely ask where the code came from; we just run the program.

The Leadership Impact: This internal programming doesn't vanish when we get a promotion; it sits at the head of the conference room table or the dining room table.

Consider the standards we hold for success. Who defined them? Carrying this into the business arena, ask yourself:

- "What is my definition of a loyal employee?"
- "Does my definition differ between men and women?"
- "Do I subconsciously reward people who are deferential (like a 'good child') and punish those who challenge me?"

So much of our leadership energy is spent obeying these invisible, archaic rules. The work of this book is to bring that operating system online, audit the code, and rewrite the lines that no longer serve you or your organization.

Healthy and Unhealthy Loyalty Contracts

There are specific and quite dramatic differences between healthy and unhealthy Loyalty Contracts. These contracts show up in the workplace as well as within family systems, and they not only have an effect on individuals, but they affect workplace morale, productivity, and efficiency.

Healthy Loyalty Contracts are what bind us to each other; they are what enable us to put the greater good ahead of greed, aggression, or personal self-interest. And yet, healthy contracts also value the unique characteristics of each individual. They do not demand a "force fit" into one standard mold.

Just as we come to understand the components of what constitutes healthy Loyalty Contracts, it is important to also understand the negative long-term effects that unhealthy or unfair Loyalty Contracts have on individuals, families, organizations, and the culture at large.

HEALTHY & UNHEALTHY LOYALTY CONTRACTS	
+	-
• Fair	• Rigid
• Clear	• Subservient
• Functional	• Inconsistent
• Adaptable	• Manipulative
• Sustainable	• Unsustainable

Figure 1.2 Healthy and Unhealthy Loyalty Contracts.

Unhealthy Loyalty Contracts are what separate groups of people into haves and have-nots. They are the basis of the misuse of power. They put greed, aggression, or personal self-interest ahead of the greater good. They require obedience without question, and inflict punishment if rules or authority is challenged.

As you can see from Figure 1.2, there are five conditions that are required to have a healthy relational Loyalty Contract. They are:

1 **Fair:** At the heart of a healthy Loyalty Contract is the principle of fairness. Healthy contracts serve the benefit of all parties involved. They are explicit enough so that expectations are made clear, and they are based upon mutuality and equity that benefits all parties involved.
2 **Clear:** A second condition of healthy Loyalty Contracts is the principle of clarity and consistency. In order to trust in and comply with a contract, we need to rely on the fact that it will remain steady, clear, and reliable, that exceptions will not be made for some individuals at the expense of others.
3 **Functional:** A third condition is that a healthy contract needs to create a sense of functionality by providing a structure or process whereby all individuals agree to the rules and the terms.
4 **Adaptable:** A fourth condition is that healthy contracts allow room for negotiation if external or internal conditions change. How individuals are allowed to negotiate or challenge ideas in a way that feels safe, productive, and inclusive is part of what makes the contract adaptable.
5 **Sustainable:** In order for relationships or organizational systems to remain sustainable over time, it requires the ability to anticipate

changes that might be on the horizon. For corporations as well as individual relationships to remain vital, it is important to not become rigid or complacent.

As you can see, Figure 1.2 also illustrates the five conditions that constitute unhealthy relational Loyalty Contracts. They are:

1 **Rigid:** Unhealthy contracts create a kind of closed system. This is where new ideas or opportunities are not brought in to help modify or enhance stale or outdated ideas, methodologies or ways of being together or working together. Over time, rigid contracts often breed resentment, reduced productivity, hopelessness, apathy, a lack of trust, and mental or social unrest.
2 **Subservient:** While healthy relationships must make room for some degree of sacrifice, one important condition of unhealthy contracts is that they force individuals to sacrifice important parts of their authenticity in order to remain a part of the group. This imbalance is not in the service of mutual well-being. It is an act of domination of one person's wishes and demands over another's.
3 **Inconsistent:** In the business setting unhealthy contracts show up in the form of favoritism, inconsistency in how accountability measures are enforced, jumping from one strategy to the next without clear vision or explanation.
4 **Manipulative:** Unhealthy Loyalty Contracts taken to an extreme are actually a distortion of what it means to be in healthy connection. All unhealthy Loyalty Contracts are a form of manipulation that can be used to exert power and control such as scapegoating an individual or a marginalized group in an attempt to increase a sense of unity and loyalty within the dominant group.
5 **Unsustainable:** A proverbial rule of thumb is relationships that are unhealthy are not sustainable. Power imbalances, rigidity in thinking and actions, and inconsistency or unreliability if ignored for too long create tension within the system. Eventually, that tension reaches a breaking point where there is some form of collapse, whether that be the ending of a relationship, increased job turnover, or losses in revenue.

Loyalty Contracts as a "Quid Pro Quo" Engagement

A further way to understand the power of Loyalty Contracts is to think about them as Quid Pro Quo arrangements. Dating back to the 16th century, the Latin term quid pro quo means "something for something" or "this for that" (Merriam-Webster, n.d.). Quid Pro Quo engagements by their very nature are transactional. This is all fine and good when it comes to the business world, that is if the conditions offered to both parties are fair and equitable. However, when it comes to raising healthy children, unconditional love and acceptance need to be at the core of the relationship. This is not to say that healthy parent/child relationships shouldn't have rules that define expectations, but love, acceptance, and a sense of mutual respect and fairness need to be the guiding principles.

An example of an unhealthy transactional Quid Pro Quo arrangement between a parent and a child is one where the child has to sacrifice many of their own needs in order to maintain the care giver's affection. The parent's verbal and non-verbal messages might sound something like this (see Figure 1.3).

As we can see, the conditions of this Quid Pro Quo arrangement are not only completely in the service of the parent's needs, but they also send a message that it is the responsibility of the child to attend to the parent, and the child's needs are secondary. But what if the child has a legitimate need for their own? Generally, the consequence of unfair Quid Pro Quo arrangements is that the child will be punished as shown in the following example (see Figure 1.4).

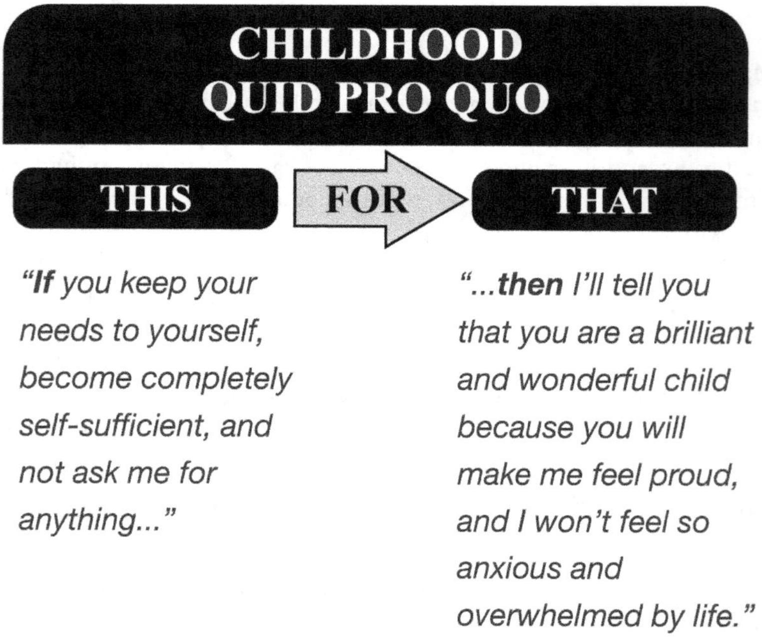

Figure 1.3 Unhealthy Quid Pro Quo – Childhood 1.

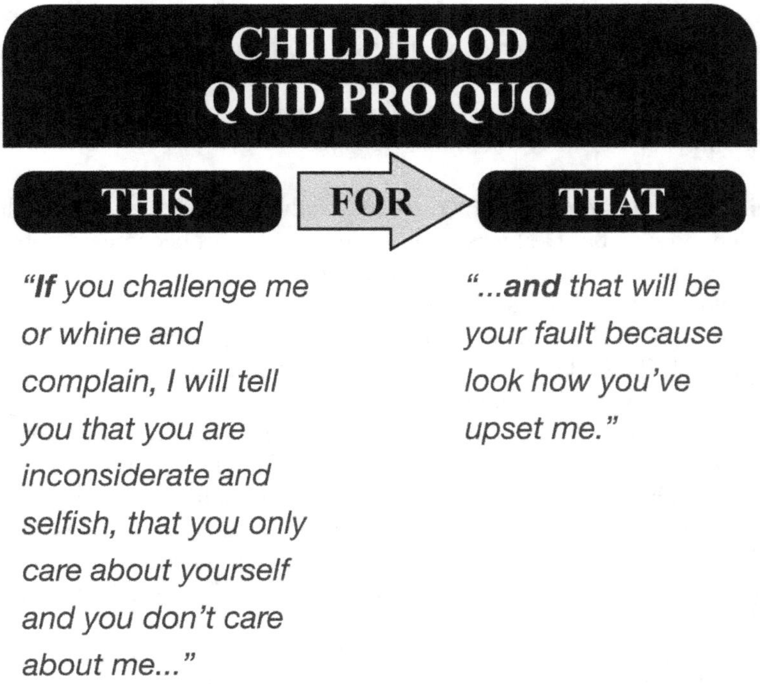

Figure 1.4 Unhealthy Quid Pro Quo – Childhood 2.

Parents (or those in authority) feel justified in this type of behavior because in their view a child making *any* request or demand is seen as disobedient. Rather than questioning if the rules are fair to the child, parents justify their behavior by saying "you broke the rules therefore deserve to be punished."

Obviously, a young, vulnerable child will do anything to try to maintain love and connection. Imagine the fear, confusion, and shame associated with early verbal and non-verbal parental cues that are based on a child's acceptance only being measured by how well that child attends to the parents' needs.

Children cannot afford to question the parameters of Loyalty Contracts because doing so feels too perilous. If the child consciously remains aware of the fear and danger of losing the attachment that his/her very life depends upon, this awareness will threaten to flood the nervous system. The child would go into a panic or become emotionally dysregulated.

As an adaptive, survival reflex, the child normalizes the parental message, accepting it as a given. The child says to himself,

> *Oh, I must be really bad. That's why mommy and daddy are angry. I'll do whatever I can to make them happy.*

In this way, the parent remains the good, stable caregiver, and the child is the one who is at fault. This is how parental messages become accepted as the truth, thus becoming internalized as beliefs that shape *who I am* and *how I must behave* in relationship.

An example of this carried into adult relationships would be as follows (see Figure 1.5). While business relies on clear exchanges (salary for work), an unhealthy workplace contract mimics the dysfunctional childhood dynamic: it demands you trade your voice and dignity for safety, rather than just trading labor for pay. Let's imagine this same person (Mary) with these early Quid Pro Quo conditions who now enters the work force as a young woman in her mid-thirties. She is part of a team where the other members are all men, including her supervisor. As a general routine Mary's supervisor would often ask her to bring coffee for the group before every meeting.

At one point she spoke up and said, "Isn't it someone else's turn to get coffee?" At which point, Mary's boss accused her of being too sensitive and told her she wasn't being a team player. In addition, he said that if she

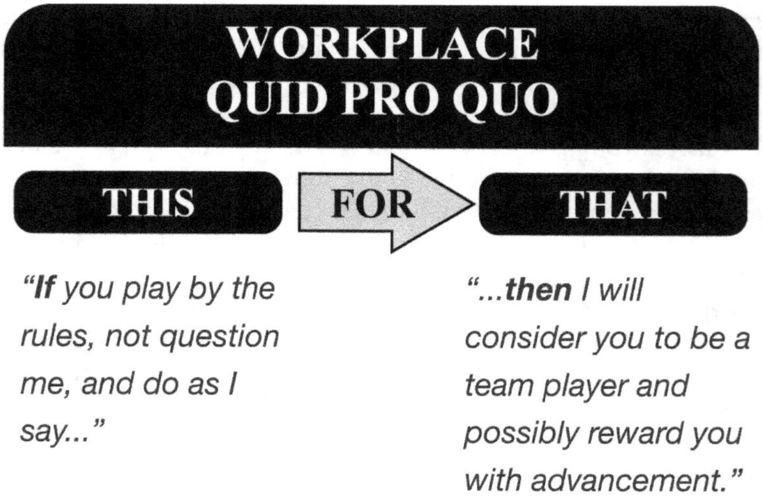

Figure 1.5 Unhealthy Quid Pro Quo – Workplace 1.

wants to get ahead in this organization, she has to pay her dues and play by the rules.

Triggered by the messages of her old Loyalty Contract, Mary immediately became afraid to push back any further. She had been caught in a Quid Pro Quo double bind (see Figure 1.6). She knew she was being treated differently than her male colleagues, but her old fears of disappointing others made her feel paralyzed to advocate for herself any further.

Inconsistent messages ingrained from early childhood create a specific hypersensitivity or pain point which helps explain why our tolerance for inconsistency and unfairness in adulthood continues to erupt. Psychologists explain this as "learned helplessness" (Maier & Seligman, 1976), where a healthy sense of outrage against unfairness is consistently suppressed. Never having permission or the opportunity to practice saying no is a behavior that begins with a childhood Loyalty Contract. The effects of that contract extend well into adulthood showing up at work and in our personal relationships.

However, using the same example, if Mary's supervisor heard her request from the vantage point of a desire to maintain a fair work-place environment, the Quid Pro Quo response would read something like this.

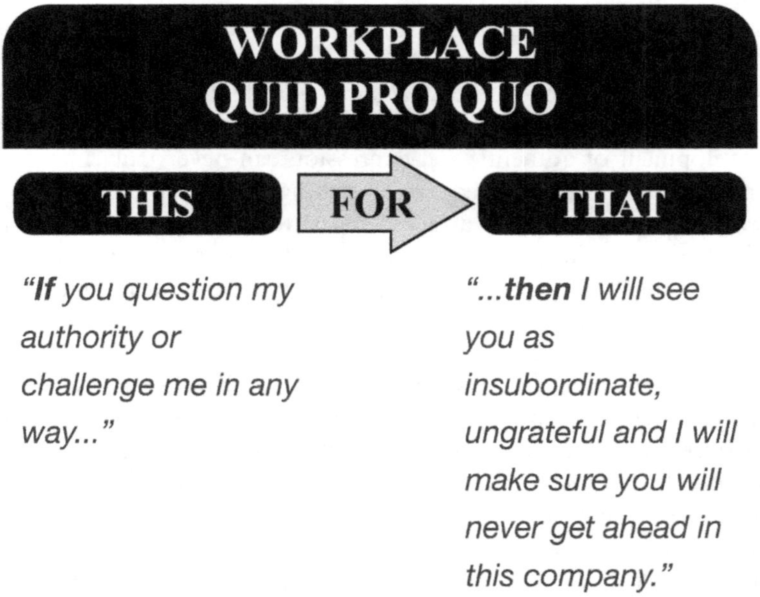

Figure 1.6 Unhealthy Quid Pro Quo – Workplace 2.

Gosh, thank you for pointing that out. Of course, we shouldn't fall back into old stereotyped roles here. Going forward, please continue to keep me honest.

A comment like this, where her supervisor listened to the employee's concern, not only sends a message that changes cultural expectations, it also could have the power to address an old Loyalty Contract, enabling the employee to speak up with more trust in herself.

Outcomes of Healthy and Unhealthy Contracts

In this next section we explore the outcomes of healthy and unhealthy Loyalty Contracts, specifically what they look like as *repeated patterns that are carried into adulthood.* We have created a chart that lists key attributes or specific qualities that individuals possess that are the outcomes of either healthy or unhealthy Loyalty Contracts (see Table 1.1).

By listing specific attributes, we create a picture that explicitly illuminates the long-term effects of early attachment conditions and how those conditions shape behaviors and the rules we live by. The list serves as a developmental guide for coaches and leaders to help identify the behavioral patterns that support or hinder professional growth.

The table below describes the behavioral outcome of healthy and unhealthy contracts.

As a point of clarification, the Loyalty Contract messages individuals receive about what it means to achieve success vs how much energy must be expended in order to achieve what society deems as successful often creates a paradoxical double bind. In an effort to be seen, valued, and loved, the development of authentic self-expression can never truly materialize when individuals feel pressured to be anything other than perfect.

In other words, insecure attachment patterns that create unhealthy Loyalty Contracts don't just happen when a child grows up in an environment of abuse or neglect. Well-meaning parents can at times create unintended consequences. Jean Lipman-Blumen (2005) refers to this as "The Achievement Ethic." Different cultures and societies have their own achievement ethic and define what is deemed worthy of real achievement. Lipman-Blumen cautions us that when a society or well-meaning caretakers obsessively push individuals to perform beyond reasonable levels, these individuals "become driven and distorted into an endless pursuit of unattainable achievements (p. 133)." This is often rewarded by a culture which in turn creates a value system and ethic that is difficult to challenge.

This ethic is carried into business and political arenas as well. If we continue to value, reward, or promote people into leadership positions whose behaviors reflect unfair or harsh loyalty standards, the eventual result

Table 1.1 Outcomes of early attachment experiences

Outcomes of early attachment experiences			
Check	*Insecure attachments*	*Secure attachments*	*Check*
	Interrupts others, dominates conversations, jumps to conclusions before getting clarity.	Listens carefully and reflects back what others say for clarity and understanding.	
	Over-compensates by trying to prove self-worth or devalues others to assert a position of pseudo-superiority.	Expresses opinions without ridiculing, devaluing, or discounting those with differing views.	
	Sets unrealistic/relentless standards of perfectionism for self and/or others.	Sets reasonable goals and objectives for self and others.	
	Demonstrates unwillingness to modify ideas, approaches to tasks or tolerate different opinions.	Creates fair, consistent rules and standards that are equally applied to self and others.	
	Desires special treatment, needs to receive continual praise for accomplishments.	Demonstrates ability to reinforce accountability standards that are equally applied to all.	
	Displays hypersensitivity to criticism/shame, without desire or skills to repair relationships.	Brings up hurt feelings without projecting blame onto others, works to repair relationships.	
	Seeks revenge when disappointed or criticized; sees others as competitors. Jealous of others' accomplishments.	Willingly supports loved ones and co-workers to achieve their own unique potential often without being asked.	
	Avoids conflict. Often projects blame onto others. Can become emotionally explosive when pushed or challenged.	Demonstrates comfort with handling conflict and the skill sets required to resolve conflict wherever possible.	
	Lacks self-care and lifestyle balance; over-use of substances, poor sleep, poor eating habits.	Creates a balanced life-style that includes self-care, rest, and renewal of body, mind and spirit.	
	Unable to ask for help, micro-manages projects, own approach is always the best approach.	Demonstrates a willingness to ask for help, able to delegate responsibility.	
	Lacks a sense of humor; humor and sarcasm used to devalue others.	Displays a sense of humor and ability to not take oneself too seriously.	
	Hypersensitivity to hurt, holds grudges, takes disappointments personally, retaliates.	Able to forgive, does not hold grudges, moves beyond disappointments in life.	

will be a weakening of the very conditions that create safety and trust. Tolerating bad behavior because a leader or a board of directors is more interested in the bottom line is short-sighted. Disrespectful leaders who impose unfair conditions and expectations (Loyalty Contracts) on employees create an atmosphere that will implode upon itself. If we are to move forward as a culture, it is imperative to insist on behaviors that reflect the standards represented in the right-hand column of the above chart.

A caveat belongs here. We do not mean to suggest that early attachment injuries are fixed in stone for a lifetime. There are many successful, happy individuals who experienced less than ideal childhoods, and yet they were able to thrive and make meaningful contributions as adults.

This is because the human spirit is resilient.

Many resourceful children, adolescents, and young adults find mentors, teachers, or other extended family members who are able to provide loving support. Having access to these individuals allows people in their formative years to find the strength and permission to buffer the hardships and challenges of difficult family environments and maintain hope because they were able to have positive relational experiences with others.

Chapter Summary

The quality of our early attachments is reflected in our Loyalty Contracts that we live out each day. They are an important dimension of what comprises healthy, vital relationships in the workplace and at home. Contracts can be spoken or unspoken, subtle or extreme. Unhealthy Loyalty Contracts might not necessarily involve punishment or trauma, or strict rules. They can also be crafted around how much of a voice a person is allowed to have; how much they are allowed to declare a preference, voice a difference, ask for attention, have the freedom to say "No," or to say, "I prefer this instead."

We all need to feel that who we are matters and that we have an impact on the world and those around us. Therefore, when it comes to understanding the foundation of healthy Loyalty Contracts two essential needs must be gratified.

The need for connection and the need to assert oneself in a way that is accepted and supported. If these two conditions exist, individuals grow up with a healthy sense of self as well as the capacity for give-and-take mutuality in relationship.

Loyalty Contracts are carried into adulthood in the form of:

- The rules we live by,
- Our values,
- Our standards for performance,

- Our ability to trust others,
- Our capacity for self-determination, and
- Our ability to connect with others in fair and mutually respectful ways.

It is quite remarkable that there is such a universal absence of curiosity and self-reflection about something that has such a huge significance in one's life – at work and at home.

It is also important to note that familial Loyalty Contracts are shaped and reinforced by cultural norms. Different cultures around the globe might emphasize or value specific characteristics over others. For example, in traditional, collectivist cultures (parts of Asia, the Middle East, Africa, and Latin America) Loyalty Contracts might lean toward prioritizing group harmony over personal needs, making renegotiation, self-advocacy, or standing out difficult. Whereas individualistic cultures (e.g., North America, Australia, and much of Western Europe) might lean toward independence, which can create tension when collaboration requires compromise (Hofstede, 2011; Minkov et al., 2017; Triandis & Gelfand, 2012).

Finally, in multicultural workplaces, conflicting Loyalty Contracts between employees from different cultural backgrounds can create hidden tensions that are often not processed or acknowledged directly. The intersection between organizational norms and a person's individual Loyalty Contract allows us to examine how specific corporate values can either reinforce unhealthy contracts or help renegotiate workplace Loyalty Contracts in the direction of greater fairness, consistency, and accountability. More on the topic of cultural differences as they pertain to Loyalty Contracts will be covered in Chapter 5.

Adulthood gives us the opportunity to choose new strategies. Making the connection to the messages that we received in childhood with what we bring forward in terms of our values, beliefs, and how we navigate life is at the heart of effective leadership. Once we understand the power of Loyalty Contracts, for ourselves and those around us, we have access to creating the leverage needed to effect positive change. This is only possible when we become consciously aware of the costs and limitations that these old coping strategies have had on our lives.

Key Takeaways

1. Our early rules of relational engagement were formed by the Quid Pro Quo modeling and imprinting from our caretakers.
2. Automatic relational response patterns are one of the most significant factors and driving forces in a person's life.

3 Healthy models of leadership are based on creating fair expectations on both sides of the equation. This is what we call "workplace Loyalty Contracts".
4 We can rewire our brains and change old patterns through new mutually fair experiences.
5 Healthy Loyalty Contracts must be fair, clear, functional, adaptable, and sustainable to ensure mutual benefit.

Next Level Reflections

1 What new take-aways do you have on the concept of loyalty after reading this chapter?
2 Describe how the idea of loyalty has possibly affected the choices you have made in life.
3 List instances when you didn't speak up for fear of making someone angry or disappointing them.
4 What feedback have you received about certain aspects of your personality that you have a difficult time changing?
5 How might this difficulty reflect early messages in childhood or part of a Loyalty Contract that still operates within you?

Chapter 2

The Ties That Bind

Identifying Your Own Loyalty Contract

Having explored in Chapter 1 the foundations of Loyalty Contracts – their source, manifestations, and psychological impact – we now turn our focus to practical application. The deeper value of understanding Loyalty Contracts only emerges when we see how they operate in everyday decisions, workplace dynamics, and how we navigate relationships. By examining Loyalty Contracts in concrete examples showing practical strategies, we move from the cognitive to the behavioral. We advance from simply knowing something to effectively doing something about becoming a Self-Differentiated Leader.

Let's turn your attention to the conditions and early messages that shaped your own Loyalty Contract that are still at play today. Doing this helps you understand why you might hesitate to give critical feedback, overly accommodate, stay in unhealthy relationships, or why you engage in micromanagement. Doing this is a way of looking at the DNA of your leadership style. This is not about dwelling on the past; it is about debugging your current operating system to improve leadership performance.

We invite you to enter "The Way-Back Machine" – not to stay there, but to conduct a root-cause analysis of your current leadership behaviors. You cannot debug a system if you do not have access to the original source code.

As you begin this journey, try to remember what typical day-to-day situations were like in your childhood home or apartment. Perhaps, you see yourself sitting at your kitchen counter or dining room table and it's right before supper, or you have just come home from an afterschool activity, or you remember a time when you got into trouble at school and the teacher told you she needed to speak to your parents.

DOI: 10.4324/9781003621393-2

> Let your mind drift until you land on your own specific scenario and let yourself gradually slip into that memory. How old were you? What were you wearing? Remember the conditions of the neighborhood that you lived in. Let yourself go into the feelings that come up for you as well as the actual visual memories.

As you picture the scene in your mind, please reflect on these questions:

- What was the atmosphere like in your home?
- Did your neighborhood feel safe?
- Who greeted you when you came home?
- Did you feel grateful, happy, safe to be home?
- Were you frightened, lonely, or even depressed?
- In general, was there laughter in the house?
- Did you have to walk on eggshells around anybody?
- Were there situations where you had to be careful fearing that you would upset mom or dad or one of your siblings?
- How protected did you feel?
- How were you treated if you started to cry?
- What happened to you when you were punished?
- Did punishments seem fair?
- What did people expect from you as a member of this family?
- Were there things that couldn't be talked about?
- Were there favorites in your family?

Now, take a deep breath, and bring yourself back to the present moment. Look at the scene you just visualized with the eyes of a leader, not just a participant. It is natural to feel a mix of fondness or discomfort when recalling these memories, but do not get stuck there. Instead, recognize that the environment you just pictured was your first corporate culture. The survival strategies you learned there – how to stay safe, how to get approval, how to handle anger, and how to deal with disappointment – are the source code for how you lead today.

Take some time to jot down your impressions.

- What memories were most prevalent for you?
- As you remember the child part of yourself, what emotions came up?
- What if any parts of yourself felt unsafe or had to go into hiding?
- What feelings of gratitude or appreciation came up for you?
- To what degree did you experience any longing or regret?

The scenario you visualized in the above exercise will hopefully help you understand the conditions or framework of your own familial Loyalty Contract. Identifying the feelings and conditions of our early contracts offers new insights which in turn create opportunities to change the assumptions that inform each of our own personal narratives.

Now, connect the dots to your P&L (Profit and Loss). If you grew up walking on eggshells, are you currently tolerating chronic underperformance because you fear the conflict of holding people accountable? If you felt you had to be the hero to save your family, are you currently bottlenecking innovation because you won't delegate? The emotional blueprint you just identified is likely the invisible ceiling on your team's productivity. Recognizing it is the first step to raising that ceiling.

Consider a leader who refuses to reassign or manage performance of an underperforming friend because their family Loyalty Contract values loyalty above competence. This isn't just a psychological quirk – it is an operational liability that degrades the team's respect for leadership.

So, the purpose of this exercise was to help you connect the dots from past to present. As you reflect on this exercise, now ask yourself:

> *In what ways has this exercise help me realize the costs in terms of time, talent or capital in my team, organization, or my family?*

It's All About the Loyalty Contract

As we explored in Chapter 1, our behaviors are continually impacted by our early attachment agreements. The first step toward Self-Differentiation is simply recognizing which Loyalty Contract is at play – paying particular attention to how you react when you experience disappointment or when plans go awry.

To illustrate how these hidden contracts dictate our leadership trajectory, we turn to two case studies: Carlos and Cynthia. Ironically, both are deemed successful by the outside world. But the difference between their levels of happiness and a life well lived is immeasurable.

Carlos – Carlos is 42 years old with a 20-year successful career at a global high-tech firm based in Japan. Carlos' roadmap to becoming a Self-Differentiated Leader was initially an emotionally precarious one. Born in Spain into a religious family with four siblings, his childhood was rich with familial connections that also included strong friendships, good grades through college, and an active physical life. We could articulate Carlos' Loyalty Contract as:

Your family, your faith, and our community traditions are what connect us together. Please make us proud as we have struggled and worked hard to give you the opportunities in life we never had.

For Carlos, this bond (Loyalty Contract) was inviolate. He could never imagine not being true and deferential to the needs of his family and close friends. When Carlos graduated from college twenty years ago, he applied for an internship at a Japanese high-tech company in Osaka, Japan. He had little faith – but high hopes – that he would land this position.

When he was offered the position in Japan was when Carlos first came face-to-face with something he never had anticipated – having to choose between his loyalty to his family and friends and what he, for himself, dearly wanted. Now facing the thought of leaving the family he loved and his long-time sweetheart, and entering into a totally foreign culture, he became quite anxious. His entire sense of self was linked to and dependent upon that which he knew in Spain.

Some of Carlos' internalized self-talk sounded like this.

What will my family think of me if I leave? I have never known a life without them. I will be a disloyal son if I leave them. Who will I be in Japan without the me I have always known in Spain?

Carlos feared having to confront his family's disappointment of him leaving and, in his head, betraying his culture. He just could not imagine taking such a huge leap into a new life and making his family angry with him. His fears of how his friends and family would react resigned Carlos to think that he had to turn down this opportunity.

Carlos faced a couple of challenges. His Loyalty Contracts with his family, his friends and his culture were incredibly strong. Too, his fear and anxiety of how his family and friends will react put Carlos in a tough emotional situation. Does he go for what he wants, or does he allow his fear of how they will react force him to turn down this opportunity in Japan? While at the time he didn't recognize it as such, Carlos was facing a critically important and hugely developmental fork on his road. This was Carlos' first encounter with the idea of Self-Differentiation.

Seeking the guidance and wisdom of his former teacher, he shared his dilemma with her. She said to Carlos,

If your family and friends really love you, of course they will miss you, <u>and</u> they will want you to do what your heart calls you to do.

Besides, if your family and friends don't want what is best for you, then why stay?

These words from someone Carlos trusted and respected, like an epiphany, told him it was ok to let what he wanted to take precedence over what other people might feel or want from him.

Permission to Break a Loyalty Contract

In most cases where there is a strong loyalty bond there is almost always some form of permission needed to break the old contract and create a new one. In family situations where a healthy contract is at play, this permission is experienced as a negotiation whose outcome is usually accepted by all parties involved. In unhealthy Loyalty Contract situations, permission is generally not given, and the ability to break free of the binds of that contract in order to self-differentiate is much more difficult.

In Carlos' situation even if he had been given full permission from family and friends, it would be emotionally challenging for Carlos to accept the position because his love (not his loyalty bonds) was so strong. He needed to grieve the loss of leaving the familiar and all that he cherished. In addition, he needed to put aside his fear of how others might react if they tried to stop him from getting what he dreamed for himself. With the help of his former teacher Carlos received the permission he needed through hearing her reassurance that changing the parameters of the Loyalty Contract didn't mean the relationships would be lost. When he realized that truly loving connections meant that contracts could be adaptable, this enabled him to take his first step towards becoming self-differentiated.

It is important to note that Carlos was able to preserve the healthy aspects of his Loyalty Contracts even as he took steps to self-differentiate. He and his family and friends did what they could to keep as close as possible with letters, cards, Zoom calls, and return trips to Spain at least once a year. Some friends and family members have even traveled to Japan keeping their connections intact and in so doing, shared increased perspectives and learning. They all paid attention to the three criteria we shared in Chapter 1 for healthy Loyalty Contracts.

- A need for fairness.
- Steadfast in care and love.
- Room for negotiation for the Loyalty Contracts to evolve.

With these, Carlos was able to learn how to become a self-differentiated son, brother, significant other, friend, and leader. By learning to negotiate boundaries with those he loved most, he developed the capacity to set clear, fair boundaries with his relationships without guilt. He didn't succumb to his fear and anxiety of how people might react to putting his needs first. This is a huge lesson for every leader and every human being to learn.

Cynthia – And then there is Cynthia. She is a retired professional who had a very successful corporate career in the international hotel industry.

Cynthia was a shy, really smart, somewhat skinny, socially awkward kid from Seattle, Washington. She attended public schools while growing up in a wealthy suburban community. At an early age, she was heavily imprinted upon by her very anxious mother who had standards of perfectionism and lived in fear of what the neighbors would think. Cynthia, the oldest of three kids, was fiercely independent often going against what her parents, specifically her mother, said.

Paradoxically, as independent as Cynthia behaved, she was always in search of her mother's approval and expression of love. Cynthia's independent streak stymied both parents, and her mother didn't quite know how to relate to her. Because of that, her mother insisted that Cynthia should watch what she said and not speak up to avoid bringing attention to herself and upsetting other people.

We could articulate Cynthia's Loyalty Contract as follows:

> *You will never be accepted for who you are because you're too fresh and you're an embarrassment to this family. If you think you can leave us and find new friends, you're wrong. You're awkward, skinny and not that attractive, and you'll just end up alone.*

Cynthia's lack of confidence for being body-shamed by her mother never left her. Even though Cynthia thought her mother was "nuts" and sometimes even mean, there was nothing she could say to calm her mother's ever-present anxiety or stop the unrelenting micromanagement of her life. One of the reasons for this is she never received the permission from her mother to become her own person and the reassurance that she was loveable and accepted just the way she was.

So early on and over time, Cynthia's self-talk remained unchanged and sounded like this:

> *What's the matter with me? Why can't my mother love me as much as my siblings? I can't stand her, but that just proves I'm difficult. No wonder the kids at school don't like me. They make fun of me because I'm too skinny. I really wish that Dad was here to be a buffer between me and Mom. But I will show them. I'll use my brain to get the best*

grades, to get ahead in the world and make lots of money. If I do this, I won't need to depend on them or anybody else, and then nobody can ever make fun of me again. Maybe then they will like me.

And that's exactly what she did. She became extremely successful, made lots of money and retired at 50. During those years before retirement, she had two failed marriages, an estranged and troubled kid, and felt an ever-present loneliness. She knew she had family, friends, and business colleagues. However, her sense of true connection to anyone was ever elusive.

Her internalized self-talk continued to haunt her as she thought about the task of finding a new partner hoping to shave the edge off of her loneliness:

I'm not attractive enough for that guy. I can't go swimming. I can't go on that cruise. People will see how unattractive and selfish I am. I must be a horrible person because I remember my mom saying I am awkward and I never have anything intelligent or witty to say. So, I'm better off just staying home and reading a book. I am not really worthy of being a good partner.

In spite of her internal self-talk, Cynthia realized her vow to become successful by achieving an international leadership position and accruing wealth and a certain amount of notoriety. She did this through overcompensating for the deficiencies heaped upon her by her mom and absent dad. Cynthia's wealth and her position of authority successfully served as a buffer to these feelings of insecurity, allowing her to tell herself that she had successfully protected herself from the external criticism of others, the embarrassment of two failed marriages and the pain of having an estranged son. However, these overcompensations never helped her resolve her internalized belief that she was unworthy and unlovable. Her internalized self-talk which was a reflection of the old Loyalty Contract continued to haunt her.

As an overcompensating leader, Cynthia's personal drive to prove herself spilled over into the demands she unconsciously placed upon her direct reports, demands that often crossed the line of reasonableness. Cynthia's internal need to be perfect by avoiding criticism transitioned into an external demand for perfection from her team. She wasn't just driving results; she was using her team as a shield against her own feelings of inadequacy. This became a blind spot for her. Her expectations of working beyond regular hours and having unrealistic goals for her team short-circuited any chance of full collaboration and commitment from her team.

They grew to resent the feeling that all of their work was never enough and was only designed to make Cynthia look good with very little in return.

When Cynthia reached her first CEO role, she and her leadership team agreed to a 360° Feedback process which is a quantitative and qualitative feedback report from direct reports, peers, and those reporting to you. The consistent feedback indicated that while Cynthia might be seen as a successful leader by the numbers, she was not well liked or respected because of her harsh expectations and lack of recognition and was seen as mostly interested in owning the spotlight, not sharing it.

Unfortunately, this is a familiar story for many people who fail to break free of old Loyalty Contracts. And here is the sad news. Cynthia never overcame her mother's relentless drumbeats about who Cynthia is at her core. The internal recordings of her mother's messages continued to chip away at her self-perception and her own self-worth. Helpless to turn this noise off, she continued to obey the mantra of her mom's early Loyalty Contract. She has remained trapped, and she never was able take the steps to achieve happiness in her personal life.

Cynthia embodies what it means to be NON-self-differentiated. In spite of clear evidence of her being smart, successful, highly capable, an effective international business leader, her entire life has been defined by other people, mostly her now dead mother.

Stepping Back

As a friend, leader or a professional coach, this kind of self-inflicted pain is difficult to witness. To our knowledge, Cynthia never found a way to stop her self-flagellation. Sometimes the grip of unhealthy Loyalty Contracts just won't let go. Understandably, the grip of unhealthy Loyalty Contracts can become so tight that Self-Differentiation seems impossible to achieve. These situations often require professional support to heal the underlying cause before leadership growth can occur.

Sometimes our support systems cannot undo that which requires in-depth licensed professional therapy. Those that seek help, often are able to find the path to Self-Differentiation once the damage from old Loyalty Contracts is healed. Those that do not get the needed support live lives that forever seek but are never able to grasp a full, healthy, and integrated life.

Carlos found a way to not let his fears of family and friends' reactions stop him from being who he aspired to be. This required him to be clear about what he wanted and compassionately create ways to remain connected to those he loved and who loved him. Cynthia on the other hand found a way to forge international success as a recognized leader; however, she was never able to terminate the demons in her head that she was not good enough, not pretty enough. In her more vulnerable moments, she was able to share with her coach how lonely and painful her life had been.

Cynthia's Monkey Mind

In the Asian culture early Chinese and Japanese spiritual masters originated the concept of "Monkey Mind." From the Chinese word *xinyuan* literally "heart-mind monkey", the term describes a state of restlessness, rapidly shifting thoughts and constant mental chatter. It is a metaphorical leaping from branch to branch, never still, constantly distracted and making it difficult to control. Monkey Mind rarely if ever pauses long enough to find peace or clarity, is riddled with mental chatter and distraction that arises from overthinking, overcompensating, anxiety, or emotional reactivity. Monkey Mind is the equivalent to negative internal self-talk we referred to in Chapter 1 (Buswell & Lopez, 2013).

In a leadership context, the Monkey Mind is the mechanism that enforces the unhealthy Loyalty Contract. It is the internal voice that shouts, "Run! You are not safe!" during a meeting or personal conversation, causing you to react defensively rather than rationally.

A more contemporary illustration comes from the 2019 Tony Award-winning Broadway musical *Hadestown*. In the show, the narrator Hermes offers a stark warning about the nature of fear. He tells the protagonist that the most vicious beast he will ever encounter is not a wild dog barring his path on the street, but rather the doubt that howls inside his own mind. This metaphor shows how the fears in our head do more than make us afraid; they attack the spirit.

Whether it's the monkey or the dog, this internal noise pulls attention away from the present moment, making it difficult to focus. People plagued by this internal noise likely struggle to listen attentively, make lucid decisions, or respond calmly under pressure.

In meetings, the Monkey Mind looks like the leader who interrupts constantly, doesn't track conversations well, checks emails while others speak, or reacts defensively to data. It destroys executive presence because it signals that the leader is not in control of their own faculties. Their thoughts can swing wildly from one idea to another, from past to future, driven by desire, fear, worry, or judgment.

This noise represents the unfocused, reactive consciousness that keeps individuals trapped in cycles of distraction and suffering. Given today's relentless onslaught of information overload, these concepts seem to aptly describe the overall current human condition.

Cynthia's inability to quiet her mind around her outdated Loyalty Contract derailed her from living into her full leadership potential. Likewise, for any leader, the ability to manage **any** animal in your head is essential. One of the most effective ways to manage the Monkey Mind is to cultivate a certain mindfulness that trains the mind to quiet the self-talk, slow down the mental activity, thus finding emotional balance that bolsters personal and professional effectiveness.

This essentially starts with catching yourself when you become aware of the negative self-talk, taking a pause to calm your emotions, and then bringing yourself back into present awareness. The ability to quiet the distractions and maintain presence allows leaders to engage more deeply with their team, think more clearly in complex situations, and project a sense of stability and confidence.

The leadership discipline of focus (cultivating mindfulness) and self-awareness (Self-Differentiation) helps leaders notice when their thoughts are scattered or reactive, giving them the clarity, intention, and better leadership choices with better leadership outcomes.

This book provides skills to keep your Monkey Mind at bay because Self-Differentiation staves off the demons of paralyzing concern and anxiety born from the nonapplicable or exaggerated worry of what others think or expect of you. Becoming self-differentiated quiets the monkey and scares the howling dog away.

Summary

This chapter moves the concept of Loyalty Contracts from theory into practice by showing how early influences quietly, often unknowingly shape leadership behavior, decision-making, and our emotional reactivity. By revisiting your childhood environments as your first "corporate culture," you can begin to identify the unspoken rules learned about our fears of conflict and our need for approval, safety, and belonging. These early survival strategies become the invisible source code behind behaviors such as micromanagement, conflict avoidance, over-accommodation, or overcompensation. By recognizing these patterns, leaders can see how outdated Loyalty Contracts impose hidden ceilings on team performance, trust, and accountability. This creates the foundation to begin the work of Self-Differentiation. In Chapter 9, we will formalize this reflection into a systematic tool called the UCI Process.

The contrasting stories of Carlos and Cynthia illustrated how Loyalty Contracts either evolve or imprison. Carlos learned that healthy loyalty allows for negotiation and growth, enabling him to pursue his aspirations without severing meaningful relationships. Cynthia, by contrast, remained trapped by an unhealthy Loyalty Contract reinforced by relentless negative self-talk which fueled overcompensation, damaged relationships, and prevented her own happiness despite external success. Self-differentiated leadership requires terminating unfair expectations, quieting the internal noise and renegotiating Loyalty Contracts that no longer serve you. Doing this brings you to the threshold of leading from clarity and confidence rather than fear.

Key Takeaways

1 The emotional rules and survival strategies you learned in your family of origin are the DNA for how you lead today.
2 The goal is not to relive or judge the past, but to debug your operating system.
3 Unexamined unhealthy contracts are not just personal struggles; they are operational liabilities that:
   - degrade executive presence,
   - stall decision-making,
   - lower team productivity, and
   - limit personal happiness
4 Healthy Loyalty Contracts allow for negotiation; unhealthy ones trap you.
5 Persistent negative self-talk, anxiety, and overcompensation are signs of an unmanaged Monkey Mind.

Next Level Reflection

1 What unspoken rules am I still obeying from my family of origin?
2 What repetitive self-talk still sounds like someone from my past rather than my present reality?
3 What am I afraid will happen if I choose what I want over what others expect?
4 Where am I tolerating underperformance to avoid discomfort or conflict?
5 When my Monkey Mind is activated, do I know it and how it is impacting my leadership, my behavior?

Chapter 3

Self-Differentiated Leadership

Laying the Foundation for Trust

Chapter 1 explained how early attachment experiences create the relational backdrop that shapes our beliefs, values, expectations, and sense of self. We provided you with a hidden source code that connects past experiences to present behaviors through the concept of Loyalty Contracts. Chapter 2 expanded your understanding of the power of Loyalty Contracts by applying them to your own lives. In this chapter we further illustrate how the effect of internalized messages from childhood impacts our capacity for Self-Differentiation.

As referenced in the Introduction, the term Self-Differentiation is the ability to remain steady in the face of uncertainty and to not become infected by the anxiety or biases of others. Self-Differentiation is what enables us to distinguish between our own thoughts and feelings and the thoughts and feelings of others. A person with a well-differentiated "self" has learned how to establish a realistic and healthy reliance on others. At the same time, they remain personally grounded and clear-headed in the face of conflict, criticism, or rejection.

An example of this is the story of Petrina, a South African woman of color who was recently hired by a high-tech company in the US to oversee their engineering division. Soon after her arrival, the CEO approached Petrina, announcing that he had received multiple complaints that she wasn't up to the task as a leader. Petrina listened calmly, then responded,

> *You hired me based on my talent. I need your support while we get through this transition. You warned me about the "good ole boy" network. It is going to take time to change the culture.*

Impressed by Petrina's steadiness, her boss gave her the latitude and the time to establish her authority while simultaneously containing the negative comments from the engineering team by reaffirming his vote of confidence in Petrina. By staying differentiated, Petrina didn't just survive the

DOI: 10.4324/9781003621393-3

transition; she saved the company the massive cost of turnover and cultural stagnation.

This illustration shows what can happen when two Self-Differentiated Leaders work together to change a culture where intolerance for change and possible systemic bias is at play. As you can see through this example, Self-Differentiation requires the capacity to maintain an inner equilibrium in the face of criticism. It also illustrates how Self-Differentiation enables leaders to assess both the immediate and long-term impact of any given situation. In so doing, the thinking and decision-making capability of a Self-Differentiated Leader is less likely to be clouded, influenced, or even controlled by the emotional state of others.

This is not to say that Self-Differentiated Leaders don't care about what others think or feel. In fact, they are very tuned in to the emotional tenor of their organization. The key point here is that they are not controlled or unduly influenced by the emotional reactivity of others. Because Self-Differentiated Leaders operate from this place of inner strength, they can be empathic and still make tough decisions.

The Self-Differentiation Capacity Audit

We would like to invite you to assess where you currently are on the journey to Self-Differentiation. Below are five questions that we are asking you to honestly indicate which response you tend to lean into when you are leading. We recognize that leadership is rarely an either/or activity. So, simply think of this exercise as what your current leadership tendency is overall when faced with each of the five scenarios below.

1 When things go wrong, do I ask, "Why is this happening?" and remain open to new ideas, or do I tend to ask, "Who is to blame?"
   - The key leadership Self-Differentiation Capacity is – **Curiosity First**

2 Am I able to spot the repetitive behaviors and limitations in myself and my team, or do I tend to get stuck, reacting to surface-level symptoms?
   - The key leadership Self-Differentiation Capacity is – **Pattern Recognition**

3 Can I hold two opposing truths (e.g., "We need to cut costs" AND "We need to invest in people") and manage the complexity, rather than rushing to a simple, "either/or" quick fix?
   - The key leadership Self-Differentiation Capacity is – **Holding Paradox and Complexity Mindset**

4 Do I share my thinking and future plans openly to build trust, or do I have a tendency to hoard information to maintain control?
   - The key leadership Self-Differentiation Capacity is – **Radical Transparency**

5 Can I hold my own anxiety during a crisis without dumping it onto my team or are there times when I (unknowingly) let it hijack my decision-making?
   - The key leadership Self-Differentiation Capacity is – **Emotional Steadiness**

The ability to embody these capacities ensures the likelihood that we won't be "held hostage" by the fears, demands, or the reactivity of others. At the same time, Self-Differentiation does not mean that leaders should rely exclusively on their own beliefs and assumptions. This runs the risk of creating a closed feedback loop which then leads to a narrowing of assumptions and more emboldened assertion of power. We will provide further elaboration of these capacities or skill sets later in this chapter.

Ultimately, effective self-differentiated leadership is not an EITHER/OR proposition but a BOTH/AND proposition. A truly Self-Differentiated Leader has the courage to stand apart when principles are at stake, and they have the skill to preserve group harmony to achieve a collective goal. The goal is not separation but integration. It's about achieving an internal clarity that allows you to set choiceful boundaries, moving beyond an either/or mindset to a both/and approach.

Confirmation Bias: The Danger of Only Hearing What We Believe

At this junction an important distinction should be made between self-differentiated leadership and autocratic leadership. Having a clear sense of self while relying on the feedback and counsel of trusted others is what expands the capacity to hold greater degrees of complexity. And yet, leaders who only seek counsel and information from those who agree with their opinions run the risk of falling into what researchers refer to as Confirmation Bias (see Figure 3.1).

An example of this would be a leader whose own insecurities or unquenchable thirst for power result in a narrowing of thinking, the need for continual affirmation, the need to be right, as well as holding to one's own agenda regardless of the cost to others.

> When Antonio assumed the leadership of a rapidly expanding high-tech design team, his self-confidence appeared to be an asset. He introduced innovative strategies and protocols improving "time to market" (TTM) and lowering costs. When met with resistance, Antonio defended his ideas with conviction, pointing to early successes as proof he knew what he was doing.

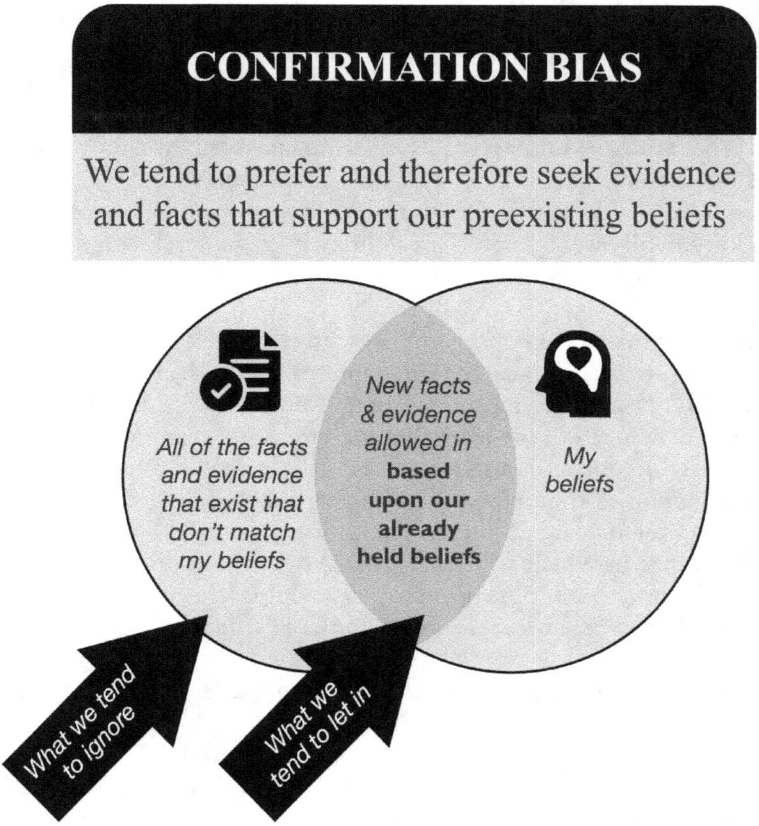

Figure 3.1 Confirmation bias.

During meetings, his presentations laden with test results and progress reports were designed to confirm his original strategies hoping to highlight them as evidence of his strong leadership. Reacting to his presentation, Courtney introduced different data points that contradicted Antonio's assertions. He dismissed them as flawed or irrelevant. He even went so far as to question the intentions or competence of those who presented contrarian data points rather than engage in the substance of the differences.

Over time, team members began to resent Antonio's selective attention towards embracing evidence that supported his ideas, having a very narrow tolerance for broader information. This dynamic began to negatively shape both the productivity and the evolution of the design team. Engineers learned that ideas aligned with Antonio's views were rewarded, while colleagues like Courtney with alternative perspectives were quietly sidelined or publicly denounced. It didn't take long for innovation and ideas outside of Antonio's narrative to fade to silence as did innovation and informed risk taking.

What Antonio interpreted as growing consensus was in reality, the result of confirmation bias. His now unchallenged beliefs reinforced themselves while innovative ideas and critical warnings went unheard and eventually went away. This ultimately created a design team Blind Spot that everyone saw except Antonio.

Confirmation bias is a slippery slope. Resentment and lowered productivity aren't the only risks associated with confirmation bias. Another danger is the possibility that team members begin to adopt the leader's views in an effort to be included in the leader's inner circle. Or, team members might (consciously or unconsciously) begin to believe that the leader's version of the situation is the *only* truth, shutting down Self-Differentiation of thought in exchange for loyalty to the leader.

The manner in which we invite, receive, and incorporate feedback is a critically important dimension of developing the capacity for Self-Differentiation. Therefore, it is important to ask ourselves:

What are the sources I draw upon to help me learn and grow in my career and in my life?

The people we turn to for support can be used to soothe our egos, or we can surround ourselves with trusted advisors that aren't afraid to challenge us in an effort to help us gain clarity and reveal possible blind spots that interfere with more effective decision-making and leadership.

In general, as people mature there is a tendency for thinking and decision-making to become somewhat more cautious or narrowed. As people age, they tend to exhibit an over-reliance on past history and have difficulty or disinterest in learning new tasks, particularly of those tasks that require higher levels of complexity (Perez et al., 2018; Ding et al., 2015).

In addition, how individuals typically process information tends to favor information that supports one's prior beliefs and values. Research experiments (Nickerson, 1998; Kenrick et al., 2018) have found repeatedly that people believe information and evidence in a one-sided way; that is, they search for evidence that is consistent with their current hypotheses or beliefs. This is how confirmation bias is reinforced.

Confirmation bias tends to be strongest when there is an emotionally charged issue, especially if that issue or situation poses a potential threat to one's deeply entrenched beliefs, or if there is a perceived fear of loss of power or control.

An example of this would be the denial of climate change in spite of the overwhelming scientific evidence. One explanation for the denial is that the topic is unsettling. It requires us to potentially change our routines. Or, it might ask us to experience some loss of comfort and convenience. This in turn creates emotional reactivity or resistance to accurately assessing the long-term costs, which then inhibits individuals from making lifestyle adjustments to take positive action.

The risks of confirmation bias can be costly, even dangerous. Confirmation bias generally leads to all or nothing thinking, unconscious overconfidence, and eventually to skewed decision-making. Confirmation bias isn't just a psychological reaction; it's an innovation killer. It is the reason Kodak missed digital photography and Blockbuster missed streaming (Lovallo & Sibony, 2010). When leaders surround themselves with "Yes Men" to feel safe (a Loyalty Contract issue), they miss the market signals that threaten their survival.

As we become more entrenched in the age of AI, there also appears to be a decrease in concern about the risks of operating from a place of confirmation bias. In large part this is due to the increase of AI-driven "algorithmic editing" in social media platforms that is designed to intentionally direct individuals to information they are likely to agree with while eliminating opposing views.

This narrowing of access to information can in turn lead to increased polarization, suspicion of others, and fear or intolerance of differences. Fear is the antithesis of Self-Differentiation. However, fear seems to be a driving force behind the tendency to slip into confirmation bias.

Individuals whose early attachment histories were filled with inconsistency, trauma, or neglect are more susceptible to confirmation bias. This is because confirmation bias unconsciously functions as an attempt to maintain a sense of stability, certainty, and safety. This is especially true when challenges, differences of opinion, or unexpected information triggers uncertainty or confusion. Individuals with a less secure sense of self are more likely to fall into confirmation bias. This can be measured by increased rigidity in thinking, the denial of critical information, coupled with increased self-righteousness.

Our Mutual Need for Connection and Recognition

The need for personal recognition is an innate desire in every human being, one that is present from birth. Being seen and valued for our unique contributions at work AND at home is of vital importance to ongoing growth across the lifespan. As we mentioned in the Introduction, personal recognition, *the act of being seen and valued*, is one of the ways we begin to develop into our full potential and thereby positively impact both work and personal interactions using our full potential. And yet, it is difficult for that potential to fully materialize unless those around us *recognize* our talents and give us the proper support and stability to access the resources we need to bring our full potential into being.

Since most of us spend the majority of our waking hours in the workplace, it is important for leaders to understand that creating healthy working environments creates a huge competitive advantage, one that bolsters productivity, effectiveness, retention, recruitment, to name just a few. One way to gain this competitive advantage is for leaders to strategically create work environments where the innate human need for personal recognition is valued and rewarded.

Axel Honneth (2014, 2019) the originator of recognition theory, states that recognition is necessary for good relationships with ourselves, and it explains how we develop our identity. Recognition, he explains can be interpersonal between two people or within a family unit, but it also occurs within non-family groups, communities, workplace departments and teams.

Psychologist Jessica Benjamin (2018) states that beginning in infancy, if a child is not sufficiently recognized by the parent, through acts of mutual cuing and mirroring, the capacity to develop a solid sense of self, the capacity for mutuality in relationship, and the capacity to achieve ethical self-consciousness is thwarted.

Acts of recognition show us that we are valued. A child who grows up in an environment of deprivation, where the self is not seen or acknowledged, creates an invisible kind of damage that is not as easily recognized, yet can be just as damaging as growing up in a traumatic or chaotic environment.

In addition to Honneth and Benjamin's findings, decades of infant research based on parent-child interactions (Beebe & Lachmann, 2005; Beebe et al., 2010; Siegel, 2020; Stern, 2007; Tronick, 1989, 2007) agree that *mutual recognition* is an important component to healthy self-development. They conclude that there are two equally important needs that must be satisfied in order to develop into healthy stable adulthood. As mentioned in the introduction, these needs are:

- The need to be seen and valued as a unique human being, and
- The need to feel a sense of belonging in a safe, secure, and loving home.

Both of these needs mutually support and reinforce one another. Research confirms that these needs continue to be important across the life-span.

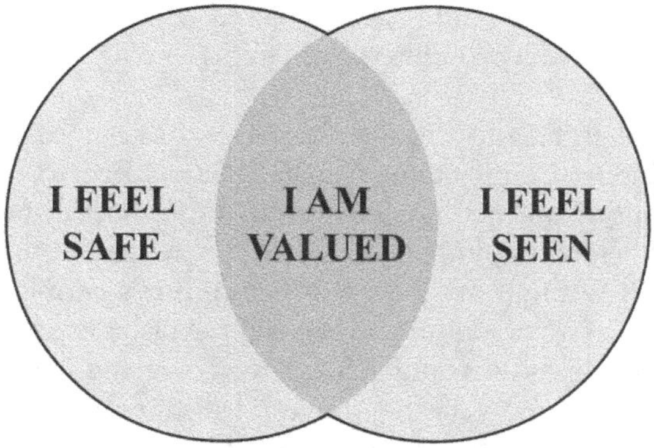

Figure 3.2 Psychological foundation.

This implies that effective leadership means taking on the responsibility of creating workplace environments that attend to these needs.

Figure 3.2 illustrates what happens at a psychological level when both of these needs are met in equal measure. The result is that the person is able to internalize a sense of self that feels valued and confident to enter the world equipped not only to take on challenges but also to discover the world's joys and opportunities. These individuals have a trust in themselves and a sense of optimism and hopefulness.

If, however, one of the needs is met and the other is minimized or ignored, the person is often left with an unresolvable conflict. Many individuals grow up in environments where the balance between these two needs has not been equally reinforced or valued.

To illustrate this further, we have provided three examples of how under-attention to either need or the stark neglect of both needs plays out in adult life. All three of the following examples, where basic needs for healthy self-development fall short, results in a core sense of self that lacks a stable foundation. This in turn leaves these individuals vulnerable to being manipulated by others, or they develop an over-determined effort to continually prove their value.

Example # 1 – Masha was the youngest child of a first-generation immigrant family. As the only daughter, Masha grew up in an environment where she was overly protected. However, she was also told that her value as a person was measured by her sense of duty to family. Growing up in a Muslim community in Chicago, Masha's extended community as well as her nuclear family reinforced the message that a woman's role was to be the caretaker. Masha was confused – she was told she was a cherished member of the family, but things didn't feel fair. She saw her female schoolmates having liberties that she was denied, and she wondered why her brothers were given privileges that she was prohibited from experiencing.

Analysis: This scenario of imbalance between the two basic needs created a specific type of internal conflict for Masha. She wanted to obey the messages of her Loyalty Contract by showing loving respect in order to maintain her sense of belonging, but she also had a need and desire to explore the outside world. Without her family or her culture's permission to be seen and appreciated as a person in her own right, Masha continued to doubt her value. In later life she would struggle with voicing her own opinions, and she would feel guilty if she conveyed disappointment or anger to her parents with regard to feeling trapped at home.

Although she remained dutiful, she never married, became depressed and withdrawn. After her parents died, without having the skills to examine the unfairness of her family's Loyalty Contract, Masha became vulnerable to outside flattery of others. She eventually met a man on an on-line dating site who had asked for money to invest in a business with the promise of marrying her once his business was established. This never happened; the man disappeared, leaving her with no way to recoup her loss of $100,000.

Example # 2 – The story of James illustrates the reverse of Masha's family environment – a situation where he was given free rein but was not given enough attention and love to feel safe and cared for. James was told that he was smart; therefore, he needed to be self-reliant because his parents were overwhelmed with work and raising three younger siblings. Fast forward to a picture of James in the work setting. Whenever James needed help with a team project, he found it difficult to ask for advice. Given his early Loyalty Contract, it was not surprising that it was extremely uncomfortable for him to depend on others. In addition, James experienced any performance feedback from his boss as a sign that he was falling short, interpreting suggested areas in need of improvement as a sign of weakness.

Analysis: Because James learned not to depend on others, and because he had to over-function in order to survive, it is not surprising that he developed into a workaholic with perfectionistic standards. Not only did he impose these standards on himself, he complained if others fell short of the mark as well. Consequently, James' work ethic and attitude had a demoralizing effect on his fellow co-workers. His lack of receptivity to feedback left him more vulnerable to a potential lay-off as his company began to experience a downturn in sales. Again, like Masha, James' professional and personal trajectory is not likely to change until he first understands where his fears and strategies of overcompensation come from.

Example # 3 – Larry is an only child of a wealthy entrepreneur and socialite mother. Although his mother continually told him that he was superior to other children, she was emotionally distant and showed little affection. Often left alone, Larry felt unworthy and unlovable. On the other hand, Larry's father had unreasonably high standards of achievement for his only son. Although he often felt that his father's rules were unfair, fighting back or voicing anger was not an option. As a young adult, Larry grew to be a successful business owner by acquiring control of one of his father's companies. But his reckless need to show his self-worth led him to extravagant spending and near bankruptcy. At which point, his father had to bail him out, only to say,

> *I knew you would never amount to anything. You ruined what I built. I knew you always would come running back to me to rescue you.*

Analysis: Here we see an example where neither of the needs for loving connection or the need to be valued and respected were met within this family's Loyalty Contract. Success was the only way of being recognized. But the Loyalty Contract also demanded that Larry could never outshine his father. His irresponsible, self-destructive tendencies led him to unconsciously "prove his father right." However, his family Loyalty Contract also left him extremely vulnerable to manipulation and flattery by others.

After his father died, Larry took over his father's business and surrounded himself with "yes-men" in an effort to never be chastised and humiliated again. Because his early Loyalty Contract was never examined or resolved, Self-Differentiation was not in his picture. His expansive need for gratification and affirmation led to yet another business collapse.

These examples illustrate what can happen when there is an imbalance between the need for safety/sense of belonging, and the need to be seen and valued for who we are. Given these three scenarios, it's not a stretch to imagine the kind of influence these early contracts have on a person's workplace behavior and personal relationship dynamics. Many cultures place enormous value on being number one, being a superstar, but there is less regard for personal safety or providing a strong and skilled human resources presence.

As leaders, it is important to develop strategies that honor and recognize employees. This can actually be a *reparative experience* for those individuals who weren't valued or recognized by family members. Examples of this would be companies that honor employees through appreciation dinners or awards ceremonies, not just end of year bonuses. Or the manager who gives a public thank you at a team meeting to specific individuals who completed a project on time or ahead of schedule. Or developing mentoring programs for new employees to grow their talent and build confidence.

A Two-fold Perspective

The ability to recognize and make sense out of repeating patterns is one way a leader can discover how to tap into a person's motivation as well as what might be blocking a person's ability to achieve their full potential. In order to get a handle on key components of motivation as well as predictive patterns, this requires a two-fold approach.

- **Self-Examination:** The first centers on the need to understand our own motivations and fears from the lens of attachment injury. At the same time, it requires us to become aware of our own potentially under-examined patterns or Loyalty Contracts. Once we gain clarity of our own patterns and vulnerabilities, this moves us from a place of reactivity to a place of intentional and productive action.
- **Intentionality:** Operating with intention allows leaders to assess how the corporate culture is impacting performance, motivation, and morale with greater accuracy. The corporate culture of any organization is, in actuality, an embodiment of the group's *shared* Loyalty Contract.

This aligns with Edgar Schein's (2010) definition of culture as the "basic underlying assumptions" that a group has learned and shared. For the Self-Differentiated Leader, intentionality means discerning and then naming what the shared Loyalty Contract is from your own perspective. It means making the "unwritten agreement" explicit (Rousseau, 1995), and then inviting employees to give their version of what values and priorities the corporate culture's Loyalty Contract reflects.

Using the same conceptual framework, we can apply this to workplace motivation and initiative of employees as illustrated in Figure 3.3 below. And taking it one step further, we can see the impact this concept can have on our personal relationships.

Bottom line, if workplace expectations become clarified through the lens of mutual fairness, the contracts we make with one another can be more intelligently examined and intentionally modified, not simply accepted by default. We have found that by using the framework of Loyalty Contracts, identifying patterns that are beneficial vs detrimental, people become more willing and able to let go of unconscious and/or unhealthy expectations of self and others. Examples might be creating a workplace environment that values collaboration over competition, or letting go of unreasonable, perfectionistic demands, or refusing to push oneself to the point of collapse in order to prove you're a valued employee.

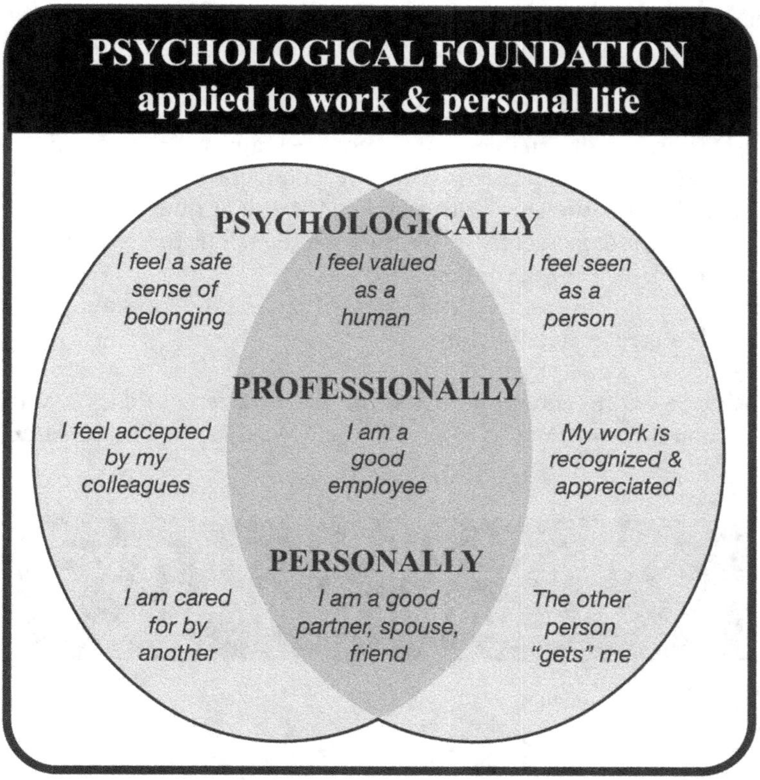

Figure 3.3 Psychological foundation applied to work and personal life.

The Skill-Sets Required for Self-Differentiation

In this next section we will highlight the skill sets required for self-differentiated leadership. Taking a pause to objectively evaluate how we choose to interact at any given time is the solid foundation upon which Self-Differentiation rests. This also requires a willingness to challenge some of the expectations, values, and messages that we were told in terms of being seen as successful and "good" members of our families and our communities.

All remaining skill sets required for Self-Differentiation rest on how well we are able to objectively evaluate how the costs of our early upbringing continue to limit our present assumptions, beliefs, and behaviors. When we are able to do this, we are then more easily able to differentiate our own emotions from those of others.

For example, Self-Differentiation allows us to be able to discern when someone else's emotional reactivity is caused by our own carelessness or insensitivity vs something that is based on another person's unrealistic or unfair expectations unfairly being placed upon us.

Self-Differentiation enables us to not feel guilty or responsible for another person's hurt or anger when we take action to say "No" or to end an abusive relationship or to simply do the right thing. We are able to act and decide independently of whether people tell us that we are wrong, inept, or to blame for their misery.

Figure 3.4 illustrates five skill sets of Self-Differentiation. Each is explained in greater detail below.

Curiosity: Self-Differentiation begins with having a genuine curiosity about why we and those around us behave in the ways that we do. Unexamined,

Figure 3.4 Skill sets required for Self-Differentiation.

this lack of awareness can be a leadership fatal flaw. Remaining curious allows us to find new and creative options when challenged with a difficult situation. Curiosity is what also allows us to keep an open mind in order to adapt to differing viewpoints. Leaders or partners who are able to adopt an attitude of curiosity and mental agility, are able to demonstrate a more informed viewpoint and are able to make choices from a wider array of options.

Recognizing Patterns: The second skill set is the ability to recognize repeating patterns. Doing so, we are better able to assess if those patterns sustain organizational or relationship stability or whether they drain resources and derail trust. Identifying destructive patterns within or between individuals deepens a leader's understanding and increases decision-making effectiveness. In addition, it is important to seek feedback about your own repeated patterns because this is what allows you to make necessary adjustments in order to develop into a more effective, skillful leader.

Paradox and Complexity: We are defining paradox as holding what appears on the surface to be contradictory pieces of information. Yet, when examined more closely, you discover that they are actually connected in a meaningful way. Once the connection is seen, you are then able to hold a more complete picture of the complexity of what's actually going on. This capacity is what leads to integration. For example, think of a conductor leading a full orchestra with close to 100 musicians who must direct the distinct sounds of each instrument and each musician (complexity) while simultaneously ensuring they all serve one unified piece of music (integration).

Transparency: Self-Differentiation is also reflected in our ability to be transparent. For example, Self-Differentiated Leaders do not avoid difficult conversations for fear of conflict. They let people know (appropriately) what they are thinking and planning and are able to explain what makes sense for the greater good for the organizations they lead. Hiding key information for fear of how people will react eventually creates an atmosphere of uncertainty or suspicion. Clear communication and the sharing of information are foundational elements to being seen as trustworthy and transparent at work or at home.

Emotional Steadiness: At the heart of self-differentiated leadership is the ability to manage our own emotional reactivity. This means not being held hostage to what others think of us if we disagree or hold them accountable for bad behavior. Self-Differentiated Leaders, friends, and family members trust in their capacity to talk things through and attempt to repair misunderstandings whenever possible. And, they are also able to assess when another person is not able or interested in putting the effort into making that repair.

A word of caution here: there is a difference between emotional steadiness and emotional rigidity. Steadiness conveys a flexibility and curiosity to let new information in. Rigidity might appear steady, but there is an impenetrability to rigidity, reducing the ability to hold complexity. Leaders who hold a more rigid stance eventually create a closed system, where important information is missed or not factored into the long-term sustainability of that system. Consider the difference in how two leaders handle a project that is falling behind schedule:

- **The Rigid Leader** says, "We agreed on this deadline three months ago. I don't want to hear excuses; I want results. We are sticking to the plan."
  - The Result: The team stops sharing bad news to avoid the leader's anger. The system closes, and the project fails because the leader refused to accept the reality of the situation.
- **The Emotionally Steady Leader** says, "I remain 100% committed to our launch date (Steadiness), but the current data shows we are off track. I need to know exactly (Curiosity) what obstacles are getting in the way so we can solve them together (Flexibility)."
  - The Result: The team feels safe to share the "ugly truth." The leader holds the tension of the deadline without denying the reality of the obstacles, allowing the system to adapt and succeed.

We see a powerful, real-world application of this distinction in the story of Alan Mulally, a leader so transformative that *Fortune* (a well-known American magazine) ranked him third among the world's greatest leaders (Colvin, 2014), just behind Pope Francis and Angela Merkel. When he took over as CEO of Ford in 2006, the company was losing billions, yet the culture was paralyzed by a "survival of the fittest" mentality. Executives hid problems protecting their careers, meaning that in his weekly Business Plan Reviews, every chart was green, depicting a company in perfect health even as it burned cash.

Then came the moment of truth. Mark Fields, then the head of the Americas, displayed a single red slide – a production halt due to a tailgate actuator issue (a mechanical device that controls the locking mechanism of SUVs and hatchbacks). The room froze. In the old culture, which relied on rigid leadership, this admission was professional suicide. The team waited for the explosion.

Instead, Mulally clapped. He smiled and said, "Thank you, Mark, for that visibility. Who can help Mark with this?"

By refusing to be hijacked by the anxiety of the failure, Mulally demonstrated profound emotional steadiness. He didn't just fix a tailgate; he fixed the nervous system of Ford. By refusing to react with anger – the standard unhealthy Loyalty Contract of the past – he made it safe for the truth to enter the room. In the following weeks, the charts were speckled with red and yellow – the truth was finally on the table. Mulally proved that a Self-Differentiated Leader's primary job is not to punish the problem, but to make it safe enough to solve it (Hoffman, 2012).

Chapter Summary

Self-Differentiation is at the heart of effective leadership. One of the keys to Self-Differentiation lies in understanding the shadow side of our own histories and working to liberate ourselves from the triggers that cause our ineffective or unhealthy reactivity or impulsive decision-making. This chapter has highlighted key attributes of self-differentiated leadership. We also connected those attributes to understanding the components of healthy Loyalty Contracts.

Self-Differentiated Leaders at work and at home have an opportunity to repair and create new Loyalty Contracts by ensuring conditions that hold to standards of fairness, mutuality, and consistent accountability practices across the entire system. The human spirit never gives up the hope that things can be better, that making things better is possible.

This chapter covered the concept of Self-Differentiation on more of a macro-level. Chapters 9 through 11 will focus on the specific processes and micro-skills required to become a Self-Differentiated Leader. Our final chapter, Chapter 12, has three case examples highlighting Self-Differentiation.

Lost in Translation: A Global Framework

We understand that some readers from different cultures might wonder how to translate this book's key terms – Loyalty Contracts and self-differentiated leadership into their own languages. It's a valid concern that the nuanced meaning of these concepts might be lost in translation.

Untangling Loyalty Contract: We've received feedback that the word "contract" can sound overly legalistic or transactional. It's important to clarify that we are using it metaphorically. A Loyalty Contract is not a business arrangement but rather the unspoken rules of engagement that dictate how we show loyalty in exchange for connection and safety, first with our parents and later with others.

There's a reason we pair these two words. While "loyalty" is an emotionally charged concept, "contract" is intentionally dry and neutral. This distinction is the very point. By reframing loyalty as a psychological contract, we lessen much of the culture's power of dictating the rules we live by without question. This shift in perspective empowers us to change, revise, and negotiate the terms of our loyalty, allowing us to build healthier relationships.

Reframing Self-Differentiation: Similarly, the expression of Self-Differentiation manifests differently across cultures. In low Power Distance cultures – where members are encouraged to value equality and challenge authority – it might look like a bold, independent path of creating one's own identity. In high Power Distance cultures, however, where respect for hierarchy and authority is more ingrained, it's often a more nuanced process of navigating expectations while maintaining connection (Hofstede, 2011). We will delve much deeper into these distinctions and their impact on leadership in Chapter 5.

Key Takeaways

1 Self-Differentiation is at the heart of effective leadership.
2 The more you calm your own emotional reactivity, the less likely you are to act on impulse or be swayed by other people's demands.
3 Creating healthy, fair, and equitable organizational Loyalty Contracts is a key component to creating a healthy organizational culture and motivated employees.
4 Beware of Confirmation Bias: Insecure leaders often seek only the information that supports their existing beliefs, which creates a "closed loop" that kills innovation and leads to skewed decision-making.
5 There is an important and critical difference between emotional steadiness and emotional rigidity.

Next Level Reflections

1 What insights do you have on the concept of Self-Differentiation after reading this chapter?

2 Describe how the two mutually important needs for personal recognition and a sense of safety are at play within your organization or your family system.
3 How might you implement measures to correct any possible imbalance between the two?
4 Identify the components of Self-Differentiation that might need further development in your personal life in terms of your actions, beliefs, and behaviors.
5 Imagine a plan of action that has the conditions of a healthy organizational Loyalty Contract. What might be some of the components of mutual recognition that you would want to add or reinforce within your organization and/or within your family system?

Chapter 4

Navigating Conflict

Turning Friction Into Flow

Introduction

In the Introduction, we defined the four cornerstones of leadership that enable you to fully realize your personal and professional potential which are the core components of this book.

Healthy Loyalty Contracts
Self-Differentiation
Psychological Adulthood
Integrated Life

Chapters 1 and 2 introduced in depth the significance of our Loyalty Contracts. Chapter 3 made the connection between our Loyalty Contracts and our ability to Self-Differentiate. Each of these chapters provided solid psychological research and real-world examples to support the connection between how the formation of our early relationships affects how we behave at work, with our loved ones, and how we lead.

In this chapter we focus on the third cornerstone of leadership – Psychological Adulthood. From Chapter 1 we remember that Psychological Adulthood emerges when we are aware of the causal relationship between our Loyalty Contracts and how self-differentiated we are. But it goes beyond awareness. To be a psychological adult, that consciousness must show up consistently in our behaviors. While our inherited sense of obligation to our past might still tug at us on some level, the psychological adult is able to move beyond these emotional tethers to where we act with healthy intention rather than unconscious and unhealthy agreements with our past.

Nowhere does our ability to show up as a psychological adult get challenged more than when we are confronted by adversity, difference of opinion, disappointment, sabotage, or betrayal. Operating from a place of Psychological Adulthood means that instead of reacting with an autonomic response, you are able to pause long enough to clear your head so that you can choose a response that creates more clarity than negativity, more

DOI: 10.4324/9781003621393-4

curiosity rather than adversity. When your reactions are in fact conscious choices aligned with who you are, not inherited reflexes shaped by who you were told to be, this is when you recognize your own Psychological Adulthood.

This chapter examines how we can, as psychological adults, respond to the inevitable daily conflicts that punctuate our lives. What we mean by conflict is not necessarily fighting or arguing. For this discussion we expand our definition of conflict to include any situation that feels confusing or even threatening in ways that we don't completely understand. This is important because whenever we don't completely understand, we tend to slide into a state of confusion, resistance, or inaction. That state tends to create a degree of friction that demands our emotional attention and diminishes the ease (flow) we need as leaders operating from a place of grounded, Psychological Adulthood.

When conflict gets triggered, people become confused or afraid to speak. Here are a few examples of when this might happen.

- I disagree with the CEO about the strategy going forward.
- Someone gets the promotion that I should have gotten.
- My supervisor spends more time with my co-worker than she does with me.
- I got yelled at by my friend or my manager.
- My significant other forgot my birthday.
- We argued over who should do the dishes.

This list could go on forever. And for many of us, this list repeats and multiplies throughout our lives. Avoidance or not understanding the underlying source of the conflict creates RUPTURES in our relationships that in turn undermine and interfere with our needs and our goals in life. Let's take a closer look at the role and the toll of ruptures beginning in early childhood.

The Relationship Between Conflict, Rupture and Repair

In 1975, Edward Tronick and colleagues from UMass Boston's Infant-Parent Mental Health Program introduced the "Still Face Experiment" which illustrated the power of early attachment connection (Tronick et al., 1978). The experiment consisted of a mother engaging with her infant in a mutual cuing and response pattern, followed by the instructor's command which ordered the mother to make an abrupt shift in her behavior, directing her to remain non-responsive and expressionless in front of the infant.

Video observations of these interactions reflected infants trying to elicit their mothers' attention through eye contact, verbal articulations, crying, and reaching out physically. Consistently, after three minutes of the infants' failed attempts, the infants would then withdraw and orient their faces and bodies away from the mother with a hopeless facial expression. Watching videos of these infants collapse so quickly when there is a break in connection for even a short period of time is heart-breaking. It is also incredibly illuminating in terms of the power of relational attunement.

One of the conclusions drawn from this experiment was that there seemed to be a strong correlation between the baby's experienced loss of connection and an ensuing loss of their sense of "personal agency." Personal agency is having the ability to initiate, execute and control one's actions in the world. In other words, when infants are able to get their mothers to become responsive to their efforts, a sense of personal agency begins to develop. As one matures, this turns into self-esteem coupled with having a sense of confidence and optimism in relational interactions, as well as the ability to move through the world successfully.

As a second conclusion, they assumed that secure attachment patterns were the result of less frequent ruptures in connection between the parent and child. However, continued study of data collected over decades of video-taped observations revealed an even more significant discovery. In 2020, Ed Tronick and Claudia Gold published findings that essentially corrected their earlier conclusions. Secure attachments didn't appear to be created by *less frequent* ruptures between parent and infant. In fact, securely attached and non-securely attached infants and their caregivers were actually moving into states of mis-attunement on average of *70 percent* of the time. The difference was that in securely attached relationships, the parent quickly took action to repair the ruptures.

Conversely, when there was little opportunity for repair, over time those infants did not make the same efforts to reengage with the parent as contrasted with infant/parent dyads where repair was consistently forthcoming. Repeated failures of repair over time resulted in more anxious and/or withdrawn behaviors coupled with a less confident sense of self.

In the corporate world, the "Still Face" is the manager who never gives feedback, the leader who checks their phone during a one-on-one, or the executive who ignores a team's win. Just like the infant, employees eventually stop trying to engage. We call this "Quiet Quitting" (Harter, 2022). It is not laziness; it is a psychological defense mechanism against a lack of connection.

Tronick and Gold concluded that one of the ways infants and children *learn* to develop personal agency is through the process of reengagement and repair. Learning how to repair ruptures is a skill that builds over time. Much like any other skill, it takes continued practice. Reinforcement of successful repair builds hope, and it confirms that repair is possible through one's own efforts.

Ruptures, conflicts, and misunderstandings are inevitable in any relationship. The ability to observe and acknowledge a rupture and to take responsibility to move toward repair and reconciliation is a fundamental skill of being a psychological adult.

Conflict Is Inevitable, Combat Is Optional

As author Max Lucado (1993) famously observed, "Conflict is inevitable, but combat is optional." And because conflict is uncomfortable for most of us, it is not usually seen as an opportunity for growth; therefore, we tend to avoid it or react in less than productive ways.

In our work with clients, we have come to realize that when it comes to people being confronted with conflict, one of three reactions typically show up.

- *Overly Aggressive:* This reaction can show up as an angry outburst, blaming, shaming, or even rage. It's as if the person is saying with raised voice,

  "How DARE you disagree with me!" or possibly, "Look, stay in your lane. You don't know what you're talking about!"

  Or, possibly this is where *passive* aggressive behavior secretly launches a smear campaign behind your back.

- *Measured and Collaborative:* This reaction, usually shows up in psychological adults, where they seize conflict as an opportunity, a puzzle to solve, an intrigue worthy of their time, or a situation that needs their expertise to help resolve or manage it. Some enjoy the challenge of facing conflict as a way to learn and develop. In a healthy way, some behave as if to say,

  Bring it on!

- *Avoidant:* The third typical response to conflict is avoiding it. People tend to resort to avoidance for a couple of reasons. First, very few of us are trained to effectively deal with conflict. Hence, it tends to remain an unwelcomed visitor in our lives. Second, when conflict erupts, we are, at least for the moment, caught off guard.

  I just don't know what to do, so I'll just wait and see what happens.

We often are stymied because there is a lack of understanding of conflict and a lack of knowing how best to respond.

So, in order to better understand from where conflict comes, let's take a moment for a brief exercise.

> Think about a situation where you have experienced conflict. It could have been a work situation where you got into a disagreement or felt misunderstood or disrespected. Or maybe think about someone in your personal life that you care about. Perhaps that person disappointed you or hurt you. As you recall this scenario:
>
> - In what ways did you feel surprised or ambushed, and if so, what caught you off guard?
> - What did you feel like saying, but perhaps couldn't find the words to say?
> - What other emotions do you remember feeling at the time?
> - How did you react that you might possibly have regretted afterwards?
> - How did you make sense of the interaction in terms of what happened, why it happened and who was to blame?

Most conflictual situations come from one of two conditions and often both.

1 You were missing some information, you had bad information, or perhaps you had no information. We call this ***lack of clarity***.
2 The conflict caused you to feel unsafe on some level, which we call ***lack of safety***.

In the situation that you just recalled in the above exercise, were either or both of these conditions present? Perhaps you feared letting someone down, or maybe you feared that they would retaliate. Were you afraid of losing face, or were you worried you made a mistake? Sometimes lack of safety shows up as people being embarrassed, being shown up, or shamed. In some situations, they might even be worried about their physical safety. In most cases the two culprits beneath the surface of conflict are: *Lack of Safety and Lack of Clarity*.

Let's look at both separately.

The first reason conflict arises is *Lack of Clarity*. What this means is you were missing some information, you received bad or inaccurate information, or you lacked any information. When this happens, our innate need for clarity causes a form of tension that we experience as conflict. Because of the lack of information, we find ourselves saying to ourselves:

"I don't understand why this is happening!"
"Why would he act that way towards me?"
"That promotion should have been mine!"
"How is it that I got left out of that conversation?"
"She didn't call me."

We don't like not knowing or being confused about something. Aristotle is quoted as saying, "Nature abhors a vacuum." In Latin this is called, *horror vacui* or a fear of the empty implying that an empty space is scary, and it must be filled. Isn't it interesting that when we are confused about something, and we are missing some important piece of information, what happens? Because the vacuum of not knowing creates tension or stress, we fill in the missing information with our own information (assumptions) even if we don't know if it is accurate.

"Oh, she must have been in a hurry."
"I must have done something wrong."
"I bet he knew this would bother me!"
"She just doesn't like me."
"He just doesn't care about relationships."

It is almost as if we can't help ourselves. For most of us, this is an autonomic response.

The second place that conflict originates is *Lack of Safety*. This means that the conflict I am experiencing is causing me to feel emotionally and sometimes physically unsafe – unsafe as in a fear of loss of something like opportunity, recognition, love, appreciation, or even fear for our life.

When we feel a lack of safety, it sends a trigger to our brains that activates earlier memories of attachment failures (Loyalty Contracts) when safety was lacking, and we were helpless to change our environments. These triggers from the past are felt in the present. Our emotions are stimulated. But what the thinking part of our brain is telling us is coming from more of a child's memory of lack of safety and lack of options. In that moment we aren't using our full adult capacities to rationally problem solve. Once triggered, our internal self-talk might sound like:

"I can't believe he got credit for this and not me!"
"If I don't set the record straight, I won't be considered for the next promotion."

"Gosh it hurts that they think I would actually do that!"

"How could they not know it was my 10th work anniversary. My manager must not care."

One of the best things we can do when faced with conflict is to ask two simple questions.

"What's not clear?"
and
"What's not safe?"

Asking these two questions creates a pause in our reactivity and allows our adult brain to come back online. Taking this pause and inviting the other person to also take a pause to answer these two questions can change the conflict resolution playing field immediately and dramatically. When we are able to find honest and candid answers to these two pivotal questions, we make a huge leap forward in resolving or at least better managing the conflict.

Doing this resets the context for moving forward. Quite often these two questions allow solutions to emerge making the movement towards resolution much easier, sometimes faster, and usually less combative.

In Figure 4.1 we illustrate the relationship between Safety and Clarity and our various internal reactions depending on how much clarity and how much safety we have. Rather than viewing these states as static labels, view them as diagnostic zones that tell you where to focus your leadership energy:

1 **The Paralysis Zone (Low Safety/Low Clarity)**: This is the "Fight, Flight, or Freeze" basement. In this state, the brain is hijacked. A leader cannot explain their way out of this zone; they must first re-establish safety before any information can be processed.
2 **The Anxiety Zone (Low Safety/High Clarity)**: Here, the problem is understood, but the environment feels threatening. This is common in toxic cultures where an employee knows what to do but fears the consequences of doing it. The missing ingredient is psychological safety, not more data.
3 **The Confusion Zone (High Safety/Low Clarity)**: This is often a failure of communication, not intent. The relationship is strong, but the directive is vague. This is the easiest zone to fix: simply provide the missing information.
4 **The Caution Zone (Moderate Safety/Moderate Clarity)**: This is the "wait and see" middle ground. While not disastrous, staying here creates organizational or relational drag. It requires a deliberate push – either a candid conversation or a clearer directive – to move the team toward action.

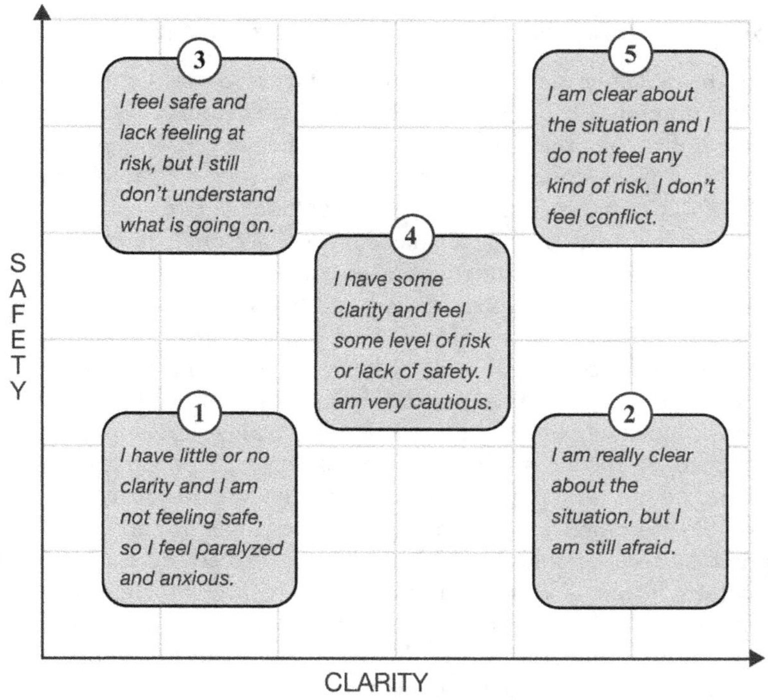

Figure 4.1 The clarity/safety conflict matrix.

5 **The Resolution Zone (High Safety/High Clarity)**: This is the target state for the Self-Differentiated Leader. Here, the two primary drivers of conflict have been neutralized, liberating energy for creativity and problem-solving rather than self-protection.

One way to achieve this level of safety and clarity is to seek outside feedback before making a move to confront the situation at hand. This could come from:

Trusted co-worker
Trusted friend
Family member
Coach
Mentor
Therapist

We have heard many stories of someone sitting next to a stranger on a flight or in a waiting room and that stranger provides an unexpected moment of clarity or safety as a result of a serendipitous conversation.

Becoming Comfortable NOT Being Comfortable

Each of the reactions experienced in the conflict scenarios described above are quite common. We often tell our coaching clients that if your goal is to remain comfortable, there is not much of a chance you will ever change. Personal and professional growth only happens when we stretch ourselves outside of our familiar comfort zone of avoidance or over-reactivity. This means that for professional advancement or personal development, at some point in the process there will be discomfort.

The most effective self-differentiated and psychologically adult leaders no longer fear or avoid discomfort. Many of them have actually come to embrace not being comfortable. They have come to realize the energy and the rewards of being comfortable with being UN-comfortable. Remember that on the other side of discomfort, there is learning, learning that cumulatively becomes the heart of self-differentiation.

The good news is there are steps you can take to gain clarity and safety by beginning to practice new behaviors. For example, if part of the sticking point in a conflictual situation is that you received bad or missing information, now you know that you need to get the information to gain greater clarity. And if you are experiencing fear or a lack of safety as you face this specific conflict, identify what those fears are. Take a pause, then seek advice, feedback, coaching, organizational support, even therapy. Each of these is an appropriate action to help you move forward.

If you feel unsafe or frustrated because you are continually left out of receiving key information that others in your organization have access to, identifying the source of your fear is a required first step to correcting the situation. Identifying that fear can also have a calming effect because it allows you to become proactive. It can enable you to ask for what you need or find ways to change the situation.

Being stimulated by lack of clarity or lack of safety is likely to be connected to a spoken or unspoken Loyalty Contract from the past. For example, a parent and child might have the kind of healthy relationship where – in general – there are no surprises and when there were, the parent intuitively saw the surprised child and addressed the rupture in a healthy caring way. This early imprinting, where someone has consistently protected us or helped us work through difficult situations doesn't leave us. We internalize that sense of safety in the form of trust in ourselves and in others, and we develop a trust that we can resolve whatever misunderstanding comes up.

Fast forward to our work years or dating years. We look for and arguably need a similar kind of relational contract from our manager, our peers, and those in our personal lives. If someone at work surprises you or leaves you out of something, you are likely to speak up and ask for what you need in order for an unhealthy contract to become a more balanced and fairer one.

Imagine if your early upbringing (Loyalty Contract) was one where your parents were inconsistent, and you were kept in the dark about why you were left out or why you didn't feel seen or appreciated. Fast forward to now when someone surprises you with a work assignment or inadvertently leaves you out of an important decision. Chances are you are likely to have a strong reaction. What makes this fascinating is that the conflict then becomes more about you and less about the other person whom you see as having left you out of the loop.

The degree to which we are able to successfully manage each and every conflict that knocks on our office door or our front door is based on our clarity about our Loyalty Contracts and our level of Self-Differentiation. What we are saying is that we need to look inward first. The key to understanding what causes our inability to effectively manage starts right here. Then, we need to choose reactions that are rooted in Self-Differentiation and Psychological Adulthood.

What Do We Mean by Friction and Flow

The concept of friction and flow comes from the science of Tribology. Very briefly, tribology attempts to understand what happens when two physical forces come into contact with each other (Bowden & Tabor, 2001).

Interestingly, the term tribology comes from the Greek "I rub" (Bhushan, 2013). So, when I say, "You rub me the wrong way." I am talking about the human side of tribology of how you and I are interacting. When things between us are good, we have flow. When one of us rubs the other the wrong way, we have friction. The more conflict, the greater the friction, which in turn creates the unease, the resistance, the emotional overload, the difficulty of getting through something.

For a leader, friction isn't just annoying; it is expensive. Every unresolved conflict, every confusing directive, and every passive-aggressive meeting is a tax on your organization's speed. "Flow" is the absence of this tax, allowing your resources to go directly into performance rather than managing resistance. Less friction allows for a more reliable and dependable flow, meaning things in general are easy or easier, less stressful, less threatening, even more enjoyable.

Friction and Flow can be likened to the difference between walking against a strong wind and walking with a strong wind at your back. Walking against the wind (friction) slows you down, pushes you backwards and can force you to change your intended course, and at times even your destination. Walking with the wind (flow) is when you feel the wind at your back nudging you, sometimes pushing you, encouraging you to move toward the direction you want to go. It aids in your movement. It propels you forward.

For this book, we use the term flow as any relational interaction that feels and is supportive of what you want or need. Flow is affirming. Flow is acknowledging who and what you are. Flow is collegial. Flow is collaborative. Flow is non-competitive. Flow feels like you have a partner at work or at home to help get you where you are trying to go and to grow into your full potential.

Think about the last year or even the last month of your life. If you could count how many times you have felt flow and how many times you have experienced friction, what would that ratio be? Try and add it up for yourself. Numbers don't lie. Look for which ones had the more frequent pattern or which ones happened more.

For flow in our work and our personal lives, we can use this simple tri-level measuring device. The key here is to have a work life and a personal life that has as a pattern or a regularity of more flow than friction.

Starting with the right half of the Figure 4.2:

- If the flow happens once, (something someone said or did that felt supportive and affirming) it could be a fluke or a one-off, but it is important to note it.
- If the flow happens a second time, it might be a coincidence. Hopefully this gets your positive and appreciative attention as you possibly say to yourself,

  "Wow, that is the second time he remembered what I needed."

  or

  "Wow, she put my needs ahead of hers."

  If the flow is healthy for you and helps you in a meaningful way, make sure you say,

  Thank you for acknowledging my input in today's meeting.

  You want to clarify what you are thankful for hoping this would become a healthy and welcomed pattern. Doing this increases the likelihood of the flow becoming a pattern, a positive one.
- If the flow happens three or more times, you more than likely have a pattern. Recognizing that this is not the first or second time something has happened is key to creating or reinforcing healthy Loyalty Contracts

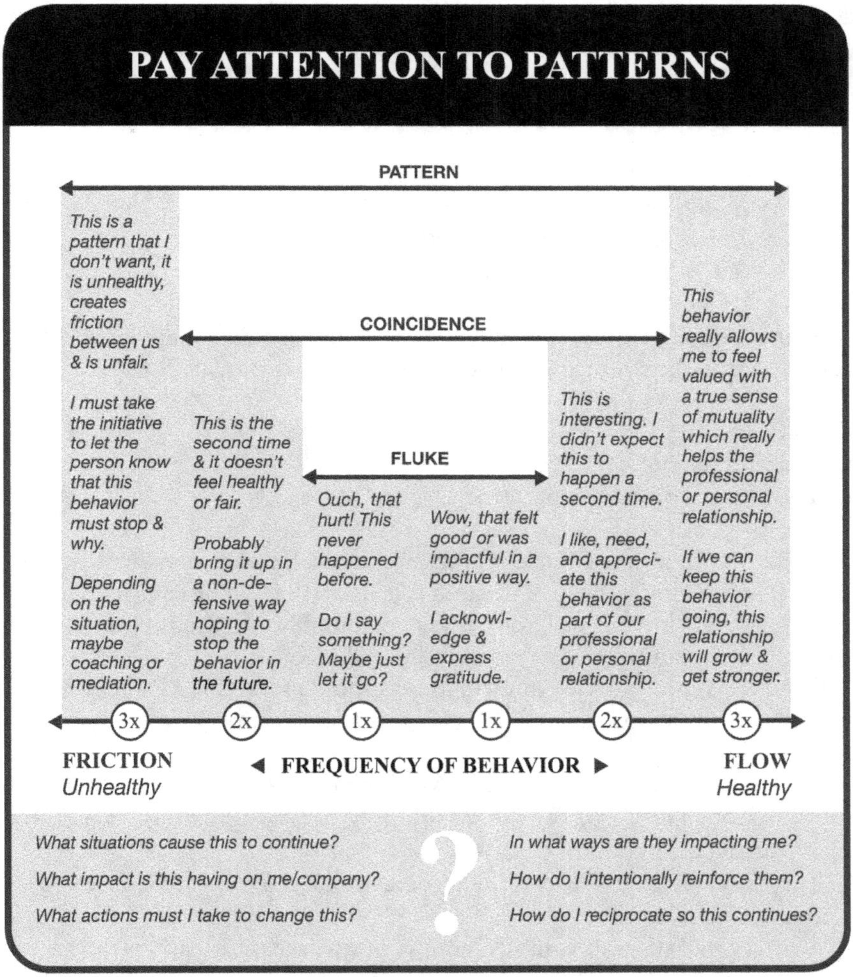

Figure 4.2 Patterns, friction, and flow continuum.

that are about fairness and mutuality. Regardless, if something creates more flow than friction, it is really important to understand the importance of an emerging or an established pattern of behavior.

If you want to reinforce flow when it shows up, let the other person know that you noticed what she did and that you are appreciative.

Shifting to the left half of the Figure 4.2, friction feels much different. Friction is anything that goes against you or moves you away from what you need or want at work or in life. Friction can show up as someone who doesn't listen to you, is overly controlling, is mean to you, minimizes your input, demeans you; and we are sure you can think of many more. Most of us recognize friction on an emotional or intuitive level, where we find ourselves saying inside,

"Ouch, that hurt!"
"Why would she react that way to me?"
"Geeze, that felt very disrespectful!"
"Oh my God, I am so embarrassed!"

Of course, none of us is immune to these kinds of things happening periodically throughout our lives. The rule of thumb is this...

- Once let it go.
- Twice take note.
- Third time you have a pattern.

For each of these, please note: judgment must be part of your discernment. If something happens once and it is a safety issue or some egregious behavior at work, you really don't have the luxury of letting it go to see if it is a pattern. You would have to act immediately.

To put this into practice immediately, simply apply this "Rule of 3" to any behavior that sparks an emotional reaction in you.

- **1x (Fluke): Pause.** Do not react. Assume positive intent or a bad day.
    - Action: Let it go. (This cannot apply to any egregious, illegal, or unsafe behavior.)
- **2x (Coincidence): Observe.** The data point has repeated. Is there a stressor causing this?
    - Action: Take note and heighten your awareness.
- **3x (Pattern): Act.** This is no longer an accident; it is an unhealthy Loyalty Contract in action.
    - Action: You must now address it using the conversation tools we will introduce in the remaining sections of this chapter.

When there is more friction than flow, it is important to remain open and curious. When you notice that the behavior causes friction falls into the category of a pattern, this is an indication that someone is not operating from a Loyalty Contract that values fairness and mutuality in relation to others. Learning how to change a Loyalty Contract is central to becoming a Self-Differentiated Leader which we delve into more deeply in Chapter 9.

Three Options for Dealing with Conflict

We have coached many people who live their lives in constant fear of conflict. They become stuck or figuratively paralyzed by fear or because they don't know what to do when faced with it. What seems to help is to clarify and refocus them on the three choices that always exist (see Figure 4.3). In every conflict situation, each of us has three choices. Accept, Terminate, or Realign. Let's examine each one.

One option we have when faced with conflict is to Accept the situation as is which can sometimes feel more like tolerate and less like acceptance. Perhaps we realize there is nothing we can do, or it doesn't feel safe to act, so we find ways to live with the situation. This option requires us to manage what we don't want or don't like because we believe there is no alternative.

To know if this is the best choice, we recommend doing a cost-benefit analysis, meaning is the cost of trying something different worth the risk? Is simply accepting a behavior you don't like a better choice than expending the energy and risking relational capital to change it? The point here is to recognize and name the situation for what it is. I can't change it so I choose to accept it. It is much like the old adage, "Pick your battles." Just make sure that you are not unknowingly letting any old unhealthy Loyalty Contracts decide your choice which then limits you in some way.

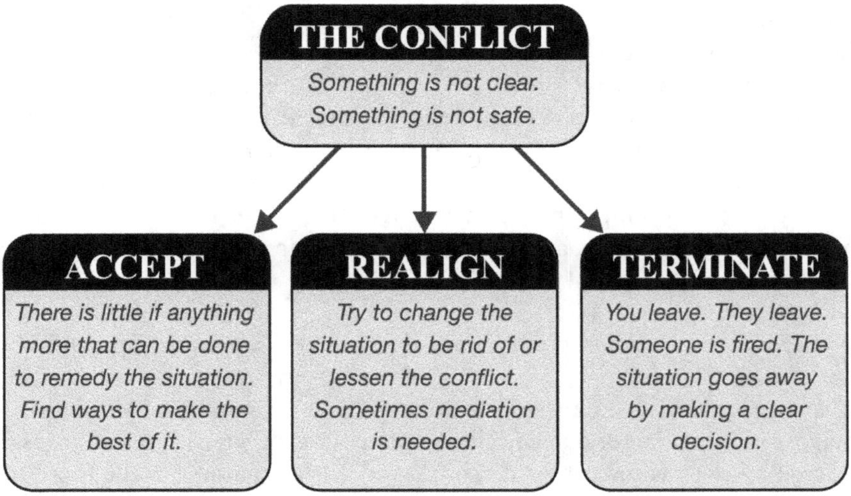

Figure 4.3 Three options for dealing with conflict.

The second option is to **Terminate,** meaning get rid of the conflict or extricate yourself from the conflict. This could mean firing someone, or you might quit or get a divorce, or find another way to remove yourself. In this scenario you might believe that there is no use in continuing to fight or deal with the conflict for a variety of reasons. The personal or professional cost of staying has become too high or too toxic. This option can feel awkward or painful in that termination of any kind is disruptive, potentially hurtful, and will require major change.

There are times when a person delays the decision to Terminate because in their mind, they see this as giving up or that they have failed in some way. However, if there is no effort to accommodate a healthier exchange on either person's part, sometimes Terminate is the very best choice you can make. And leaving doesn't need to be equated with failure on your part. In fact, it could end up being one of the more important lessons in your life.

In both options above, there is a level of avoidance that is at play. But let's be clear, not all avoidance is bad or unhealthy. Avoidance is a critical life skill that keeps us safe, keeps us within the framework of the law, and has a positive role to play. Having said this, avoidance becomes detrimental and creates even more friction if we avoid conflict for the wrong reasons. We might be afraid to deal with an important issue presenting itself as conflict because our old Loyalty Contract is telling us,

I am not worthy of something different, something better.

This might be an indication that it is time to take a leap into action that represents self-advocacy rather than obedience or subservience. It is important to be able to know the difference.

Another unhealthy reason we delay taking action might be that we are trying to convince ourselves into believing that if I leave it alone, it will go away. There are times when this is true, particularly if there is a minor disagreement, a difference of opinion that doesn't compromise our values, or if a person is simply having a bad day. However, if the conflict has any degree of substance, a foundational leadership principle that we have taught is:

Pay now or pay later. If you pay later, in most cases you will pay more.

The damage that avoidance creates is that often a small problem inevitably turns into a larger one with the ancillary cost of higher anxiety or loss of credibility to your own leadership. More often than not, if the topic is important, the time to deal with it is now.

The third option is to try and **Realign** the situation, meaning to make it better. And to make it better requires a form of "negotiation" between the people involved. This could mean taking a step toward repair by saying you are sorry, or asking to talk the situation through, or even resetting the expectations of the work or personal relationship.

Here we hold a sense of hope that things can and will actually change for the better. We hope for a greater sense of mutuality or fairness and more flow. For this to actually happen, however, all parties (stakeholders) have to want the situation or conditions to change. There needs to be a willingness to do something different going forward.

An Investment Metaphor: To apply these three options in the boardroom, conference room, lunch room, or at the dinner table, view these three options as relationship investment opportunities. Just as you manage financial assets, you must manage relational assets based on what will help the company, the team or the relationship. Put another way, it is relational return on investment or RROI.

- **Realigning** is an investment in growth; you spend time to get a higher return.
- **Terminating** is a stop-loss measure; you divest to protect the longer view.
- **Accepting** is a calculated hedge; you acknowledge the cost but decide the dynamic is currently necessary for stability.

The Self-Differentiated Leader never confuses these three options; they consciously choose one, switch to another when it makes sense to do so, and they own the outcome.

We find that the relatively straightforward process of realigning a relationship or repairing a conflict situation can easily be thwarted when one of the parties involved thinks they have more to lose than gain by making a change. If any stakeholder is invested in keeping things the same and is not willing to change, the option of realignment cannot happen without force. And rarely is forced realignment sustainable. This recalcitrant stance is a form of cancer in the workplace and relationships, the source of much friction and even relationship destruction or organizational dysfunction.

The important thing to keep in mind here is that in each of these three options, our Loyalty Contracts and our level of Self-Differentiation will show up. It is important to ask yourself the following questions.

- If I decide to tolerate something, is doing so rooted in a healthy or unhealthy contract?
- If I choose to Terminate, is this a result of over-reactivity due to my lack of or my need for more Self-Differentiation?

- When I decide to Realign, am I seeing clearly that there is real possibility for change or am I stuck in thinking "this time things will change"?

Having these three distinct options when dealing with conflict can help clear our mind and lessen our confusion or sense of feeling overwhelmed as we search for doing the right and healthy thing.

Knowing When to Walk Away

There are times when no intervention strategy is capable of changing the situation. These are generally situations where an individual holds onto beliefs or behaviors so rigidly that asking for any modifications in their behavior will simply not work.

It is as if no matter what is suggested, no matter what facts are given, there seems to be an impenetrability in the individual and no new information can get through. The person's belief system is so rigid, their insistence on being right is so strong, that no adjustment in the behaviors or beliefs can be made.

Often, this impenetrability is coupled with an air of self-righteous superiority or indignation. These individuals might actually believe they're in the right, trying to help an organization. However, they have difficulty looking at the fact that *how they are coming across* might be part of the problem. Or, they simply don't care.

There are several indicators that a situation might not be fixable.

- A lack of curiosity with regard to considering new information or another person's point of view.
- An impatience or irritation with being asked to compromise or change their approach even in small ways.
- A smugness and sense of self-righteous superiority, conveying that they know better or know more.
- When given factual information that attempts to explain or correct misinformation, they insist that their version of "the truth" is the correct one.
- An inability to hold the complexity of multiple factors simultaneously – mistaking a part of the situation for the whole situation.
- An inability to forgive, even when an apology is offered.
- Pushing the limits to get their own way – ignoring sanctions or warnings, insisting on special treatment.
- Seeing things in all or nothing terms.
- Being easily wounded and seeking revenge when crossed.
- Accusing others with an inability to take ownership for any part of the problem.

When you recognize that any one of the above indicators is at play, you are faced with a more complex situation. The more indicators you identify that are at play with the individual in question, the less likely there is a chance of reconciliation or change.

In what we believe is a seminal leadership book *A Failure of Nerve*, Edwin Friedman states,

> *The colossal misunderstanding of our time is that insight will work with people who are unmotivated to change.*
>
> (2007)

Organizations waste time and precious resources in trying to "coach" individuals who have no interest in changing their behavior. In business, we call this "uncoachable." If an employee cannot receive feedback without defensive armor, they become a liability to the team's psychological safety. Continuing to invest resources in them is often a failure of leadership courage, not a failure of patience.

And when it comes to personal relationships, the same holds true. We all too often think "This time it will be different" or "Someday they will change." Make sure there are firm accountability structures in place, with time limits and measurements that indicate change is imperative. Although terminating a relationship is difficult, not doing so creates costs to individuals, organizations, and their culture. Knowing when to Terminate a toxic relationship is a sign of your own self-respect.

Chapter Summary

With the ever-increasing challenges inherent in our workplaces, our personal relationships, our respective societies, and the continual information-overloaded, AI-confused, resource-stretched, and politically divergent world that we all share, it is inevitable that friction will show up regularly. No one is immune.

We know that pretending friction, co-mingled with mistrust and fear, doesn't exist or that it will magically disappear is an idyllic but unreal thought. It is also a fantasy that leads to organizational or personal ineffectiveness and the dehydration of the spirit. We are inviting you to no longer fight the friction or run from it. We invite you to recognize and use its value.

The more we normalize the idea of conflict as an inevitable visitor to our work and personal lives, the better able we will be at living with less stress, being less afraid, and making small and large strides towards confronting unhealthy relationships. A smooth-running automobile engine has lots of metal-against-metal moving parts. The power from those moving parts is made possible by the lubrication in between these moving parts. The skills we have shared with you in this chapter is the lubrication you need when friction flares up at work or at home.

When we decide to be intentional and committed to creating something better for ourselves, we can transform the unhealthy or limiting Loyalty Contracts that don't serve us well. This takes conscious effort, patience, and perseverance. But the good news is that change is possible if we collectively work to communicate without retaliation, punishment, or blame. Respond first with genuine curiosity, compassion, and perhaps most importantly, courage. Crossing the threshold of fear is always a wiser and more courageous you!

Listening is the first step towards expanding our understanding, giving us greater clarity around options for negotiation. Being listened to and understood is a powerful balm when it comes to repairing ruptures in a conflict resolution process. Being understood is being seen – one of the two basic needs we all require in order to thrive and engage in efforts that lead to creating meaningful lives and healthy work environments.

When leaders realize the power that they have in repairing unhealthy childhood contracts by creating fair and equitable contracts at work, they sow the seeds of transforming work, home, and their soul.

Key Takeaways

1 Self-Differentiation, Loyalty Contracts, becoming a psychological adult and the importance of leading an integrated life collectively form the cornerstone of highly effective leadership at work and at home.
2 Conflict is at the root of all friction and flow. Conflict is neutral. It's what we do with it that matters.
3 Beneath the surface of conflict are *Lack of Safety and Lack of Clarity.*
4 Nowhere does our ability to show up as a psychological adult gets challenged more than when we are confronted by adversity, difference of opinion, disappointment, sabotage, or betrayal.
5 When there is more friction than flow at work or in our personal life, usually avoidance is not an option. Avoidance is a debt. When we delay taking steps to resolve conflict, usually friction in the workplace or at home increases.

Next Level Reflections

1 Where in your work and personal lives do you experience more friction than flow? Try to be specific about the circumstances where they exist.
2 How much of the "Friction" in your life is a pattern?
3 Try to imagine small changes that you could make in your work or personal life that could eliminate friction and create more patterns of "Flow".
4 When it comes to the patterns in your life, keep, change, or jettison them. Those are your three choices – always.
5 How do the areas of your life impact the effectiveness of your leadership? Impact your happiness?

Postscript

If you recall, we received feedback from readers from all seven continents who read various chapters providing independent, constructive comments about the book's content. These global voices informed and shaped how this book evolved.

We would like to share with you Isabel Jeha's feedback from Brazil after she read this Chapter 4.

> *Finishing your chapter on rupture and repair left me with a sense of hope. If friction is inevitable – in families, in work teams, in politics, in love – then what differentiates healthy systems and healthy leaders is not the absence of friction, but how they use it.*
>
> *I loved the metaphor you offer about engines and metals: how rubbing, when managed with care and the right conditions, can actually reduce resistance and create flow. That feels deeply true. Some degree of friction will always be part of human relationships, but it doesn't have to be corrosive; it can become a force that polishes, aligns, and strengthens people and structures.*
>
> *This has made me reflect on what kind of leader I want to be, and what kind of environments I want to help nurture. Because if friction is a given, then the real work – the transformative work – lies in learning to meet it with clarity, care, emotional presence, and the willingness to repair. These qualities are exactly what differentiate leaders who perpetuate cycles of fear and pressure from those who cultivate trust, growth, and creativity.*

Even in the political environment in which I work, where the pressures are immense and the stakes are high, I can see glimpses of this possibility. I can sense how things can be if emotional safety is taken seriously; how "love as a political practice" becomes much more powerful when it's not just an external message but an internal reality.

And although I don't know exactly how my path will unfold from here. Whether or not I will continue in this job long-term or eventually terminate this chapter, I do know that I am more equipped than ever to recognize what alignment feels like, what realignments require, and when termination becomes an act of self-respect rather than failure.

Your writing reminded me that conflict itself is not the enemy. What matters is the system around it – the willingness to repair, to listen, to stay curious, to hold space for discomfort, and to move toward understanding rather than away from it. If these capacities are nurtured, friction can become something that produces movement, coherence, and even beauty. That possibility gives me courage. It gives me direction.

And it gives me a quiet, steady hope for the kinds of relationships – and kinds of politics – that I still believe we can build.

Thank you!

Isabel

Isabel wisely notes that often, "what matters is the system around it." This observation leads us directly to our next frontier. We cannot fully understand the friction between two individuals until we understand the invisible water we all swim in, the largest system of all: Culture. As we turn the page, we explore how our diverse cultural backgrounds write the rules of engagement, and how a Self-Differentiated Leader navigates them.

Chapter 5

Understanding Cultural Norms

Culture plays a leading role in shaping a person's ability to lead effectively as a self-differentiated person because it influences values, communication styles, emotional expression, and perceptions of authority. Culture, alongside our early Loyalty Contracts, tends to predispose us to certain ways of behaving and interacting with people at work and at home.

This chapter explores how cultural norms influence Loyalty Contracts and Self-Differentiation. And it also provides instruction on how to navigate these influences effectively. Here, we define cultural norms as the *unwritten rules that guide behaviors, decisions, and interactions that are considered acceptable within a given group or society* (Gelfand & Jackson, 2016). These norms are often reinforced from early childhood through family, education, and broader societal interactions. It is closely tied to a society's perception of Power Distance – the extent to which authority is distributed equally or unequally – and other cultural dimensions, shaping how individuals perceive authority, and relationships. Therefore, it influences and shapes Loyalty Contracts and Self-Differentiation.

Culture influences society in the same way memory influences an individual (Kluckhohn, 2017). Both culture and memory serve as a roadmap from the past, guiding the present actions of people and groups. Culture acts as a society's collective memory, profoundly shaping its members psychological landscape and behaviors (Triandis & Gelfand, 2012).

We begin with several stories because it is through our stories that we can best capture the tension that arises when our own personal desires clash with our past circumstances (Loyalty Contracts). When this difference is stark, the challenge of rupture and repair emerges. We will explore these dynamics by first defining the key cultural dimensions of Power Distance and Individualism vs Collectivism.

We will then examine how these forces shape our earliest family Loyalty Contracts and ripple outward, impacting critical areas like organizational

DOI: 10.4324/9781003621393-5

safety in aviation and healthcare. To conclude, we will examine powerful case studies of leaders who not only reshaped corporate cultures but also broke through rigid societal expectations to redefine leadership. Finally, we will explore how modern technology is creating new ways to flatten traditional hierarchies and support the journey toward becoming a psychological adult.

The Chef's Dilemma: When Passion Clashes with Tradition

Let us begin with Ann Kim, a James Beard Award-winning chef in Minneapolis, Minnesota, who immigrated from South Korea. After graduating from Columbia University in New York, she pursued her passion for acting for years. However, she hid this from her parents, knowing they wouldn't approve. During an interview, she described their reaction when they eventually found out.

> *I remember sitting in the living room. My mother was crying. I could see the disappointment in my father's face. There was a certain panic, like "How dare you? We came to this country. We sacrificed everything for you. And you're throwing it all away." They told me I was a disgrace. And the profession I chose [theatre actor] was no different from being a whore. And that they'd disown me.*
>
> (Gelb & McGinn, 2022)

Then there is Yoshihiro Imai, an innovative pizza chef in Kyoto, Japan, who had to face strong opposition from his parents when he decided to be a chef rather than following his father and grandfather's footsteps to become a dentist. In Japanese society, the oldest son is expected to continue the family business. Yoshihiro explains,

> "*I thought if I followed in their footsteps, it would make my parents happy.*
>
> *However, in my heart I knew I wanted something different. When I decided to become a chef,*
>
> *I called my parents, and basically that was that.*" His mother's response to him was,
>
> "*Have you lost your mind? A restaurant is where we go to get food, not to serve food.*"

His mother couldn't understand why he chose that path. His father also felt worried. Yoshihiro summarized his dilemma by saying, "Well, they were fiercely opposed." (Gelb & Shiraki, 2022).

In 2022, Netflix launched a special documentary series called "Chef's Table: Pizza," featuring six chefs from around the world: Americans Chris Bianco (Phoenix, Arizona) and Sarah Minnick (Portland, Oregon); Italians Gabriele Bonci and Franco Pepe; and Korean American Ann Kim and Japanese Yoshihiro Imai.

Interestingly, the episodes featuring the two Asian chefs highlighted their struggles with parental expectations regarding their career choices, as described earlier. But what about the American chefs? While Chris Bianco's father was reportedly disappointed when he dropped out of high school, there was no mention of parental objections to their eventual career paths (Gelb & Weaver, 2022).

The Italian chefs presented a contrasting case. When Franco Pepe chose to develop his own pizza style rather than following his father's traditional methods, his family initially felt betrayed (Gelb & Hall, 2022). However, they eventually reconciled, and Pepe now encourages his own son to forge his own path in the family business.

For a global leader, this isn't just a family drama; it's a talent retention risk. If your corporate culture mirrors the rigid unhealthy Loyalty Contract of these parents, where obedience is valued over innovation, you will lose your most creative talent (your Chefs) to competitors who allow them to experiment. The cost is not just a lost employee; it is lost future market share.

While these specific stories from the United States, Italy, Japan, and Korea provide a clear and powerful illustration of this cultural tension, they are illustrative, not exhaustive. The fundamental dynamic, the interplay between Power Distance, loyalty to family/parents and an individual's drive for Self-Differentiation is a universal human theme that plays out in distinct ways across the globe.

A leader in Lagos, Nigeria, for instance, navigates a complex Loyalty Contract built on deep communal respect and hierarchical traditions that differs significantly from one in Sao Paulo, Brazil, where a vibrant mix of collectivism and personal expression shapes professional authority. Likewise, the powerful emphasis on family honor and hospitality in Middle Eastern cultures creates its own unique set of unwritten rules. We encourage you to use the Loyalty Contract and Self-Differentiation framework as a lens to examine the specific, unspoken expectations within your own cultural, familial, and organizational setting not necessarily to change them but to better understand how they impact or even pre-determine your own behaviors.

Understanding the Cultural Framework: Power Distance and Individualism vs Collectivism

While this Netflix documentary might not fully represent each culture, it suggests that parental expectations and pressure are more pronounced in

East Asian cultures. This relates to the concept of *Power Distance*. The term was defined as "the extent to which the less powerful members of organizations and institutions (like the family) accept and expect that power is distributed unequally." In the low Power Distance culture, parents treat children as equals while in high Power Distance culture, parents teach children obedience (Hofstede, 2011).

Beyond Power Distance, another critical cultural dimension is *individualism versus collectivism*. Individualistic cultures, such as those in North America and Western Europe, prioritize the "I" – personal goals, privacy, and speaking one's mind. In contrast, collectivistic cultures found in many parts of Africa, Asia, Latin America, emphasize the "We" group harmony, belonging, and interdependence (Hofstede, 2011).

While these distinctions are a useful starting point, recent data reveals a more complex picture. As shown in Figure 5.1, based on the latest research (Minkov et al., 2017; The Culture Factor Group, n.d.-a), the individualism scores for Japan (62), South Korea (58), and the U.S. (60) are surprisingly similar.

This represents a dramatic shift from the "legacy" data, where the U.S. scored 91, Japan 46, and South Korea a mere 18 (The Culture Factor Group, n.d.-b). These changes reflect not only methodological revisions but also significant societal shifts, such as changing family structures – Japan and South Korea have the world's lowest birth rates (McCurry, 2024; Takahara, 2024) – and evolving generational values.

Both Eastern and Western cultures show trending patterns of disharmony that we believe is moving the world toward disillusionment and apathy. While they might manifest differently culture by culture, symptoms of distress basically stem from a lack of mutuality within individual and cultural Loyalty Contracts.

For example, South Korea, a nation that emphasizes the importance of obedience to authority and respect for the collective as a cultural Loyalty Contract, has one of the highest suicide rates of young people in the world (World Health Organization, 2021). The shadow side of this contract is that the self is often crushed by the weight of the expectations of others.

The United States on the other hand, a country that still views itself as a "global superpower", has a cultural Loyalty Contract based on the over-emphasis on independence and personal freedom. One can only wonder how this might be connected to the US being a statistical outlier among wealthy nations regarding violence. According to the 2025 Global Peace Index, the United States ranks 128th out of 163 countries – falling behind nearly every other developed nation and sitting in the "Low Peace" category alongside countries with significant instability (Institute

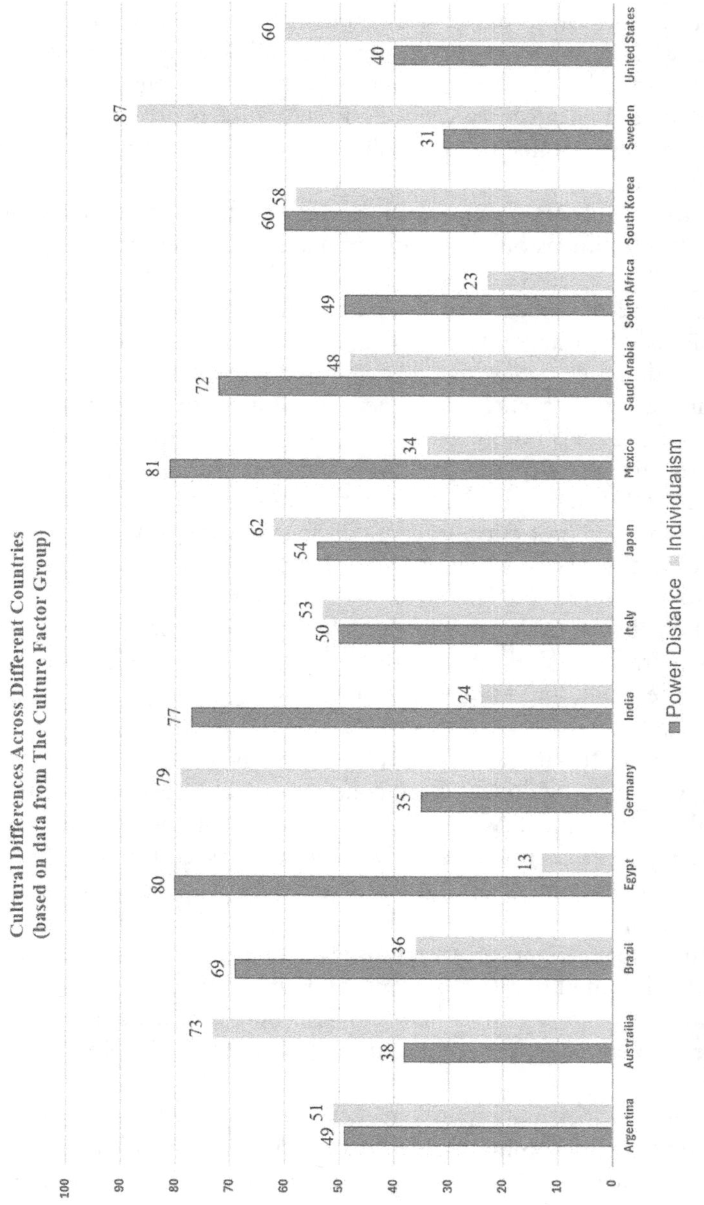

Figure 5.1 Cultural Differences Across Different Countries (based on data from The Culture Factor Group)

for Economics & Peace, 2025). When the contract prioritizes the individual over the whole, the social fabric begins to tear.

Both of these cultural examples illustrate the long-term toll that a lack of mutuality has on its citizens. Imagine if this trajectory continued, what the potential consequences would be for us all. We believe the concepts in this book provide clear and actionable options to potentially and dramatically change the trajectory we are all on. While as professionals it is not our nature to be fatalistic, we would be irresponsible if not foolish not to be concerned.

The stories of chefs Ann Kim and Yoshihiro Imai perfectly illustrate how these cultural dimensions play out often across a generational divide.

- Individualism-Collectivism explains the "Why": This dimension explains why the conflict occurred. The parents held traditionally collectivistic values, viewing their children's careers through the lens of family duty. The chefs, however, chose a more individualistic ethic, prioritizing their unique passions over parental expectations.
- Power Distance explains the "How": Power Distance (Japan: 54, South Korea: 50, US: 40) explains how the conflict unfolded. Their parents' reactions were not curious. They did not have two-way conversations; instead, they issued one-way commands fueled by disappointment. ("How dare you?", "Have you lost your mind?"). For the chefs, raised in high Power Distance cultures, this was not just a disagreement; it was a transgression against authority that triggered deep feelings of pressure, guilt, and even rejection.

Understanding the impact of culture is crucial in today's interconnected world, where individuals often collaborate with people from diverse cultural backgrounds. Whether managing multinational teams, coaching international clients, or simply working with colleagues from different cultures, awareness of cultural differences is essential for successful collaboration.

Cultural norms operate at various level – national, organizational, and familial – shaping Loyalty Contracts and influencing Self-Differentiation. The following figure shows how cultural norms and Loyalty Contracts can be linked to three different stages of Self-Differentiation (see Figure 5.2).

Becoming a Self-Differentiated Leader requires us to examine the unspoken rules we inherited from our culture. In cultures with high Power Distance, for example, respecting hierarchy is a foundational rule. This can lead us to passively accept unequal relationships and unhealthy Loyalty Contracts out of a sense of duty to authority. The goal is to move from unconscious acceptance to conscious choice. The Quid Pro Quo formula introduced in Chapter 1 helps us map the emotional past. We can

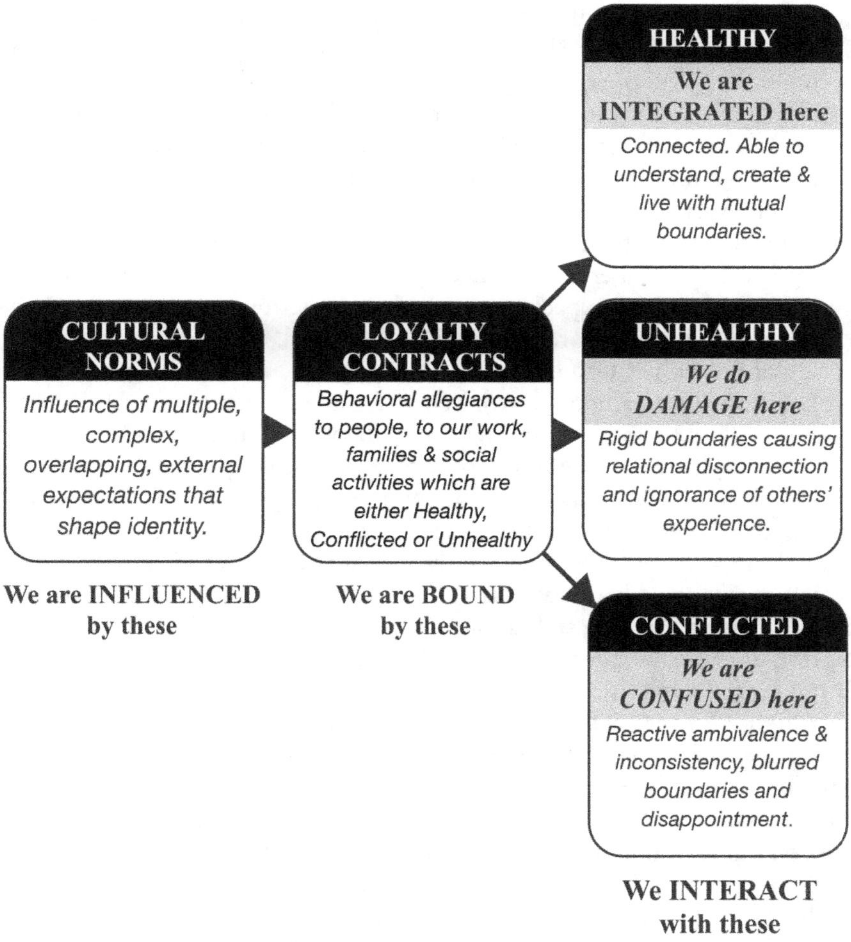

Figure 5.2 Cultural norms, Loyalty Contracts, and Self-Differentiation.

reject reactive patterns, negotiate healthier Loyalty Contracts and establish choiceful boundaries, which enable us to remain connected to others without losing ourselves (Bushe, 2001a, 2001b). And the capacity to not lose one's sense of self and personal desires in the workplace and home is how one self-differentiates into Psychological Adulthood.

Power Distance, the Most Important Cultural Norm for Loyalty Contracts and Self-Differentiation

At its core, a Loyalty Contract reflects the distribution of power in a relationship, which can range from a shared agreement to forced compliance.

When the contract is unfair and one party is forced to comply, then Self-Differentiation and the choice to move into Psychological Adulthood becomes a process of reclaiming your own power within that dynamic.

Accordingly, the most important cultural dimension to consider is Power Distance. If you lead, manage, live in another country, or coach a client from a different culture, understanding how Power Distance manifests will be crucial.

According to Hofstede (2011), Power Distance is the extent to which less powerful members of families, schools, organizations, and communities accept and expect unequal power distribution. Higher Power Distance cultures are more hierarchical. As noted above, Hofstede's data (The Culture Factor Group, n.d.-a) shows that the U.S. (40) has the lowest Power Distance among the four countries mentioned previously. South Korea (60) has the highest, followed by Japan (54) and Italy (50).

Interestingly, Northern Italy prefers more equal power distribution than Southern Italy, making the latter more hierarchical. Franco Pepe, who spoke about family expectations, is from Caiazzo in Central Italy, but culturally closer to Southern Italy. Nisbett, a pioneer in cross-cultural social cognition, also found that Southern Italians, unlike Northern Italians, have a thinking style similar to the Chinese (Lee, 2017). Globally, North America, Northern Europe, and Oceania exhibit the lowest Power Distance, followed by South America, then Europe, Africa, and Asia.

In higher Power Distance societies, Self-Differentiation is more challenging because less powerful members are more accustomed to accepting unequal power distribution. This tendency can lead to violations of the fairness requirements in healthy Loyalty Contracts and reinforce the sacrifice conditions found in unhealthy Loyalty Contracts.

It is important to note that each cultural dimension has its own strengths. High Power Distance cultures, for example, often excel at creating social order, clarity in roles and respect for generational experience. Conversely, low Power Distance cultures often thrive on innovation and agility, creating environments where open dialogue is encouraged, and the best ideas can surface regardless of the speaker's rank. The challenges arise not from hierarchy itself, but when it becomes rigid and prevents necessary communication, reasonable autonomy, or personal growth.

When Culture Impacts Safety: From the Cockpit to the Operating Room

In extreme cases, unhealthy Loyalty Contracts associated with high Power Distance can have fatal consequences. Malcolm Gladwell's "Cockpit Culture Theory," based on airline crash data from the late 1990s, illustrates this point. In an interview with *The Atlantic* (Ohlheiser, 2013), he stated:

> *Korean Air had more plane crashes than almost any other airline in the world for a period at the end of the 1990s. When we think of airline crashes, we think, oh, they must have had old planes. They must have had badly trained pilots. No. What they were struggling with was a cultural legacy, that Korean culture is hierarchical. You are obliged to be deferential toward your elders and superiors in a way that would be unimaginable in the U.S.*
>
> *But Boeing and Airbus design modern, complex airplanes to be flown by two equals. That works beautifully in low-power-distance cultures [like the U.S., where hierarchies aren't as prevalent]. But in cultures that have high power distance, it's very difficult.*

In business terms, we call this The Silence Tax. In high power-distance cultures (or companies), silence is expensive. The Tax you pay is hidden risks, covered-up mistakes (like the VW emissions scandal which we will discuss later in this chapter), and preventable accidents. As a leader, your job is to lower this tax by artificially lowering the Power Distance during critical feedback sessions, making it cheaper for your team to tell you the truth than to hide it.

Gladwell's analysis wasn't just a critique; it was a diagnosis of a communication breakdown. The solution came when David Greenberg, a former Delta Air Lines executive brought in to run Korean Air's flight operations, instituted a radical protocol: He mandated that English be the language of the cockpit (Kirk, 2002).

Greenberg didn't do this just because English is the language of aviation. As Gladwell (2008) notes, English served as an "alternate identity." It allowed pilots to step out of their rigid cultural roles and speak as professional equals, free from the hierarchical baggage of Korean honorifics. This shift didn't just change how they spoke; it changed how they thought.

Even in lower Power Distance societies like the U.S., some organizations can exhibit high Power Distance in certain areas. For example, after the fatal Boeing 737 Max crashes in 2018 and 2019, Boeing's safety culture, particularly after its merger with McDonnell Douglas, came under scrutiny. Former and current employees reported being unable to speak up about safety concerns due to fears of being ignored or facing retaliation (Chokshi et al., 2024; Godlewski, 2024; Isidore, 2024; Kennedy, 2022; Kim, 2022; Picchi, 2024). This raises questions about the quality of communication and recognition between management and employees, especially engineers.

As Edgar Schein argued (2010), real corporate culture is not so much about artifacts or espoused values, but about underlying assumptions. The *Quid Pro Quo* of Loyalty Contracts we introduced in Chapter 1 is a useful tool for uncovering these assumptions. Figure 5.3 illustrates a dangerous underlying assumption in a manufacturing context. Here, the *Quid* (the

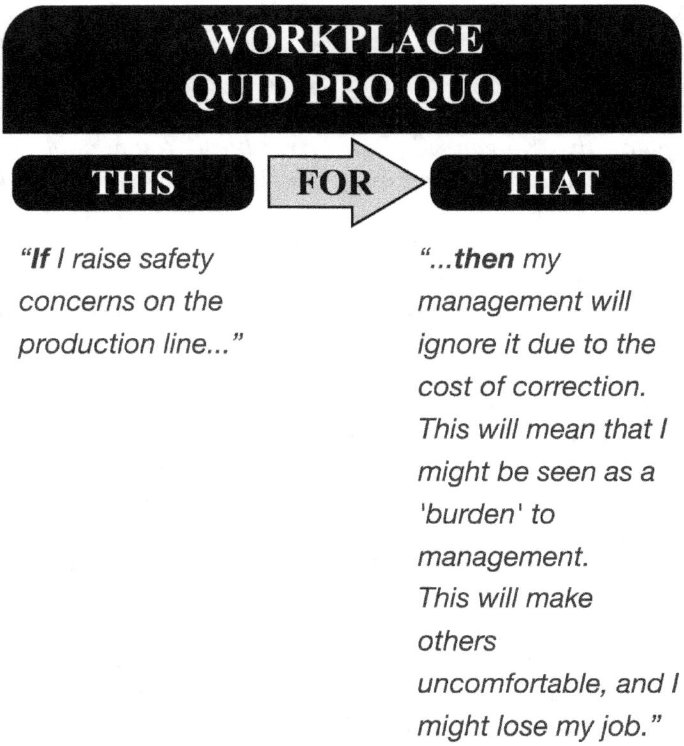

Figure 5.3 Quid Pro Quo – Workplace 1.

action) is raising a safety concern, but the employee's internalized *Quo* (the consequence) is not gratitude, but fear of being labeled a "burden" or losing their job.

Self-Differentiated Leaders who genuinely want to understand their employees' reality can use this framework to audit their culture. For example, using an anonymous survey, leaders can provide a specific *Quid* prompt (e.g., "If I challenge my manager's idea in a meeting...") and ask employees to honestly fill in the *Pro Quo* (e.g., "...then I will be labeled as difficult and sidelined"). This reveals the invisible rules that are actually driving behavior.

A similar principle applies in other high-stakes environments, particularly in medicine, where team communication can be a matter of life and death. Edmondson's research on 16 medical operating room teams found that "team leader coaching, ease of speaking up, and boundary spanning" were crucial for the successful implementation of new cardiac surgery technology (Edmondson, 2003).

Imagine a scenario where a new surgical technique, like robotic-assisted surgery, is introduced. Team leader coaching in this context means the leader actively builds a learning space where anyone can ask questions to increase the level of understanding. This often involves pre-op briefings where the leader makes it clear that everyone is on a learning curve, so asking "dumb" questions is encouraged, not punished. This fosters a sense of shared learning and cuts down on mistakes.

Ease of speaking is all about making sure everyone feels safe to voice their concerns, share ideas, or even question assumptions. For instance, if someone notices a potential equipment glitch, even if they're not sure, they should feel comfortable saying something. The team leader should welcome this and check it out, preventing small problems from becoming big ones.

And then there's "boundary spanning," which is simply good communication between all the different experts in the room. When everyone shares information and talks about potential issues, you avoid errors caused by miscommunication between different specialists.

These factors are essential elements of psychological safety, which allow members of an organization to feel safe in exchanging feedback and ideas, offering help, taking risks, and experimenting collaboratively (Edmondson, 1999).

Corporate Culture: When Power Distance Silences Ethics

In 2015, the automotive world was rocked by the "Dieselgate" scandal. The Environmental Protection Agency (EPA) in the US discovered that Volkswagen had installed software in millions of diesel vehicles designed to cheat emissions tests. The software was able to detect when the car was being tested and temporarily reduced emissions to meet legal standards, only to switch back to high pollution modes during normal driving.

How could a company renowned for German engineering excellence allow such a massive ethical breach? The answer lies not in a lack of technical skill, but in a toxic culture of high Power Distance.

Under the leadership of then-CEO Martin Winterkorn, Volkswagen was driven by an ambitious goal: To overtake Toyota as the world's largest carmaker. Winterkorn was known for a leadership style that demanded perfection and did not tolerate failure. He was described by insiders as an exacting authoritarian who created a culture of fear.

In this high stakes, high Power Distance environment, the engineers faced an impossible technical challenge: creating a diesel engine that was powerful, fuel-efficient, and clean enough to pass strict U.S emissions standards – all within a limited budget.

When the engineers realized the physics didn't add up, they couldn't manage up. The Loyalty Contract at VW then was rigid and unhealthy: Loyalty meant delivering the target, no matter how. To admit that the goal was impossible was to admit incompetence, which, in that culture, was professional suicide.

The engineers didn't cheat because they were inherently corrupt; they cheated because the cost of telling the truth to a high Power Distance leader was too high. They chose to protect the hierarchy and their jobs rather than the company's integrity.

The VW Loyalty Contract at the Time (Quid Pro Quo)

We can map the unhealthy agreement that governed the VW engineers at that time using our Quid Pro Quo framework (see Figure 5.4).

This disaster illustrates that when Power Distance is too high, it severs the feedback loop between the engine room and the boardroom. The

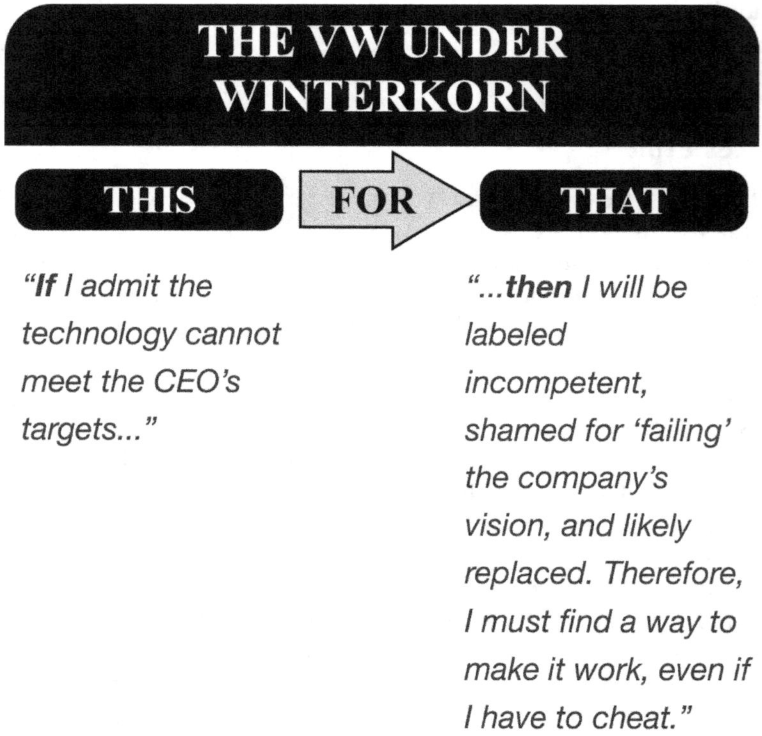

Figure 5.4 Quid Pro Quo – VW Under Winterkorn.

leaders at the top set the vision. But because they had created an environment where "no" was not an acceptable answer, they were shielded from the reality of what their demands required. The result was $30 billion in fines and settlements and a tarnished reputation, a catastrophic price to pay for an unhealthy Loyalty Contract. (Cavico & Mujtaba, 2016; Edmondson, 2018; Ewing, 2017; Ordóñez & Welsh, 2015; Rhodes, 2016).

As a footnote: Immediately after the scandal broke in 2015, Mr. Winterkorn resigned as CEO, taking responsibility for the crisis, yet denied wrong-doing. In September, 2024, Mr. Winterkorn's German trial was suspended after suffering an accident which deemed him unfit to stand trial. As of late 2025, the proceedings remain on hold.

Renegotiating Your Inner Script: A Framework for Self-Differentiation

Jieun was raised in a hierarchical society. One of her parents' mottos, especially her mother's, was well reflected in a Korean proverb:

There is nothing wrong with what adults say.

Whenever she felt uncomfortable with something her parents said or did and she tried to speak up, their response was,

Do you think I'd do that to hurt you?

Jieun's parents never asked what made her uncomfortable. Her childhood survival strategy was to be a "good girl" according to her parents' definition, without having the opportunity to develop her own. She was praised by her parents in front of others for being a good "errand girl" who always obeyed their orders. Her Loyalty Contract in early childhood can be summarized in the following *Quid Pro Quo* example (see Figures 5.5 and 5.6):

Of course, no parents are perfect. Many people carry some form of unhealthy Loyalty Contract from their childhood. Her mistake was not being aware of the specific Loyalty Contract she had internalized and how it influenced her adult relationships and leadership behaviors.

When she first became a manager of a small team, and even later as a corporate executive, she equated "good management" and "good leadership" with being nice, praising, and pleasing those around her. She didn't consider how to give constructive feedback or address areas needing improvement in her team members to avoid any conflict.

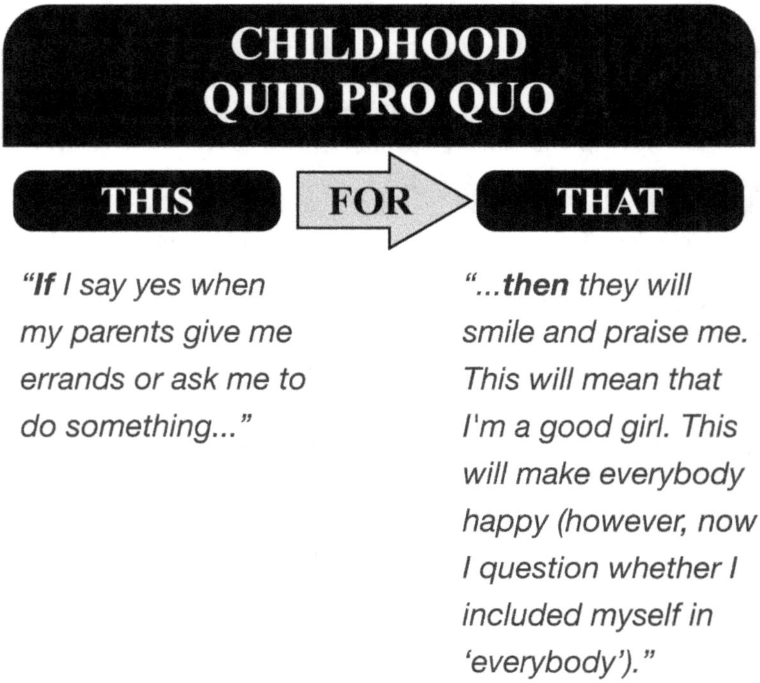

Figure 5.5 Quid Pro Quo – Childhood 1.

In her mid-30s, she had her first executive coach. After qualitative and quantitative assessments of her leadership style, the coach told her straightforwardly, "You are not doing your job as a leader."

She was avoiding difficult conversations, such as giving constructive feedback, even when she saw areas needing improvement in her team members. She wasn't a "nice" leader; she was a naive leader. That was a turning point in her leadership journey. Although she realized she needed to change aspects of her leadership style, she wasn't exactly sure how to do that.

However, it was in the later stage of her life, with coaching, that she truly understood the Loyalty Contract she had internalized and how it had influenced not only her leadership behavior but also her relationships with others. This was an even more significant turning point in her leadership and her life journey of becoming a psychological adult.

Once she discovered her family Loyalty Contract and realized she could renegotiate it, first with herself and then with others, she could then move to changing her personal and professional relationships. Understanding Loyalty Contracts was her "ticket" to becoming a Self-Differentiated

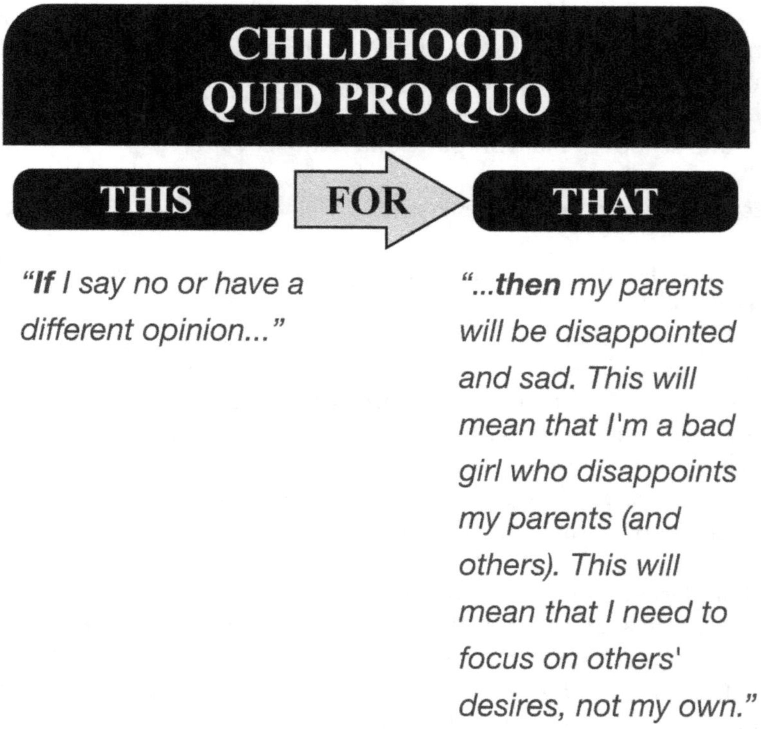

Figure 5.6 Quid Pro Quo – Childhood 2.

Leader and psychological adult. She could establish choiceful boundaries (Bushe, 2001b) in her relationships, achieving a balance between being separate and connected, knowing when she needed her own space while remaining curious about others around herself.

The ABCDE Framework

Bushe (2001b) proposed five elements of "acts of differentiated leadership," which we've adapted into five keywords, using the acronym ABCDE, to review Jieun's journey of Loyalty Contract renegotiation and Self-Differentiation.

This framework isn't just for unpacking childhood memories. Leaders can use it to audit their current team dynamics. Ask yourself: In your quarterly reviews, are you inadvertently reinforcing a contract that says, "If you agree with me, you are a team player; if you challenge me, you are difficult?" If so, you are building a team of followers, not future leaders.

A – Awareness: The crucial starting point was recognizing the Loyalty Contract Jieun had developed in childhood and understanding how it still influenced her adult behavior, particularly in her relationships. This involved reflecting on the broad cultural influences she has had, from family and school to the workplace and national culture.

Reflecting on your own awareness:

- Begin with articulating the Loyalty Contract messages from your childhood.
- Beyond your immediate family, what broader cultural proverbs, sayings or societal expectations did you internalize about authority, obedience, or pleasing others in your formative years?
- How has your understanding of "success" or "being a good person" been shaped by these early Loyalty Contracts?
- Ask yourself if any of these messages are influencing you in your current situation, either emotionally or in terms of taking action.

B – Boundaries: Once Jieun understood her Loyalty Contract, she could start setting new boundaries. This required her to say "no" more often, which was initially uncomfortable because she feared hurting others' feelings. At this stage, while aware of her Loyalty Contract and beginning to set boundaries, she was not yet fully self-differentiated, as her feelings were still intertwined with others.

Reflecting on your own awareness:

- What boundaries are being violated in your current situation and what emotions are initially being triggered?
- In what specific situations do you find it most challenging to say "no," and what fears are associated with that difficulty?
- How do you typically react when a boundary you've attempted to set is challenged or ignored?
- What concrete steps can you take to begin asserting a new boundary and whom do you need to consult with to get help with your confusion?

C – Curiosity: While respecting boundaries, she became more curious about others' perspectives and experiences, using inquiries like, "I'm curious to understand..."Setting clearer boundaries gave her more choice and control in building and managing relationships. She shifted from a reactive mode to a proactive and initiating mode.

Reflecting on your own awareness:

- Ask yourself, how clearly do you understand what led to this situation? Are there pieces of factual information that the other person might be missing?
- Sit with the person to hear their point of view, using statements such as, "I'm curious to understand ..."
- When faced with conflict or disagreement, what is your initial tendency – to assume ill intent or to seek to understand the other person's perspective?
- How can you reframe a challenging situation from a judgment-based perspective to a curiosity-driven inquiry?

D – Description: She learned to describe her own experiences and perspectives more openly, rather than reacting with judgment. Instead of losing her temper and focusing on blaming others, Jieun focused on her needs and expectations, communicating them clearly and assertively.

Reflecting on your own awareness:

- When you feel upset or frustrated, do you tend to focus on blaming the other person/situation or on articulating your own needs or expectations?
- How can you shift from reactive and judgmental interpretation ("They are X and I feel Y") to descriptive language that differentiates your experience from situation ("When X happens, I feel Y")?
- Think about a recent challenging interaction. What specific needs or expectations are not met in that situation?
- How does clear, descriptive communication contribute to fair boundaries?

E – Emotion: Jieun tended to worry excessively, becoming hijacked by her emotions. Even with self-awareness, she still tended to catastrophize. Her work as a legal advisor for many years might have exacerbated this tendency. Her coach advised Jieun to use a "countering" technique. Whenever she is overwhelmed by worst-case scenarios, she should imagine a boxing ring with two versions of herself: one consumed by worry, the other countering with positive possibilities. This helped Jieun calm down and differentiate "her open self" from her "worrying self." Even Jieun, like Cynthia in Chapter 2, suffered from Monkey Mind.

Reflecting on your own awareness:

- When do you find yourself "catastrophizing" or "imagining worst-case scenarios?"
- What physical reactions or thought patterns accompany these overwhelming emotions?
- How can you apply the "countering" technique (or another mindfulness practice) to create distance between your "worrying self" and your "open self?"
- What positive possibilities or alternative outcomes could you consciously bring to your mind when you feel emotionally hijacked?

With this new ABCDE framework in mind, you can renegotiate your inner script.

A Positive Model: Leading the Shift from "Know-it-All" to "Learn-it-All"

While this chapter focuses on navigating cultural conflicts, it's equally important to highlight positive models of self-differentiated leadership. A powerful modern example is Satya Nadella, CEO of Microsoft. Raised in India, a culture with a relatively high Power Distance, Nadella famously led a monumental shift in Microsoft's notoriously sharp-elbowed corporate culture from a "know-it-all" mindset to a collaborative, "learn-it-all" ethos.

This wasn't just a mission statement; he re-engineered the company's core processes to reflect this new Loyalty Contract. A prime example is how he transformed Microsoft's performance evaluations (Kim & Lee, 2023). Instead of rewarding lone-wolf achievements, the new framework asked employees to reflect on their collective impact by considering:

- Your results that built on the work, ideas, or efforts of others.
- Your contributions to the success of others.
- Applying a growth mindset, what you could have done differently and what you learned.

Notice what Nadella did here: He didn't just give speeches about culture; he changed the incentives. He rewrote the Loyalty Contract by literally paying people differently – rewarding collaboration over individual genius. He proved that culture change isn't a poster on the wall; it's a change in how you measure success.

These questions are a masterclass in organizational change and directly apply the principles of Self-Differentiation. They shifted the unspoken contract from "I succeed by outperforming my peers" to "We succeed when I empower and build upon the work of others." This new framework actively fosters:

- **Awareness:** Nadella recognized the toxic, "know-it-all" culture was a liability. He understood the old loyalty contract stifled innovation.
- **Boundaries:** He set new boundaries by dismantling the stack-ranking system. He redefined success as collaborative impact, not just individual wins.
- **Curiosity:** He championed a "learn-it-all" culture to embed curiosity. He valued inquiry and customer empathy over internal certainty.
- **Description:** He shifted from judgmental labels to descriptive impact. His new review questions focused on articulating contributions and learnings.
- **Emotion:** He replaced the corporate emotion of fear with empathy and psychological safety. He reduced internal threats to focus energy on external innovation.

By applying this framework, we can see that Nadella's success wasn't just about business acumen; it was a profound act of self-differentiated leadership that reshaped an entire organizational culture.

Rewriting the Rules from the Factory Floor to French Luxury. Consider Leena Nair, the Global CEO of Chanel. Growing up in a small town in India, the cultural Loyalty Contract presented to her was explicit: an arranged marriage and a life of domestic stability. To choose otherwise was to risk being seen as a rebellious outlier. Nair broke this contract not through reckless rebellion, but through purposeful Self-Differentiation.

She pursued electronics engineering and insisted on taking a job on the factory floors of Hindustan Unilever – a gritty, male-dominated environment where there were literally no restrooms for women. She refused to sign the unspoken Loyalty Contract that whispered, "This is not a place for you." By consistently choosing her own internal drive over external expectations, she rewrote her narrative, rising from the factory floor to the pinnacle of global luxury. Her journey proves that breaking an unhealthy Loyalty Contract doesn't just free the individual; it paves the way for a more inclusive style of leadership that challenges the status quo of entire industries (Global Indian, 2022; Semuels, 2024; Taluja, 2024).

The Role of Technology. It is also worth noting how technology has become a powerful force in reshaping cultural dynamics. In many organizations, digital tools like Slack, Microsoft Teams, or anonymous feedback platforms such as Culture Amp or Officevibe are beginning to flatten traditional hierarchies. Junior employees might hesitate to challenge their manager in a meeting, but they might feel safer sharing a different perspective in a shared document or a dedicated channel. This technological shift can act as a catalyst, creating new avenues for communication and slowly renegotiating the unspoken Loyalty Contracts around authority.

Chapter Summary

When writing about Cultural Norms we wrestled with how deeply we would be able to delve into this complex topic in one chapter. We recognize that there are many other systemic elements like gender bias, socio-economic factors, racism to name a few, that impact one's ability to become self-differentiated. We chose to focus on culture as it seemed to address the broadest spectrum of Self-Differentiation impact.

This chapter explored how cultural norms, particularly Power Distance, are directly related to Loyalty Contracts and Self-Differentiation in leadership. In high Power Distance cultures, such as those in East Asia, the strong emphasis on group harmony and respect for authority can present unique challenges to the Western concept of Self-Differentiation. This environment might contribute to the formation of unhealthy Loyalty Contracts, where individuals feel immense pressure of prioritizing obedience and sacrificing over personal needs. This can lead to negative consequences, including safety issues in aviation and healthcare, limited career choices, and even personal safety and well-being. This chapter cautioned against imposing our own cultural leadership concepts without adaptation.

Diverse cultural perspectives can create misunderstandings, conflict, or discomfort where individuals usually struggle to balance personal authenticity with organizational demands and group harmony. Or, varied cultural perspectives can bring a wealth of ideas, perspectives values, and communication styles that can foster creativity, innovation, empathy, deeper understandings, and broader worldviews all of which can enhance and exponentially propel an organization or a personal relationship forward.

Cultural differences in the workplace and at home play a determining role how individuals understand themselves and interact with others, directly influencing their ability to become or to remain self-differentiated.

Recognizing and renegotiating ingrained Loyalty Contracts is crucial for developing self-differentiated leadership. As we read from the chapter, even people in higher Power Distance culture can overcome ingrained cultural norms to become more effective and authentic leaders with the longer-term impact of cultural harmony.

We can only imagine what might be possible if each of us, when faced with a professional problem or personal concern, would ask a very simple and perhaps obvious question:

I wonder if there is a different perspective on this?

This, we believe, is the opening we need for less friction and more flow – everywhere.

Key Takeaways

1 Power Distance is a critical cultural dimension that shapes "Loyalty Contracts."
2 In conflicts, Culture influences the "why" (the values at stake) and the "how" (the dynamics of the confrontation).
3 Effective self-differentiated leadership is an "AND" proposition – balancing personal conviction with relational connection – not an "OR" proposition.
4 Cultural norms directly impact our psychological or physical safety whether it is in an airplane at 35,000 feet, in the workplace, or at the dining room table.
5 With cultural sensitivity, leaders can actively renegotiate unhealthy Loyalty Contracts to build relationships that are mutually fair to all parties.

Next Level Reflections

1 What is your level of tolerance with challenging authority or expressing dissenting opinions in your workplace?
2 What cultural factors contribute to elements and impact of cultural intolerance?
3 How have cultural norms and expectations at any level (from family and schools to organizations, politics, and societies) influenced your leadership style and decision-making?
4 How might you adapt your leadership style to effectively support team members with different cultural backgrounds and expectations regarding Power Distance?
5 How can companies and organizations with a mix of cultures, generations and genders foster a greater sense of Psychological Adulthood?

Chapter 6

The Seven Archetypes of Non-Differentiated Leadership

On the way to becoming a Self-Differentiated Leader there will be frequent roadblocks, some visible and others hidden from view. While many leadership challenges appear to be unique, there are surprising similarities among them. These similarities can be organized into recognizable patterns that are often referred to as archetypes.

The term archetype has an interesting origin going back to the Greek language. Comprised of *archein* meaning a beginning or a place of origin and *typos* for pattern, model or type, put together we have "the origin of a pattern."

There has been extensive research into personality preferences and patterns viewed through the lens of archetypes. Jungian-Based psychology (Jung, 1981) identified 12 different personality characteristics organized into distinct patterns of behavior that he labeled as archetypes. Manfred Kets de Vries (2006, 2013) built upon Jung's theory and identified eight leadership archetypes that focused on assessing the impact of a leader's decision-making and temperament on the corporate culture, productivity, and overall success of a company.

Expanded definitions of various leadership archetypes include: *the transformational leader* (Bass, 1990; Burns, 2004), *the servant leader* (Greenleaf, 1970, 1977), *the charismatic leader* (Adair-Toteff, 2005; Joosse, 2014; Weber, 1947) and *the Self-Differentiated Leader* (Friedman, 2007) and Peter Senge's groundbreaking book, *The Fifth Discipline* (1990) built upon Jay W. Forrester's (1961, 1969, 1971) groundwork on systems archetypes. Archetypal patterns have even extended into examining how archetypal categories can be used to improve branding and marketing by matching company products with personality preferences of consumers (Pearson & Mark, 2001).

In this chapter we explain the concept of archetypes as *patterns of behavior that people learn in response to their early childhood environments.* We categorized them into seven clear types, each representing a

DOI: 10.4324/9781003621393-6

specific set of behavioral patterns. These patterns, learned in childhood, were once adaptive strategies. Carried into adulthood, they now continue to influence how people relate to others, how they make decisions, and how they navigate conflict throughout their lives.

The Research Behind the Archetypes

The descriptions of each of the archetypes illustrated in this chapter are based on the work of Karen Horney, an early psychoanalyst and forerunner in research on personality development. Her contributions succinctly capture a descriptive picture of strategies that children adopt in an attempt to manage anxiety stemming from early attachment injuries.

Horney called these strategies "neurotic solutions" (1950) which is a clinical way of describing behaviors that people use to preserve self-worth and maintain connection. Because these solutions are learned overcompensations to hide feelings of inadequacy, they are highly reactive, compulsively driven, and are at times subject to adversely influencing beliefs and behaviors at home and at work. She labeled these solutions, "Moving Toward, Moving Away, and Moving Against." We have integrated and expanded Horney's descriptors into seven archetypes that are based on these solutions, revealing with greater specificity how these limiting patterns of behavior show up in interpersonal relationships at home and the workplace.

To further validate research supporting our seven archetype descriptors, we refer to the Hogan Developmental Survey (HDS; Hogan, 1997). The HDS is a psychometric tool, designed to assess behavioral tendencies that adversely affect workplace performance or career advancement. Robert Hogan's design of this non-clinical assessment inventory was also largely inspired by the work of Karen Horney. The HDS, frequently used by coaches and supervisors, measures eleven "dark side" tendencies or patterns of behavior that emerge under stress, resulting in decreased workplace effectiveness. Hogan's eleven descriptors are in alignment with the seven archetypes presented in this chapter.

The Hidden Cost of Leadership Overcompensation

In his book *A Failure of Nerve* Edwin Friedman (2007) made the distinction between differentiated and non-differentiated leadership. Our archetypes continue to build on Friedman's important contributions by illustrating seven distinct types of non-differentiated leadership and how each of these leadership styles interfere with workplace practices and efficiencies.

It is important to distinguish between specific types of non-differentiated leadership for a number of reasons. First, if we gain a clearer understanding of predictable over-reactions that interfere with interpersonal relationships or workplace effectiveness, we can become more effective at managing them. Second, if we identify specific archetypal patterns, we can then employ individualized accountability measures to better contain the negative behaviors.

These archetypes are not just personality quirks; they are an "organizational tax." They slow down decision-making, increase turnover, reduce productivity and trust, and create a culture of fear. For a leader, identifying them is the first step in stopping the drain on your company's resources.

The Figure 6.1 below visually displays the seven unique archetypes. And yet, each has the following two core things in common:

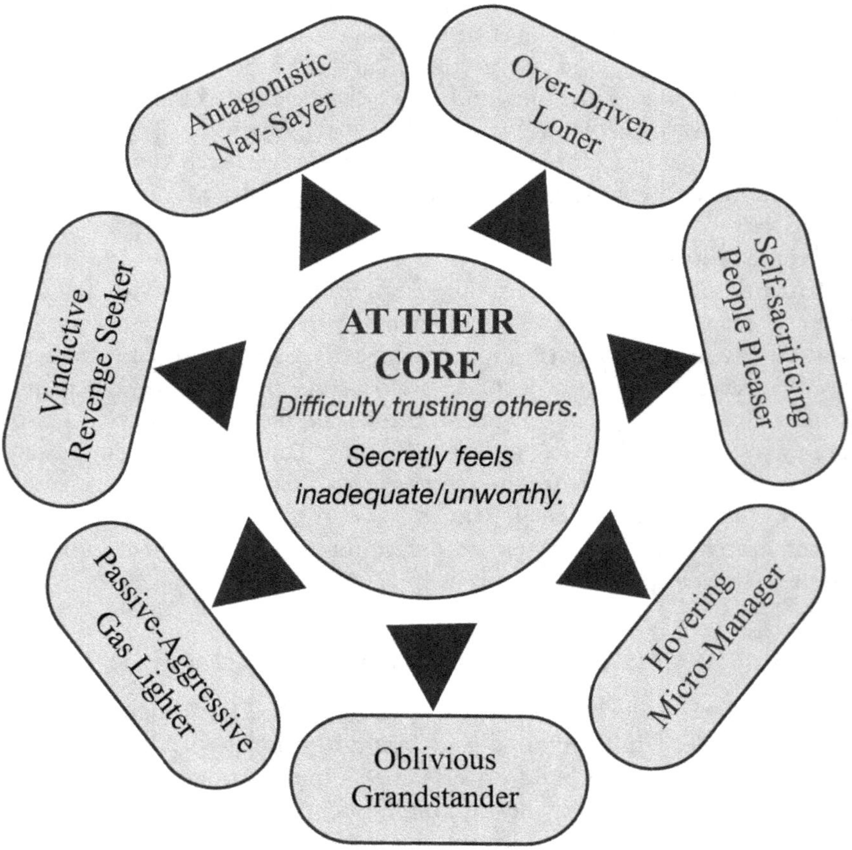

Figure 6.1 Common core over-compensations.

Difficulty trusting others
and
Secretly feeling some form of inadequacy or unworthiness

Unfortunately, there are many people in positions of power that are unconsciously governed by these core vulnerabilities. Their assumptions, demands, personal ambitions, and impulsive decision-making style create a ripple effect that negatively impacts personal relationships and organizational stability.

Healthy, well-adjusted leaders, on the other hand, have found ways to shed the shackles of these early defense mechanisms or overcompensations. We can recognize well-adjusted, effective leaders because they seem to have a palpable sense of emotional equilibrium that, like a north star, underpins their actions.

An example of this would be to compare leaders who are facing an economic downturn. Self-Differentiated Leaders are able to command a steady, calm presence offering reassurance in the face of anxiety. They do not succumb to their own anxieties, or to criticism, or group hysteria. They are able to offer clear communication as to how the organization is able to weather the storm.

However, individual leaders who are either susceptible to criticism or have a strong need for approval would often react in a number of ineffective ways. They tend to:

- change course or direction based on personal criticism,
- overcompensate by adopting an overly intellectual, authoritarian approach,
- remain aloof or withdrawn in times of crisis,
- criticize or respond dismissively to people who show emotions.

These personal responses might have a momentary stabilizing effect on the leader's own mental state. They might also appear to give the person the upper hand in terms of strength and self-esteem. However, the greater the degree of reactivity and rigidity, the less effectiveness the person has in creating a sense of trust in others. Too, their problem-solving and creative thinking become compromised.

When behavior is defensively driven, the person's motivation for action isn't grounded in stability, intentionality, or the greater good. There is more of a rigid or reactive quality to their decision-making and their leadership style, which often results in suboptimized effectiveness.

Defensively driven patterns and/or overcompensations are the opposite of Self-Differentiation. And yet, it is sometimes difficult to determine the line in the sand when a positive attribute crosses over into a self-absorbed, over-determined effort. Let us take the example of ambition. The desire to achieve our highest potential is, in itself, a positive attribute. And yet, ambition can also be used as a way of proving you are better than others or attaining power or wealth so no one can harm you, or to make up for areas where you feel inadequate.

The following chart illustrates the difference between aspects of the personality that reflect the motivation that drives healthy ambition and those learned behaviors that are meant to make up for or hide core feelings of inadequacy.

Ambition

As you can see from Table 6.1, defensively driven ambition is often at the expense of others. And no matter the extent to which the desired ambition is achieved, it never seems to satisfy. According to Human Synergistics International (Cooke & Lafferty, 1982), highly competitive individuals tend to view interactions through a "win-lose" lens. For instance, upon hearing their partner say, "Oh, I had a tough day at work," they might defensively respond, "Oh, my job is way tougher than yours," attempting to "win" the argument of whose life is harder. This exemplifies aggressive-defensive behavior.

In contrast, individuals with a strong achievement orientation focus on their own goals and progress, rather than trying to outperform others. While a highly competitive person might follow a competitor down a wrong path, fixated on winning against them, someone with a healthy achievement drive, though not avoiding competition, remains focused on their own objectives and direction. Achievement, seen in this light, is a constructive behavior.

In a corporate setting, we call this the difference between Sustainable Drive (Achievement) and Toxic Drive (Competition). Sustainable Drive builds momentum; Toxic Drive burns out the engine. It erects organizational silos, where departments hoard resources and information to "win" against their internal colleagues rather than the external market.

Caretaking

A second illustration that often creates a similar type of confusion is the example of caretaking. Most of us would agree that expressing care for others is a positive attribute, a sign of empathy, or an expression of gratitude. However, compulsive caretaking can be used as a way of manipulating others to gain the advantage or feel a sense of control.

With micromanagers, caretaking can be a mask for hiding feelings of inadequacy. Or caretaking can also be a means of continually proving

Table 6.1 Healthy and over-determined ambition

	Qualities of healthy ambition		*Qualities of over-determined ambition*
1	Celebrates other people's accomplishment as well as one's own.	vs	Feels resentful and envious of other people's accomplishments.
2	Does not feel threatened by or have a need to undermine others' accomplishments.	vs	Feels threatened by other people's accomplishments and needs to undermine or destroy them.
3	Holds an accurate perspective of one's own contributions relative to the larger whole.	vs	Holds an inflated sense of one's own accomplishments relative to the accomplishments of others.
4	Is able to maintain a sense of humility in the face of external achievements.	vs	Craves praise and rewards for external achievements.
5	Can receive constructive feedback without becoming defensive.	vs	Becomes defensive and angry in the face of constructive criticism.
6	Learns from mistakes and can readily admit them.	vs	Has difficulty admitting mistakes or learning from them.
7	Takes responsibilities for one's actions, both successes and failures	vs	Blames others for mistakes and often defers responsibility onto others.
8	Gives credit to others when credit is due.	vs	Takes and rarely offers credit for other people's ideas and accomplishments.
9	Keeps a balanced perspective and can walk away from a project when it becomes too much.	vs	Is driven to achieve success at all costs and has difficulty knowing when to stop.
10	Comfort in sharing vulnerable feelings, including the awareness of appropriate boundaries.	vs	Difficulty in sharing intimate feelings, including no apparent ability to understand mutuality and reciprocity.

Note: It is completely normal to feel or display some of the behaviors in the right-hand column. When these behaviors become patterns and compulsions over which a person lacks or exercises control, this is when they become unhealthy.

self-worth in an attempt to receive external validation and reassurance. And yet, when people feel unworthy at their core, no amount of reward or reassurance will quiet their inner anxiety to the point that they are able to stop the compulsive pattern of over-caregiving (Horney, 1945, 1950; Danielian & Gianotti, 2012).

For those in coaching or leadership positions, given both of these examples, it is important to assess whether the person you are working with is able to modify their over-determined behaviors when they receive negative feedback or when they are in a coaching situation. Assessing whether an individual is able to recognize and then modify behavioral patterns or they stubbornly stick with their same strategies, regardless of the hurt or damage being done, is a key factor in assessing employee improvement plans and the overall effective management of employees.

Mapping the Seven Archetypes

In the following section, we explain each of the **defensively based archetypes** in greater detail. What we mean by "defensively based" is specific behaviors or patterns of behaviors that are driven (motivated) primarily by a sense of threat, insecurity, or a need for self-protection, rather than by calm reasoning or genuine preferences.

Because each of the seven archetypes represents a type of non-differentiated leadership, the descriptions listed below only highlight the negative impact that the over-compensations have on others. The following Table 6.2 gives a brief synopsis of each of the archetypes and their core features.

Core Characteristics of Each Archetype

In the following section we provide a more detailed explanation of each of the seven archetypes, showing the core characteristics of each. At the end of each archetype description we then provide an example of how the archetype could manifest in a present-day context.

The Over-Driven Loner – Usually preferring to function as an independent expert, these individuals often prefer isolation, solitary tasks, individual hobbies, or activities. Over-Driven Loners present as either shy and awkward in social situations, or by contrast, they can appear as aloof or somewhat defiant in an attempt to present as confident. Both of these seemingly opposite presentations reflect an underlying awkwardness around people, which often stems from the fear of being controlled or disappointed by others. Over-Driven Loners are propelled by a relentless drive to maintain their rigorous internal standards.

The Leadership Cost: While often technically brilliant, this style becomes a liability at scale. By hoarding information and refusing collaboration, this leader creates a key person risk, where they become the single point of failure for the entire organization. Their reluctance to delegate inadvertently silos data and slows decision-making velocity, turning the leader into the ultimate bottleneck.

Table 6.2 The archetypes: Brief descriptions

The archetype	*Brief description*
Over-Driven Loner	Isolated, intense focus on personal goals/hobbies, prefers solitary activities, untrusting, emotionally guarded, self-reliant, need to prove autonomy, secretly wants (needs) approval.
Self-Sacrificing People Pleaser	Appears to be a selfless caretaker, gives to others to prove value, difficulty in delegating or receiving help, feels un(der)appreciated, holds quiet resentments, martyr, chronic self-neglect.
Hovering Micromanager	Excessive hyper-vigilance, perfectionistic standards, reluctance to delegate, constant oversight, lacks trust in the innate capacities of self or others, frequently second-guesses decisions, views their behavior as protective/helpful.
Oblivious Grandstander	Craves the spotlight, is a know-it-all, constantly interrupts, violates boundaries, pushes the limits, takes credit for others' accomplishments, rationalizes or minimizes own inappropriate behaviors.
Passive-Aggressive Gaslighter	Disavows their own negative emotions, has a hidden competitive edge, projects aggression onto others while appearing concerned and/or helpful, doesn't confront directly, exhibits indirect resistance, sabotages outcomes through inaction or half-hearted effort.
Vindictive Revenge Seeker	Highly competitive, continual need for praise/validation, hypersensitive to perceived slights, values own opinions over others, threatened by success of others, externalizes blame, holds grudges, retaliates, can't apologize.
Antagonistic Nay-Sayer	Armchair critic, cautious, resistant to change, quick to explain why something won't work, challenges ideas of others, stifles innovation, rarely satisfied, seems to enjoy and takes pride in being the opposition.

Core Characteristics

- *Intense Inner Drive*: They set high goals for themselves, are prone to perfectionism, and do not rely on approval from others. Although they have strong convictions, Over-Driven Loners are subject to a narrowing or rigidity of thinking because they don't seek feedback from others.
- *Preference for Solitude*: Over-Driven Loners find relief and respite by being alone. Their internal emotional life can be vivid and intense, where fantasy, competitive online gaming, or solitary sports often replace the need for relational connection.

- *Sensitivity to Criticism:* While outwardly appearing stoic or indifferent, they are often highly sensitive to criticism.
- *Reluctance to Delegate*: Trust issues or perfectionistic standards can make delegation difficult. They fear that others' efforts will fall short or that collaboration will dilute their vision.
- *Overly Controlling*: If left in charge of a project, they will likely become overly controlling, and they have difficulty taking feedback from others. Their attitude toward those in authority is one of deference or complete indifference. In terms of occupation, they often acquire specialized skill sets that are uniquely valuable to the organization, thus making them beyond reproach or outside the normal accountability checks and balances within the system.

Example: With decades of commercial experience, Thomas, the Commercial Business Unit Head of a European multinational pharmaceutical company, is leading a new product launch with a tight deadline. It requires close cross-functional collaborations with different expertise. Thomas views himself as the most capable leader for the critical new product launch, often underestimating the expertise within his marketing, sales, medical, regulatory, and legal teams. His fixed approach threatens to override the necessary cross-functional collaboration.

He struggles to delegate, constantly second-guessing and imposing his own methods, creating tension in meetings where he impatiently dismisses others' ideas. In addition, overall productivity within his division as compared to other pharmaceutical divisions begins to lag behind, drawing attention to how Thomas's behavior is affecting productivity. Rather than lose Thomas as a valued employee, he is offered coaching in hopes of creating new insight and strategies for Thomas's leadership style. After speaking with Thomas, the coach recommended that he might be better suited for an individual contributor role.

The Self-Sacrificing People Pleaser – Acting as the devoted caretaker, these individuals put others' needs in front of their own. They present as polite, cooperative, and empathic. As easy as it is for Self-Sacrificing People Pleasers to give assistance and advice, it is quite difficult for them to receive help or delegate responsibility. They exhibit a repeated pattern of taking on too much, becoming overwhelmed and resentful, which puts them at risk for burnout. When they reach the breaking point, reactions can range from having an emotional meltdown to exhibiting martyr-like symptoms. This might include letting people know that they don't feel appreciated, or they might choose to go "underground" by withdrawing in silence, or suddenly resigning from commitments, leaving people scratching their heads saying, "Wow! I didn't see that coming!" or "What the heck happened?!"

The Leadership Cost: This style is often the root cause of team mediocrity. By prioritizing harmony over accountability, this leader avoids the necessary conflict of candid feedback, leading to "grade inflation" in performance reviews. The cost is a measurable erosion of talent density: Under-performers stay because it's comfortable, while high achievers leave because they are frustrated by the lack of standards.

Core Characteristics

- *Need for External Approval:* Self-worth is tied to pleasing others and being applauded for a job well done. If praise is not forthcoming, they become easily wounded and might withdraw or break down in public.
- *Difficulty Setting Boundaries:* They struggle saying *no* to requests, even when they are overwhelmed or when tasks fall outside of their job description.
- *Chronic Self-Neglect*: Because they habitually put others' needs ahead of their own, they tend to neglect self-care and have a secret resentment toward others.
- *Under-developed Sense of Identity*: Because of their constant adaptation to others' needs, this can lead to confusion about their own preferences, ideas, or their ability to creatively problem-solve.
- *Difficulty Receiving Feedback*: Any constructive criticism from a manager, friend or spouse is experienced as a personal injury. It will either lead to an increased promise of compliance, coupled with feelings of guilt, profuse apologies, or they will assume too much of the blame and not push back to assert their own rights and desires in a situation.

Note: This archetype manifests in two primary ways depending on cultural and relational dynamics. Vertical people-pleasing often appears as unquestioning obedience to authority (a parent, an elder, a teacher, or a boss), which is common in more hierarchical country cultures (e.g. East Asia, Latin America, or the Middle East) or organizational cultures (e.g. a company led by a boss with the Vindictive Revenge Seeker archetype). In contrast, horizontal people-pleasing manifests as excessive caretaking among peers to maintain group harmony and to be liked.

Example: Emily, a well-regarded individual known for her helpfulness, recently took the lead on a critical cross-functional project team of six. Driven by a desire for both project success and team harmony, Emily initially defaulted to her familiar pattern of over-giving. She took on many tasks that could have been delegated, offering valuable growth opportunities for her team members. Emily began working excessive hours, becoming overwhelmed as the tight deadline approached. She found herself thinking:

> *I've taken such good care of the team, why aren't they stepping up to help me?*

The irony was that she had never explicitly asked for their assistance. The project began to fall behind, causing Emily significant, though unexpressed stress. This situation stemmed from her repeating an ingrained "Loyalty Contract", which drove her to internalize pressure, avoid delegation, and not seek help. While outwardly focused on pleasing her team, she harbored resentment and secretly blamed her teammates as the risk of project failure increased.

The Hovering Micromanager – Driven by the instinct of the exacting perfectionist, this archetype not only oversees tasks but scrutinizes every detail. While they believe they are being helpful, their demeanor conveys a combination of hypervigilance coupled with an underlying sense of anxiety and fear of failure. Highly shame sensitive, they attempt to avoid losing face by either controlling others or being obsessed with details and not making a mistake for fear of appearing imperfect.

The Leadership Cost: This leadership style is the enemy of scale. While it may ensure quality on small projects, their obsession with control creates a massive decision-making backlog. It stifles innovation because staff stop offering new ideas, knowing they will be overruled. Ultimately, this drives up recruitment costs, as autonomy-seeking high performers will not stay in an environment where they are not trusted to execute.

Core Characteristics

- *Constant oversight:* Because of their underlying anxiety, and because success and self-worth are measured by how they appear to the outside world, they feel compelled to impose their agenda and perfectionistic standards onto others.

- *Obsessed with details:* Their tendency to focus on minutiae makes it difficult for them to step back to gain a larger perspective.
- *Difficulty delegating responsibility to others:* If they do delegate, it is usually coupled with continual double-checking and monitoring, inserting themselves to "fix" what others have produced.
- *Dismissive of others' ideas and opinions*: Because they believe that the responsibility for success falls on their shoulders, they are quick to cut people off, dismiss their ideas, and they are not good listeners.
- *Fosters dependency in others*: By making themselves indispensable by fixing problems and constant advice-giving, their behavior eventually discourages others from displaying self-initiative.

It should be noted that there are two distinct sub-types of the Hovering Micromanager. One sub-type is centered on a preoccupation with self that states, "I can't fail; if I fail or fall short of being the best, I will bring shame onto myself." These core characteristics center on fear of making decisions, over-analysis of data, and worry that something will be missed. As managers, this sub-type tends to delay decision-making, often resulting in a paralysis when it comes to taking action.

The second sub-type is centered on over-focusing on others within their relational circle, such as a family member or employee. Their internal self-talk might say, "I need to make sure that my team (my family) lives up to my expectations. I don't trust that they will succeed unless I keep a careful watch." This second sub-type is not unlike the often joked about "helicopter parent" by Dr. Haim Ginott (1969) or the Chinese "tiger mom" by Professor Amy Chua (2011) of Yale Law School.

Example: Prakash, a newly appointed ESG (Environmental, Social and Corporate Governance) Regional Manager from India, was tasked with launching a new, high-stakes sustainability reporting program across Asia. His intense fear of presenting flawed data to global headquarters was noticeable. He spent the first week paralyzed by over-analysis, creating complicated spreadsheets and demanding excessive data points from his country leads, which significantly delayed the project's start.

Once the data collection began, Prakash's focus shifted to controlling his team. Convinced that his team in Japan, Korea, and Singapore are not yet capable enough, he scheduled too many check-in meetings across multiple time zones to carefully examine every entry. He dismissed a streamlined reporting process proposed by his manager in Japan, stating;

My method is more thorough and leaves no room for error.

He frequently re-versioned their reports overnight, leaving the team feeling demoralized and redundant.

Prakash's behavior blended both subtypes. His initial paralysis stemmed from a preoccupation with his own potential failure, while his subsequent intervention was driven by a conviction that his regional team couldn't meet his expected standards. He believed he was ensuring flawless execution, but instead, he fostered resentment and disabled the local initiative his program was meant to empower.

The Oblivious Grandstander – Often appearing as the charismatic visionary, this is the person who needs to command center stage and dominate the conversation. They are the "know-it-alls" of the world and never seem to tire of showing you how smart they are. Their demeanor is either jovial, well-meaning advice-givers, or they can present with an air of smugness or condescension when offering their help.

The Leadership Cost: The cost here is a silence tax. By dominating every room and taking undue credit, this leader sucks the oxygen out of meetings, causing introverted or junior talent to shut down. This results in a significant loss of cognitive diversity, as the team learns that contributing value only leads to it being co-opted by the leader.

Core Characteristics

- *Expectation of Reward Without Effort:* Regardless of how they perform in the work setting, they believe they are entitled to promotions and recognition.
- *Inability to Keep Confidentiality:* They have a difficult time keeping confidentiality because of their need for attention and to show others how smart they are.
- *Difficulty Maintaining Appropriate Boundaries:* They often dismiss other people's upset with their boundary violations, calling them trivial. Or they will tell you they meant no harm and were just trying to be helpful.
- *Manipulative or Disruptive Behavior:* When limits are set with their behavior or when praise is not forthcoming, they are apt to create some

sort of drama in the workplace. This can include spreading gossip, making threats, or having an emotional tantrum if their expectations aren't met.
- *Non-collaboration*: Oblivious Grandstanders are not team players. They rarely make an extra effort but are quick to take credit for the team's success.

On the personal side, we can see how the entitled Oblivious Grandstander might overshadow or infringe upon another person's life by having a disregard for healthy boundaries and not being an attuned listener. Their partners or children might feel that they can't voice a differing opinion, or they might feel somewhat violated because their personal privacy is not respected.

Example: Sergio, the division manager, is known company wide as a know-it-all. He predictably is the person that leads the meetings and rarely gives credit beyond his role as leader. Using humor as a cover to hide his insecurities, he will often make sarcastic comments about others' missteps all the while saying,

> *Oh, I was just kidding! Can't you take a joke?!*

When Sergio needs something, it is quite common for him to interrupt a private conversation or enter a meeting in progress to get what he wants.

In his personal life Sergio is a loving father, encouraging his sons, coaching them on the ball field, and patiently advocating for his family's needs. His Loyalty Contract is one where he puts family first, and he is able to show his tender side at home.

It is quite likely that an effective coach, colleague, or trusted friend could help Sergio see the two different Sergios (at work and at home) and help him develop his work style to be like the integrated psychological adult he is at home.

The Passive-Aggressive Gaslighter – Presenting as the composed rationalist, these individuals almost make you feel like you're the one who is going crazy. Often soft-spoken and reasonable, Passive-Aggressive Gaslighters are masters of insinuation and projecting blame. Their demeanor is such that they never seem to get ruffled emotionally and exhibit an aura of rational reasonableness. They will often deny having said or done something after the fact, and they will respond by saying that your beliefs are a distortion of the truth or that you are over-reacting.

Note: The term "gaslighting" comes from a 1938 British play by playwright Patrick Hamilton (1938) about a husband who isolates and manipulates his wife with the goal of driving her insane. Gaslighting is a form of emotional manipulation. It involves someone making you question your beliefs, behaviors, and perception of reality.

The Leadership Cost: This style acts as organizational rust, silently corroding trust and speed. By agreeing in meetings but sabotaging execution in the hallways, this leader creates a "shadow culture" of confusion. This slows down execution speed significantly, as team members are forced to waste valuable energy deciphering mixed messages rather than driving business outcome. In very subtle ways Passive-Aggressive Gaslighters sap the energy out of others, causing them to begin to doubt themselves or lose confidence, which directly and indirectly affects productivity and business outcomes.

Core Characteristics

- *Feigned Concern:* Passive-Aggressive Gaslighters express outward concern if you are upset, but they will also suggest that you misheard what they said, making you question whether you read the situation correctly.
- *Indirect Hostility:* Rather than openly confront or criticize they express their anger, disappointment, or displeasure by withholding information, or spreading rumors indirectly.
- *Conveniently Forgetting:* Forgetting a conversation or stating that they don't remember is one of the ways they can indirectly undermine project completion as well as individual or team morale.
- *Sabotage:* Passive-Aggressive Gaslighters will subtly do whatever it takes to wear someone down. This is often done in secret where accusations, misinformation, or the failure to convey information is difficult to pin down or when there are no other witnesses to track the behavior over time.
- *Applying Inconsistent Standards:* If gaslighters are in a leadership position, they will apply rules, rewards, and performance expectations unevenly, thus keeping the entire team feeling unsure of what is expected.

While Passive-Aggressive Gaslighters profess that they are not interested in getting ahead, there is a highly competitive edge to them. It is difficult to hold these individuals accountable in work situations as they are quite adept at shifting the focus of blame or concern onto others.

Example: Edward, a corporate lawyer heading legal and government affairs at a startup, consistently undermines Sarah, the marketing manager leading a new campaign. Edward subtly blames the design team for delays after agreeing to deadlines for his analysis. When communication issues arise, he feigns misunderstanding:

> *Oh, I thought it was finalized... my mistake!*

His seemingly helpful legal advice often adds unnecessary steps, while subtly positioning himself as the ultimate risk mitigator.

He might casually mention to the data analyst his concerns about the marketing team's unrealistic projections, later feigning ignorance when the analyst brings up these concerns in a team meeting. Sarah increasingly questions her team's efficiency and morale due to these interactions. Rather than staying in this passive aggressive dance with Edward, Sarah decided to go to HR. As it turned out, numerous complaints had been made against Edward, none of which were clear violations. However, HR began to recognize a pattern, directed Edward to an Executive Coach, and placed him on a performance improvement plan.

The Vindictive Revenge Seeker – Operating as the intense competitor, Vindictive Revenge Seekers demand continual attention and praise. Lack of an ego boost is perceived as a slight. Because of this, they are easily manipulated by flattery. As leaders, they seek adulation and they demand absolute loyalty. In the workplace, they put people's loyalty to the test, often placing high demands on employees. They are prone to changing their minds mid-stream and expect others to fall in line without voicing a complaint.

The Leadership Cost: The primary cost is a culture of fear that hides critical risks. Because this leader punishes dissent, employees will hide mistakes and bury bad news to avoid retaliation. This blindness leaves the organization vulnerable to catastrophic failures – legal, financial, or operational – that could have been prevented had the leader fostered psychological safety instead of compliance.

Core Characteristics

- *Highly Competitive*: Vindictive Revenge Seekers don't take losing well. If someone does outshine them in any arena, they will secretly or overtly seek opportunities to undermine them.
- *Holds Grudges*: If they experience a wound or a slight, it cannot be let go *until and unless* the person who caused the grievance suffers in equal or worse measure. Dwelling on perceived wrongs, they are prone to use angry outbursts as a means of intimidation and often wait for the right moment to retaliate.
- *Lack of Accountability:* They live by the motto that the rules don't apply to them. They refuse to accept responsibility for their actions and instead blame others. This in turn fuels their justification to retaliate.
- *Inability to Apologize:* Because Vindictive Revenge Seekers are highly shame sensitive, they rarely apologize. Apologies are viewed as an admission of failure, a sign of weakness, and a loss of power and control.
- *Emotional Volatility*: They are prone to anger and use angry outbursts to intimidate others.
- *Lack of Empathy:* Because everything is about "me", they exhibit minimal ability to see a situation from another person's vantage point. Their extreme self-focus either blinds them or allows them to be indifferent to the harm they cause others.

Vindictive Revenge Seekers believe that they are entitled to more than their fair share because they are special, intelligent, or gifted, which stems back to parental messages of entitlement. Vindictive Revenge Seekers can be charming but beware of that charm. It is always used in the service of satisfying their own needs or agenda. This charm is not trustworthy, so allow yourself some healthy skepticism when you are dealing with people that show these characteristics.

Example: *Mi-Kyung is a high-tech operations manager with 20 years of experience as an engineer. Part of her success is that she is seen as a winner in a very competitive environment. Losing for her is losing face and losing status, something she clearly loathes. Her "win at all costs" has distanced her relationally, and not many people like her.*

In fact, people are afraid of her and are reluctant to give Mi-Kyung feedback believing they are at risk should they disagree with her, especially if it is in public.

When you first meet Mi-Kyung, there seems to be this magnetism that is intriguing and seemingly unique. She appears to be generous, willing to help, and offer expertise. Later people realize that Mi-Kyung's generosity comes with a price. That price is an unspoken demand of loyalty. Mi-Kyung is often volatile, with the exception of her direct manager, the CEO. Because of this, no one can give her feedback or suggest any changes to her leadership style which has a negative impact on individual employees, team morale and the corporate culture.

From a coaching perspective, Mi-Kyung would be a big challenge. If she was willing to acknowledge some of her difficult leadership patterns, there might be hope. The challenge for a coach as well as managers of Vindictive Revenge Seekers is to assess the willingness to recognize and commit to changing behaviors. It is also important to make sure that the system is willing to put accountability measures in place to keep negative behaviors in check.

Antagonistic Nay-Sayer – Self-styled as the critical analyst, these individuals always see the glass as half empty. In business and social settings, they often take the position of armchair critic and are the first to say "yes, but." Priding themselves on their ability to debate, their own cynicism remains unexamined. What remains unspoken but felt by others is their attitude of disdain or smugness underneath the surface.

It is important to note that Antagonistic Nay-Sayers are not simply doing their due diligence by exhibiting critical thinking. Their learned Loyalty Contract reflexively compels them to point out flaws or risks, and they rarely offer solutions or constructive ideas. As a result, they have a corrosive effect on team culture and productivity over time.

The Leadership Cost: This style creates "analysis paralysis." By reflexively focusing on why new ideas will fail rather than how they could work, this leader kills innovation in the cradle. The cost is missed market opportunities and a demoralized creative team that stops proposing solutions, resigning themselves to the stagnant status quo.

Core Characteristics

- *Feedback Aimed at Putting Others Down*: Quick to point out risks or flaws, they do so with phrases such as, "That won't work", or "You don't know what you're talking about."
- *Lack of Constructive Solutions:* Antagonistic Nay-Sayers rarely offer alternative constructive suggestions to help solve the problem.
- *Dampens Creativity and Innovation*: With their continual pessimistic attitude and rejection of new ideas, this can have the effect of discouraging team members from contributing their own thoughts or new ideas.
- *Undermining Leadership*: Their negative comments can eventually erode confidence in leadership, specifically around the organizational initiatives that require changing the course of action.
- *Playing Armchair Critic to Excess:* Every organization needs individuals who aren't afraid to ask tough questions and voice objections or concerns. Antagonistic Nay-Sayers do so reflexively and excessively. Eventually, this can cause leaders and subordinates to tune these individuals out or avoid engaging with them.

On some level, successful, adventurous people remind nay-sayers of what they have missed, which produces feelings of envy and/or regret. As a way of diminishing these feelings, a nay-sayer attempts to level the playing field.

Example: *Alan has been a middle manager, working for a global manufacturing company for 25 years. He leads a core group of salespeople who are responsible for 80% of the company's revenue. As you might imagine, a huge amount of stress falls upon Alan to make sure his team delivers the numbers which, in Alan's mind, justifies his criticism of others.*

Some say Alan has been there too long because he is known as "Alan No." New ideas and innovation are often shot down by Alan's fear of risk-taking, his "Yes but, what if..." responses and analyzing things to where decisions are often delayed or not made. Because his team is comprised of younger adults, he doesn't think they have enough experience to really know what is going on in the marketplace so he has to impose his vision and direction upon the team.

Currently, Alan's CEO is pointing to unimpressive sales figures demanding a different kind of leadership from Alan. While not having yet voiced it, the CEO seriously doubts if "Alan No" can find a "Yes" to turn things around.

Chapter Summary

Changing behavior is not an easy thing to do. Entrenched behaviors that have been relied upon over a lifetime do provide some degree of comfort and predictability. How many times have coaches and therapists heard: "Things are going well for me right now, why change?" or more concerningly, "Why should I change? I have been doing this for 20 years!?" Over time these learned strategies become like a crutch that is difficult to put down. Even when the crutch is slowing our pace, it's familiar and we have learned that it works to prevent falling on our face.

In his best-selling book, True North, author Bill George (2007) talks about events that turned around the lives of each of the 125 top executives around the world that he interviewed. He describes these events as a "crucible", defined as something we go through that exponentially challenges our old way of thinking. The result was the equivalent of an epiphany that tossed aside the unhealthy crutches. And for each of the leaders that epiphany was understanding that being an effective leader is not about "me" but it is about "us" – what makes "the us" work. Being stuck in one of the archetypes tends to make everything about "me" causing everything and everyone else to be secondary, irrelevant or worse, toxic, or even dangerous.

Our recommendations for addressing challenging and dysfunctional archetypal behaviors are illustrated in greater detail in each of the seven chapters that follow. In addition, a professional, either a trained coach, mentor, or a therapist, could act as a sherpa, providing additional insights, techniques, and safe confidential guidance. This type of outside support can help ameliorate potentially defensive reactivity when a person is asked to modify their behavioral responses. No one will throw away a crutch until they see a way to walk without one.

Key Takeaways

1 Understanding archetypes as predictable patterns of behavior helps leaders identify and interrupt those behaviors by developing strategies that ensure greater accountability.
2 It is also a way to invite employees to take responsibility for patterns that continue to have a negative impact on the organization.
3 Creating an invitation to change an archetypal pattern might be met with initial resistance. Therefore, it is important to provide ongoing follow-up to assess whether further accountability measures need to be put into place.

4 Leaders must distinguish between sustainable drive and toxic behaviors. Effective leadership requires recognizing when positive traits, like ambition or caretaking, cross the line into defensive over-compensations that damage team cohesion and performance.
5 While many leadership challenges appear to be unique, there are surprising similarities among them.

Next Level Reflections

1 As you think about your past managers, friends, and even family members, to what degree did any of them exhibit some of the characteristics of one or more of the archetypes?
2 What are ways that you can keep an eye open for patterns of behavior that might be traceable to one of these archetypes?
3 As you think about your own leadership at work or at home, which of these archetypes hit close to home for you?
4 Trace the patterns recognized in a particular archetype and connect them to learned messages you received in childhood. How might you challenge these messages in a way that moves you closer to a place of Self-Differentiation?
5 How might you create a plan for speaking with an employee who displays one of these seven archetypes in a way that:
   a gives permission to let go of the destructive aspects of the pattern as well as
   b offers specific behaviors that the employee could use to replace over-used and over-worn patterns?

Chapter 7

Strategies for Working with the Archetypes

Chapter 6 provided you with a description of how unhealthy Loyalty Contracts create the conditions that produce each of the seven archetypes. This chapter amplifies our understanding of the archetypes by providing an *Archetype Analysis Process*. The process lists six specific levels of analysis to help identify conditions that are likely to trigger problematic behavior. Additionally, the *Archetype Analysis Process* offers strategies aimed at correcting the conditions that allow unproductive behavior to remain unchallenged. Finally, it draws our attention to assessing whether expectations in the workplace or at home are creating standards that are impossible or nearly impossible to uphold.

Setting unreasonable standards in any context creates insecurity and pressure. As an outcome, this can cause one or more of the three response patterns that we introduced in Chapter 6:

a Too much pressure can produce an environment where individuals learn they must *overcompensate* to try to prove they are worthy/competent. (Moving Toward)
b Too much pressure might also create a *collapse*, where the person gives up and begins to withdraw and mistrust relational connection. (Moving Away)
c Too little pressure (defined by not setting appropriate limits and expectations) creates *entitlement* and a lack of respect for others. (Moving Against)

As a leader, if you create expectations that produce too much pressure or you allow toxic behavior to continue, you are paying a tax. You are signaling to your high performers that toxic behavior is acceptable. This chapter explains how to stop paying that tax.

DOI: 10.4324/9781003621393-7

The Archetype Analysis Process

Using the Archetype Analysis Process, we describe six specific levels of analysis to help understand how the archetype becomes activated. In addition, we highlight what drives the behavior, and what we can do as coaches, colleagues, family, or friends to positively impact the negative behaviors. If you follow the step-wise process provided, clarity will emerge in terms of being able to more quickly recognize specific repeating behavior patterns.

Once identified, applying specific interventions to help repair the relationship or better contain unwelcome behavior will be easier to put into place. The grid provided in this section gives you a visual illustration of the flow of how to implement this process (see Figure 7.1).

This analysis isn't just for coaching; it is the blueprint for a Performance Improvement Plan (PIP). While PIPs are often cynically viewed as merely a paper trail for termination, a Self-Differentiated Leader uses them as a genuine roadmap for realignment. However, if an employee cannot move from current behavior to improved behavior, you have the data you need to manage into a different role or possibly move them out of the organization.

We will now turn our attention to each archetype and give specific examples of how the Archetype Analysis Process can be applied. This is in no way an exhaustive list. We have provided a sampling of examples to illustrate how the analysis process works. Feel free to adapt your own strategies to the step-wise process.

The Over-Driven Loner – Because they were often left to fend for themselves in childhood, or because their home environment was chaotic with little parental consistency, these individuals learned self-reliance as a means to maintain inner equilibrium and a positive sense of self.

1 **Present-day behaviors**
   - They have an underlying awkwardness around people, which stems from the fear of being controlled or disappointed.
   - Intellectually competent, they prefer intellectual stimulation vs. emotional/relational engagement.
   - They are ideally suited to solo tasks, but if assigned to a team project they often remain silent or disengage from group participation.
   - In their personal lives, they have difficulty making a commitment and often feel awkward or confused when it comes to expressing emotional connection or intimacy.

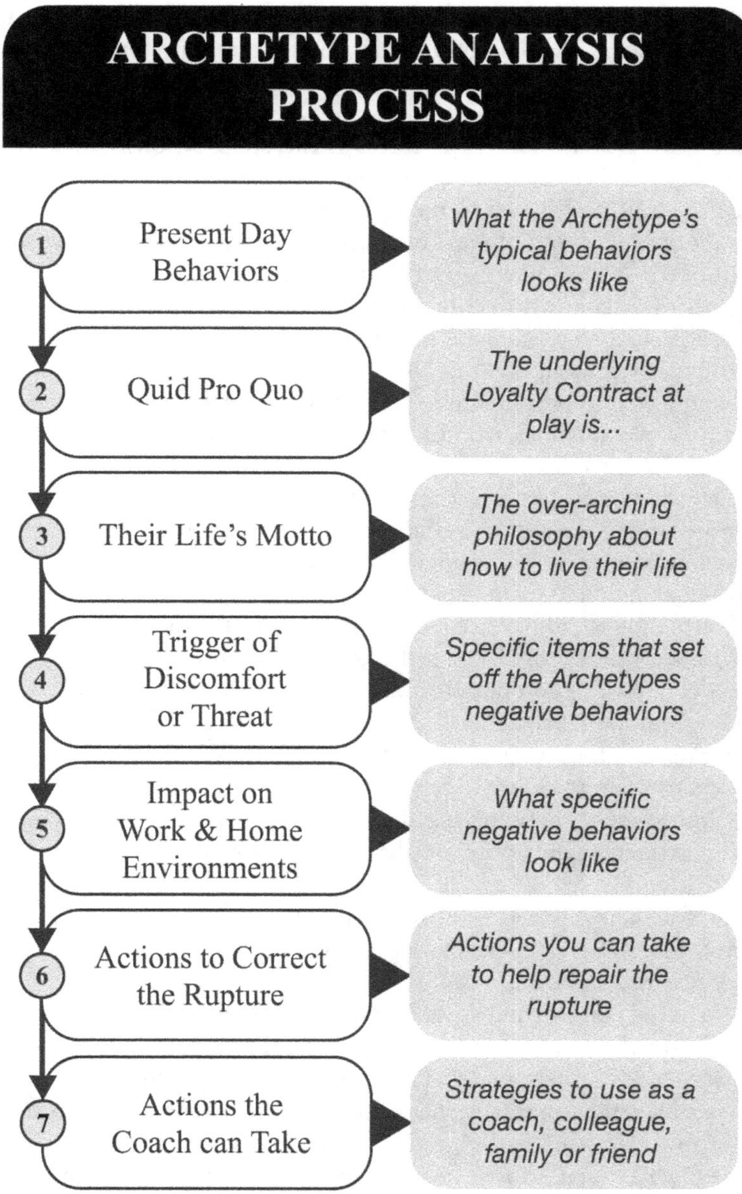

Figure 7.1 The archetype analysis process.

2 **The Quid Pro Quo could be articulated as** "You don't have a right to voice your needs or opinions directly, and if you try it won't do you any good. You will either be punished or ignored or forced to do as I say."
   - Because of this oppressive coercion, Over-Driven Loners learn that the only way to survive is through the suppression of their overt needs or by becoming fiercely independent.

3 **Their life's motto** "It's up to me to survive on my own! Emotions are a distraction and a sign of weakness. Accomplishing tasks on my own is proof of my value and a way of being seen."

4 **Triggers of discomfort or threat**
   - Being asked to participate in projects where the team leader is controlling or demanding.
   - Being asked to participate in projects where there aren't clear expectations or guidelines around deadlines and outcome objectives.
   - Not being recognized for solo efforts or accomplishments.
   - Performance evaluations that offer suggestions for improvement can easily trigger feelings of being controlled or hemmed in.

5 **Impact on work and home environments**
   - Being assigned to team projects often results in a refusal to cooperate or attempts to take control of or undermine a project.
   - Withdrawal and/or decreased participation and productivity tends to delay project completion and increase frustration in others.
   - Their emotional distancing can eventually lead to fracturing of co-worker and family relationships.

6 **Actions to address the rupture**
   - Acknowledge their expertise, hard work, and past accomplishments. This strategy calms possible shame-sensitivity that might have been activated.
   - Ask for their input as to how the situation could be improved. This gives Over-Driven Loners an opportunity to regain control by having a voice and a choice.
   - Share your concern and ask if everything is ok when there is a decline in performance. Compassionate concern can be a reparative experience for Over-Driven Loners, one that rarely or never happened in childhood.
   - Assess whether changing the external environment would correct or improve the situation. Assigning a supervisor who is respectful of the Over-Driven Loner's need for autonomy will often calm the perceived threat of being coerced. Or, assigning them to solo projects where they only report to one individual allows them to feel valued and in control.
   - The Accountability Script: "I value your expertise, but your isolation is creating a bottleneck. I need you to bring the team along, not just cross the finish line alone."

Over-Driven Loners often place themselves in organizations where their particular skill sets are invaluable or irreplaceable. This can create a situation where they don't feel that they have to play by the same rules, or they convey a superior attitude around their own intelligence or expertise. In a coaching situation it is important to help Over-Driven Loners see that performance excellence doesn't give anyone a pass when it comes to bad or disrespectful behavior.

The Self-Sacrificing People Pleaser – Because they were taught that personal value and a sense of safety were measured by how much they give to others, these individuals become overly involved in projects and are subject to burn-out and/or collapse, especially if they don't feel they are adequately noticed and praised for their efforts. This is due to the fact that being anything other than a caretaker of others raises anxiety as it threatens their perceived value, often making them feel unimportant or replaceable.

1 **Present-day behaviors**
   - Goes out of their way to keep the peace, brushing issues under the rug in an attempt to smooth over tension, suppressing own opinions.
   - Apologizes excessively for project assignments that fall short – not allocating responsibility appropriately by covering for others, promising to take on more.
   - Experiences constructive suggestions as criticism, resulting in sudden collapse, anger, withdrawal, accusations that their efforts aren't appreciated.
   - Vulnerable to the manipulation of Oblivious Grandstanders and Vindictive Revenge Seekers because remaining on their good side creates a feeling of safety and/or inclusion.

2 **The Quid Pro Quo** "We will reward you and value you if you sacrifice your needs to take care of us. You aren't allowed to ask for anything or speak up because that shows how selfish you are."
   - Because parental Loyalty Contract lacks any degree of mutuality in relation to others, self-sacrificing people pleasers measure their goodness and/or success by how much they do for others.

3 **Their Life Motto** "Other people can have needs or become frustrated, but I need to be strong enough to prove I can help others no matter what the cost. That's just who I am."

4 **Triggers of discomfort or threat**
   - When asked to delegate parts of a work project, they hear this as criticism which triggers fears of loss of control and loss of value.

- If overlooked when credit or praise for a project isn't forthcoming, they experience a rupture which becomes proof that they aren't valued.
- A hands-off boss who does not give enough structure, guidance, or reassurance can produce feelings of abandonment and/or unworthiness.
- Any form of conflict sets self-sacrificing people pleasers into over-functioning mode.

5 **Impact on work and home environment**
- Over functioning on the part of Self-Sacrificing People Pleasers often creates the under functioning of others, which eventually leads to resentment on both sides.
- Avoidance of conflict for fear of upsetting others leads to a lack of authentic self-expression, often resulting in shallow/superficial relationships.
- Conflict avoidance also limits trust and collaboration in the workplace.

6 **Actions to address the rupture**
- Continual check-ins and monitoring are critical, where the employer sets clear and specific guidelines around expectations where everyone pulls equal weight. This will act as an invitation to create a new loyalty contract for Self-Sacrificing People Pleasers. In addition, specify where their efforts are best used and where others need to pick up the slack.
- If they are still unable to delegate, individual coaching could be implemented to convey the importance of limit setting, self-care, lifestyle balance, and the establishment of appropriate boundaries.
- Invite them to express their own goals and aspirations. This exercise encourages placing their own needs in parity with others.
- Give permission to set limits. Hearing from a supervisor that they have permission to say "No" helps them set boundaries and is an important first step in moving from people pleasing to authentic Psychological Adulthood.
- The Accountability Script: "I appreciate your willingness to help, but when you say 'yes' to everything, you dilute your impact on the priorities that matter most. I need you to practice saying 'No' to low-value tasks."

The Hovering Micromanager – Driven by anxiety stemming from a fear of failure, they believe that falling short of their perfectionistic standards will result in bringing shame or humiliation onto themselves, their families, or their organizations. Because of this, they closely monitor and regulate tasks, as well as the decisions and processes of others.

1 **Present-day behaviors**
   - Over-controlling, scrutinizes every detail to the point that projects are often delayed or come to a standstill.
   - Believes that the responsibility for success of any work project or family initiative solely falls on their shoulders.
   - Does not trust that others are capable of completing tasks independently, which leads to hypervigilance and frequent second-guessing of employees or family members.
   - Tends to see things in all or nothing terms – either you achieve their goals and perfectionistic standards or you're a failure.

2 **The Quid Pro Quo** "You can never bring shame to your family. You must make us proud by always doing your best. We know what is right for you, and you must never question our authority."
   - Because of the strong prohibition against bringing shame upon the family, the ability to express autonomy and independence is seen as a betrayal or a sign of disrespect and ingratitude.

3 **Their life motto** "It all falls on me. I need to get it right, make the best impression. I can't trust others to be as attentive and as exacting as I am, so I must be there to catch their mistakes as well. But what if I make a mistake? I have to be extra careful, not take risks, and check everything to the last detail."

4 **Triggers of discomfort or threat**
   - People who challenge their directives or push back in any way.
   - Unexpected changes that require adjustments to their overall plans.
   - Highly stressful situations where the micromanager fears a loss of control or making a misstep.

5 **Impact on work and home environment**
   - People working under the supervision of Hovering Micromanagers often experience a decrease in morale and productivity.
   - In families, children often experience stunted growth because they have had fewer opportunities to learn from their own mistakes.
   - Intimate partners of Hovering Micromanagers tend to take a back seat in decision-making and often feel demoralized by the lack of mutuality.
   - If they are in leadership roles, the culture or system often experiences an increase in stress where employees show a lack of personal initiative due to continual vigilance and criticism.

6 **Actions to address the rupture**
   - 360-degree feedback from co-workers and leadership team to present a fuller picture of the Hovering Micromanager's impact on others.

- Help them practice delegation and release of control in a graduated way, starting with delegating tasks that have less visibility or create less of an impact.
- Set clear expectations for the micromanager and the team members by creating specific outcome measures, timelines, and clear delineation of responsibility.
- As a coach, you can help create a mental shift with regard to relinquishing control by suggesting catch phrases such as, "Progress not perfection", or "Empower, don't overshadow."
- The Accountability Script: "Your attention to detail is high, but your team's autonomy is low. I need you to measure success by their output, not by your oversight."

The Oblivious Grandstander – Because they were emotionally neglected in childhood and often given inconsistent rules and consequences by their caregivers, Oblivious Grandstanders learned that by making their presence known (speaking loudly, boasting, saying provocative things or even yelling) they were able to draw attention to themselves.

1 **Present-day behaviors**
   - They have great difficulty respecting boundaries and performance expectations.
   - Expert at advice giving, they come across as either well-meaning or condescending in their efforts to become the center of attention.
   - They offer numerous excuses as to why a particular situation gave them a legitimate reason for violating the rules.
   - Not good listeners, they will continually interrupt and dominate conversations.
2 **The Quid Pro Quo** "We're too busy and overwhelmed to take care of you, but we feel guilty for not being there, so we'll tolerate your interruptions and demands on our attention."
   - In childhood they learned that when they didn't receive attention, it meant they had to push harder until they got noticed.
3 **Their life motto** "Now it's my turn to get the attention I've always deserved. I have a lot to offer, and it's time people listened to me. I don't need to be bothered with fancy protocol and playing by the rules. I'm only trying to be helpful."
4 **Triggers of discomfort or threat**
   - Being cut off in the middle of commanding center stage. If and when this occurs, you might see the jovial presentation turn into overt condescension or behind the scenes gossip.
   - Constructive criticism is met with arguments and excuses in an attempt to maintain old behaviors.

- Legitimate limit setting is experienced as a betrayal where the Oblivious Grandstander will assume the victim position.

5 **Impact on work and home environment**
- Spreads rumors, which in turn creates a toxic atmosphere, leading to decreased morale within the workplace or between family members.
- Resistance to feedback when supervisors attempt to address their performance issues.
- Refusal to play by the rules; if accountability measures are enforced, they likely will accuse supervisors of unfair treatment.
- Seeks out Self-Sacrificing People Pleasers as a sounding board and as a way to gain sympathy.

6 **Actions to address the rupture**
- Because they will continue to push the limits, working with Oblivious Grandstanders requires regular and consistent check-ins to ensure that boundaries and performance standards remain in place.
- Clearly articulate the rules and expectations of behavior where boundaries around confidentiality, interruption, tardiness, and timely delivery of results are clearly specified. Often this needs to be put into writing.
- Facilitate dialogue between individuals who have been upset by the Oblivious Grandstander's behavior and then discuss ways that behaviors will be modified in the future.
- Find projects where Oblivious Grandstanders can accomplish tasks that benefit the group or organization, ones that give them credit/attention in more appropriate ways.
- The Accountability Script: "Your passion is evident, but it is consuming all the oxygen in the room. I need you to speak last in the next three meetings to let others step up."

The Passive-Aggressive Gaslighter – Gaslighters were taught to never express anger directly, being told that they didn't have a right to be upset when their needs weren't met. Using deceit and trickery, they use indirect tactics to express dissatisfaction and/or competitive envy of others.

1 **Present-day behaviors**
- Spreads misinformation, exaggerates details, or speculates about targeted individuals in ways that invite question and mistrust.
- Ingratiates themselves to authority figures in an attempt to gain favor.
- Triangulates and creates doubt and mistrust between targeted individuals.
- Likely to use Oblivious Grandstanders to intensify rumors and spread gossip while retaining their position of being the innocent bystander.

2 **The Quid Pro Quo** "You can never show your anger or challenge your parents. It is a sign of disobedience and weakness, and you will be severely punished for it. In order to be seen as good, you must be agreeable and helpful. Your needs always come second, and you must learn to be clever and fend for yourself."
   - Because of strong prohibition against expressing frustration, and the command to be agreeable, they learn to hide their anger and express their disappointments indirectly.

3 **Their life motto** "Strong, negative feelings are unacceptable, so I have to let those parts of me go underground. But I'll show them. I'll level the playing field by denying other people's reality. I'll make others look bad and appear to be helpful. In that way, I'll be seen as the good one, gain the upper hand, and get what I want."

4 **Triggers of discomfort or threat**
   - Challenging their intentions or questioning their claims of "innocence" when a complaint is made against them.
   - Being overlooked, having to witness another person's success in areas that measure performance, position, or likeability.
   - Being asked to reveal aspects of personal vulnerability.

5 **Impact on work and home environment**
   - They poison team dynamics by creating confusion and mistrust, where people become afraid to voice their opinions which in turn stifles collaboration, creativity, and problem-solving.
   - Their victims often feel a growing sense of shame and self-doubt due to the fact that it is difficult to point to the specifics of their manipulation.
   - In personal relationships, victims of Passive-Aggressive Gaslighters often become more reliant and dependent on the gaslighter's version of reality. They become meek and try to seek the gaslighter's approval which increases their sense of helplessness.

6 **Actions to address the rupture**
   - Mediate conversations between the gaslighter and the targeted individual(s) to stop innuendo or the spreading of rumors.
   - Focus on patterns, for example, the number of complaints, rather than any one specific incident. Gaslighters are masters of self-defense, and they do so through denying patterns and minimizing their involvement.
   - Challenge when they begin to deflect away from taking any responsibility, particularly when there is a repeated pattern of specific complaints within the organization or with one specific relationship.
   - Give them permission to voice concerns directly and invite their ideas for organizational improvement.

- The Accountability Script: "I am noticing a pattern of confusion around your projects and interactions with co-workers. Moving forward, I need all agreements documented in writing immediately after meetings to ensure we are aligned."

The Vindictive Revenge Seeker – Because they were raised in an environment where there was extreme pressure to excel coupled with a message that they were entitled to more than their fair share in life, Vindictive Revenge Seekers are highly competitive and believe they are justified in targeting retribution to those who challenge them.

1 **Present-day behaviors**
   - Reduces complexity by presenting conflictual or complicated situations into all or

   nothing terms, therefore missing the big picture analysis and leaving the organization more vulnerable.
   - Appearing confident, boastful, they are quick to take credit for success and are equally quick to blame others when something goes wrong.
   - Displays irritability, angry outbursts, demeaning, and devaluing of others if and when they disagree or challenge the Vindictive Revenge Seeker.
   - Insists that they have a right to express their opinions, even if they come across in a disrespectful or threatening manner.
2 **The Quid Pro Quo** "You need to be #1, and if you fall short of anything other than the best, you are a loser, and I will humiliate you. However, if anyone else tries to deny you, I will defend you, protect you, get you out of trouble because you deserve special treatment."
   - Because of the intensity of these mixed messages, Vindictive Revenge Seekers live with a thin veneer of confidence that hides an extremely high degree of shame sensitivity and insecurity. In order to protect themselves, they develop a coping strategy of assuming positions of power and then retaliating when things don't go their way. If you cross a Vindictive Revenge Seeker, be prepared for retaliation.
3 **Their life motto** "Get ahead at all costs, and don't let anyone or anything get in your way."
4 **Triggers of discomfort or threat**
   - Anything that challenges or threatens their authority or ambition.
   - Witnessing another person's success surpassing their own. There can only be one winner and everyone else is seen as losers.
   - Not being given enough attention or praise for their accomplishments.
   - Being forced to be accountable to rules, laws, and limit setting.

5 **Impact on work and home environment**
- The constant demand that others agree and follow orders often results in people

becoming "yes men" in organizations.
- Toxic work environments lead to high staff turnover, resulting in financial consequences such as costs associated with retraining and the disruption of project deadlines.
- Because co-workers, employees, and family members often feel criticized and not allowed to freely voice their opinion, this decreases motivation, mood, and morale.
- When placed in a leadership position, Vindictive Revenge Seekers create an atmosphere of rewards and punishments based on stroking their egos rather than performance and accountability.

6 **Actions to address the rupture**
- Given that this archetype frequently assumes a leadership position, it is important that any strategy you attempt is based on appealing to their sense of fair play. Although Vindictive Revenge Seekers punish those who disagree with them, they also have a high desire to be liked (adored), and might consider instituting more fair and reasonable contracts in order to gain positive approval.
- In a coaching situation, invite them to share their leadership philosophy and principles. Examine how those principles show up in their behaviors with others, or whether their behaviors are inconsistent with their principles.
- Share feedback that compares and contrasts known data and feedback from others like a 360-degree feedback process. Use this to appropriately bring unwelcome behavior to the surface as a way of challenging their blind spots.
- Determine if they are exhibiting behaviors that are contrary to HR policies or the organization's core values, using them as a point of coaching inquiry and accountability.
- The Accountability Script: "This behavior violates our core values. We can debate strategy, but personal attacks are a firing offense. This is your official notice."

The Antagonistic Nay-Sayer – Because they were raised in an environment where they always had to justify their position, Antagonistic Nay-Sayers learned to become the masters of debate or devil's advocate. In childhood, they were often told, "No" to any request that centered on pleasure or simply having fun. Therefore, they are often very serious individuals who rarely take risks, think out of the box, or possess a healthy sense of humor.

They believe that their value to an organization is to be in the role of armchair critic in order that all perspectives and options are considered.

However, rather than presenting thoughtful questions or objections, this archetype crosses the line by becoming judge and jury to obstruct others or maintain personal control.

1 **Present-day behaviors**
   - Presents as knowledgeable, quick to point out loop-holes or risks when new ideas are introduced.
   - They will be the first to say "I told you so" if a project falls short of the mark, as if these comments prove how smart they are.
   - They tend to be difficult team members as they are long-winded in their arguments, and they can quickly deplete the morale of the team.

2 **The Quid Pro Quo** "You can never count on things being straightforward and simple. There is always a catch, and people will try to fool you, so be on your guard. If you are hasty and gullible or if you make a mistake, we'll shame and punish you."
   - Because of the fear of being caught for missing an important detail or making a mistake, Antagonistic Nay-Sayers learned to protect themselves by producing enough facts and evidence to not be caught off guard.

3 **Their life motto** "In order to get the most out of life and not be fooled or made to look like a fool, I need to educate myself thoroughly and present the risks of any given situation to others. In order to protect myself from being told I am wrong; it is not safe for me to volunteer my own ideas or suggestions."

4 **Triggers of discomfort or threat**
   - Being asked to think outside of the box and come up with alternative solutions, where their own ideas might be put on the spot and challenged.
   - Individuals who push back and challenge their "yes, but" concerns.
   - Changing an agreed-upon protocol or business strategy mid-stream.
   - Dismissing their concerns or not giving their concerns enough time for group discussion or debate.

5 **Impact on work and home environment**
   - Digging in their heels, refusing to cooperate, going to upper management or HR to complain.
   - Withdrawal or failure to complete their part of projects leaves others with more work and increased resentment.
   - Their exacting nature and impatience create a general feeling of walking on eggshells.
   - Their ridicule of others creates a shut-down in the free exchange of ideas, demoralization, and frustration of team members.

Actions to address the rupture

- Ask them to summarize concerns in writing without taking up time on endless details in meetings.
- Address the summarized concerns in one-on-one meetings with their manager, not in team meetings with colleagues. Antagonistic Nay-Sayers need to know that they do not have the final say. Setting this leadership boundary helps contain the nay-sayer's desire to keep pushing for control.
- Educate them on the value of coming up with solutions not just objections. Going forward tell them that all objections must be followed by a realistic suggestion.
- An outside coach can also encourage Antagonistic Nay-Sayers to find lifestyle balance both at work and in other areas of life. Encouraging activities that reduce stress and create socialization opportunities can increase a sense of inclusion giving them the attention they are secretly longing for.
- The Accountability Script: "You are excellent at spotting risks. Now I need you to be excellent at solving them. For every concern you raise, I need you to propose two viable solutions."

The Hiring Manager's Radar: Detecting Leadership Blind Spots

Identifying these archetypes in existing employees is one challenge; preventing them from entering your organization is another. The goal here is not to play therapist or to psychoanalyze a candidate's childhood. The goal is to use behavioral interviewing to uncover how they will handle stress, authority, and collaboration. If a candidate has any of these archetypes, an effective interview process should evidence them.

Standard interviews often focus on technical competence ("Can they do the job?"). To build a self-differentiated culture, you must also assess their relational capacity ("How will they do the job?").

While this tool kit is not exhaustive, you can use it to uncover specific blind spots during the interview process:

1 **The Soloist Risk (The Over-Driven Loner)**
   - The Trap: They perform well individually but struggle to collaborate or develop others.
   - The Question: "Tell me about a time you had to rely on someone else's work to complete a critical project, and their work wasn't up to your standard. What did you do?"

- The Red Flag: "I just took it over and did it myself to make sure it was right." This reveals an inability to coach, trust, or tolerate imperfection in others.

2 **The Burnout Risk** (**The Self-Sacrificing People Pleaser**)
- The Trap: They agree to everything to avoid conflict, leading to dropped balls.
- The Question: "Tell me about a time you had to say 'no' to a key stakeholder or a boss because their request was unreasonable. How did you deliver that message?"
- The Red Flag: An inability to recall a time they said no, or a story where they ultimately just worked harder to accommodate the unreasonable request.

3 **The Bottleneck Risk** (**The Hovering Micromanager**)
- The Trap: They cannot let go, slowing down the entire team's velocity.
- The Question: "Describe the most complex project you delegated to a direct report. How did you track their progress without getting in their way?"
- The Red Flag: A lack of clear "tracking" mechanisms other than constant check-ins, or a story where they ultimately had to step back in to "save" the project rather than letting the employee solve it.

4 **The Spotlight Risk** (**The Oblivious Grandstander**)
- The Trap: They dominate the room and take undue credit, alienating peers.
- The Question: "Tell me about a recent win your team achieved. Who, specifically, was the MVP of that project and why?"
- The Red Flag: They struggle to name a specific person, or they quickly pivot the story back to their own leadership role in "guiding" that person.

5 **The Trust Risk** (**The Passive-Aggressive Gaslighter**)
- The Trap: They create confusion and avoid direct accountability.
- The Question: "Tell me about a time you made a mistake that impacted a colleague. How did you fix the relationship?"
- The Red Flag: Vague language ("errors were made"), minimizing the impact, or focusing on how the colleague "misinterpreted" their intention rather than owning the specific action.

6 **The Culture Risk** (**The Vindictive Revenge Seeker**)
- The Trap: They prioritize personal battles over company goals.
- The Question: "Tell me about a time a peer or boss strongly disagreed with a strategy you were passionate about. How did you handle it, and what is your relationship with that person today?"
- The Red Flag: Lingering bitterness, describing the other person as "irrational" or "political," or admitting they simply waited for the other person to fail.

7 **The Stagnation Risk (The Antagonistic Nay-Sayer)**
   - The Trap: They stifle innovation by focusing exclusively on risk.
   - The Question: "Tell me about a new initiative at your last company that you were initially skeptical about. How did you support the team in making it work despite your reservations?"
   - The Red Flag: A story where they "warned everyone" it would fail (and were right), rather than a story about how they tried to mitigate the risks to help it succeed.

Chapter Summary

In this chapter we elaborated on the utility of the seven archetypes by providing a step-by-step Archetype Analysis Process. This process illustrates specific ways to address unhealthy archetype behaviors so that individuals experience less stress (less friction) and are able to operate from within their productive zone (more flow). We also demonstrated ways that the Archetype Analysis Process could be used in hiring situations to spot potential Archetype risks through the Hiring Manager's Tool Kit.

Usually, people who possess negative attributes represented by one of the archetypes do know on some level that they are bending or even breaking the rules. If these infractions or boundary violations get rewarded, the culture and the system then become complicit in enabling the unhealthy behaviors to continue.

That is why "naming" is so vital in activating any change process. Being able to name what we see as a repeated pattern, specifically a pattern that causes harm to others is critically important. The Archetype Analysis Process has a powerful effect on exposing the behavior and thereby creating solid justification for how and why a specific behavior has to change.

This step-wise process provides the Self-Differentiated Leader with a form of radar, a radar for navigating those challenging or rocky employee performance difficulties. In addition to using this as an assessment instrument, we offered specific coaching suggestions to enforce new accountability measures towards repair. We should note that it is important to acknowledge the flip side of performance as well. When we see a pattern of positive behavior, naming that would be equally important as a reinforcement so that the positive behavior is more likely to continue.

Key Takeaways

1. Identifying different types of ruptures based on the seven different archetypes helps clarify specific measures that need to be put into place to create a successful plan for repair.
2. Use the step-by-step archetype analysis process to fine tune your leadership radar.
3. Not everyone wants to change. If an employee defends their archetype despite clear feedback and support, they are choosing to remain limited. A leader's job is to recognize this choice and act accordingly.
4. Ignoring or working around a rigid archetype doesn't just stall that individual; it signals to your high performers that this dysfunction is acceptable, which will begin to restrict organizational advancement and morale.
5. Hiring for skills without assessing behavioral "shadows" is an invitation for future friction. To build a self-differentiated culture, leaders must look beyond technical competence during interviews and screen for the subtle characteristics of rigid archetypes.

Next Level Reflections

1. Which archetype do you have the most difficulty understanding?
2. Which archetype do you most identify with, and how might the constraints of your old Loyalty Contract limit your ability to self-differentiate?
3. What new behavioral choices might you make in your own life or in your leadership role in your organization?
4. Are there any areas where your own leadership style might be creating unfair opportunities for certain individuals and lack of opportunities for others?
5. List specific situations where you find it most difficult to address others.

Chapter 8

The DNA of Healthy Loyalty Contracts

When Japan surrendered in World War II in 1945, Lieutenant Hiroo Onoda, remained in the Philippine jungle on Lubang Island where he had been assigned for nearly thirty years. Onoda and a small group of his comrades ignored leaflets and radio broadcasts announcing Japan's surrender, dismissing them as enemy propaganda. He continued to live as a soldier until 1974, when his former commanding officer traveled from Japan to formally relieve him of duty (Onoda, 1974).

Several factors explain why these men remained in service for so long. Communication in the scattered Pacific islands was extremely difficult at the end of the war, and many outposts never received clear orders to surrender. Equally important were the iron-clad binds of loyalty and duty that shaped Japanese military values at the time, emphasizing honor, obedience, and sacrifice. For these men, surrender was unthinkable and continuing their mission, even in isolation, was a way of upholding that honor.

This is an incredibly powerful historical example of a Loyalty Contract that for most of Onoda-san's adult life, bound him to a past that no longer existed. To be so absolute about a cultural Loyalty Contract shuts out any new information and shuts down any curiosity for something different. This was the ultimate example of being a "loyal soldier".

As we have stated earlier, a psychological adult understands that life is about creating a fair sense of loyalty to our workplace, family and friends, and finding one's own self-differentiated self. These two aspects of what it means to be a psychological adult must be integrated so that they can co-exist in a way that is subject to change and adaptation as new information is incorporated into the narrative.

According to Richard Rohr (2011), in the first half of life, we strive to be "loyal soldiers" learning the rules of our parents, teachers, and managers. Some people never question the price we pay to be a loyal soldier, so they are often unknowingly bound by these rules and in so doing, never move towards Self-Differentiation. The path of Self-Differentiation at any

DOI: 10.4324/9781003621393-8

age is about "leaving home" to find a new home for the person you are to become. This requires questioning the old Loyalty Contracts we formed in earlier years.

Becoming a psychological adult in a continuous journey leads us toward creating healthier Loyalty Contracts. Without this journey, we remain much like Lieutenant Hiroo Onoda, stuck in time, playing by the rules of a Loyalty Contract that no longer serves us, and, therefore, we cannot become self-differentiated in the workplace or in our day to day lives. Psychologically speaking, we developmentally remain the loyal soldier forever.

Components of Healthy Loyalty Contracts

How can we design a healthy loyalty contract? First, we need to know the essential components that all healthy Loyalty Contracts have in common – what we call the DNA of Healthy Loyalty Contracts (see Figure 8.1). They are:

- Fair: A sense of mutuality is a must.
- Clear: Everything is on the table.
- Functional: The "how" matters.
- Adaptable: Knowing when to change.
- Sustainable: A shared commitment to growth.

These components are built upon the concepts of healthy and unhealthy loyalty contracts that were mentioned in Chapter 1.
Let's examine each one more fully.

Fair: A Sense of Mutuality is a Must

A healthy Loyalty Contract is built on the foundation of Fairness, which is rooted in an intentional sense of mutuality. Mutuality is the shared understanding that the relationship is a two-way street where the needs and contributions of both parties are acknowledged and valued. This sense of reciprocity is crucial because it ensures that the arrangement is fair. Without it, loyalty feels like a one-sided obligation, inevitably leading to resentment, burnout, and oftentimes the destruction of the relationship. Tom's story is a classic example of what happens when this mutuality is missing and how it can be restored.

Tom was a bright consultant at the local subsidiary of a global public relations firm. He recently joined the firm from one of its competitors. His employment contract clearly stated his hours are 9 to 6, a 45-hour

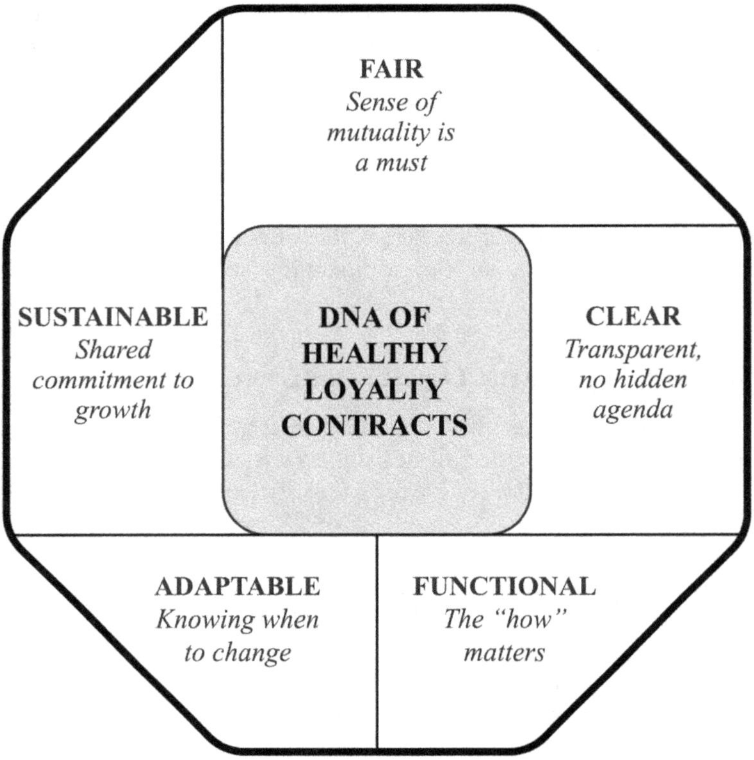

Figure 8.1 DNA of healthy Loyalty Contracts.

week, but he constantly managed "urgent" requests late at night and during weekends from his manager. There was no overtime payment. When he spoke with colleagues, the overall response was, "That's how it works here." Tom accepted this reality and tried to satisfy all the endless, urgent requests without challenging them. In this firm burnout had become a sign of a loyal worker.

The Breaking Point: One day, Tom had to delay a flight for a vacation with his girlfriend because his manager demanded last-minute changes to a client presentation. Tom had to work until midnight. His girlfriend complained about this instance of work cumulatively impacting their relationship. Tom began to harbor quiet resentment towards her for not understanding. His manager sent a 3 a.m. text message: "Thank you for your hard work and dedication to our client." With tears in her eyes, his girlfriend said, "This is never going to change!"

In that moment, Tom realized that his manager's leadership style was impacting his happiness and probably wouldn't change. Up to that point, he had never questioned this unfair Loyalty Contract. This realization, thanks in no small part to his girlfriend, was his first step toward becoming a psychological adult – the decision to stop being the overly accommodating loyal soldier and start authoring his own terms.

The Renegotiation Strategy: Tom didn't want to just complain. He decided to renegotiate his Loyalty Contract with his manager once he gathered enough evidence to show the lack of mutuality or one-sidedness of his boss's current expectations. For the next three weeks, Tom kept a detailed record of his overtime in a spreadsheet. The average was more than 10 hours per week. He then requested a one-on-one coffee meeting with his manager.

Before this meeting, Tom discussed how to best approach his boss with his personal coach. During coaching, he realized his manager exhibited characteristics of the Oblivious Grandstander Archetype, a leader who appeared concerned and helpful but often ignored or violated boundaries. When Tom practiced this conversation, imagining that he was sitting with his manager, the coach video-recorded him.

Reviewing the footage without sound, Tom observed his own non-verbal cues. "It looks like I'm apologizing..." he noted, seeing himself scratching his head with an apologetic expression. The coach reminded him that his intention was not to apologize, but to renegotiate. "You need to look and sound confident," the coach said.

Tom's strategy was to be direct, confident, and solution oriented. Here is what he said.

> *As you know, I enjoy working here, and I am 100% committed to the sustainable growth of our team and the success of our clients. At the same time, I am also committed to my own sustainable career growth. You encouraged me to speak up if I have a concern before it becomes a problem during the on-boarding process, and that's why I wanted to meet with you.*
>
> *I understand my job requires handling urgent requests, and I've been thinking about how I can manage them sustainably. The last thing I want is to burn out and suddenly quit. Because I want to work here for a long time, I took the liberty of tracking my overtime for the last three weeks and found I worked more than 30 uncompensated hours. Don't get me wrong. I'm not asking for overtime pay. Instead, I'd like to propose a "time-for-time" system. Could we agree that for every*

two hours of approved work over 45 hours, I can bank one hour of paid time off to be used within the following month? This will help me replenish my creative energy and feels fairer to me. What do you think?

Toward a Fairer and Healthier Loyalty Contract: Tom's manager didn't feel blamed or attacked. Since several high-performing consultants had recently left due to burnout, she didn't want to lose Tom. Tom's proposal made her reconsider her own best interests, as retaining talent was critical to her success. The solution was something she could implement within her authority.

She replied,

Thank you, Tom, for bringing this to the table. It sounds fair to both of us. Let's start immediately and review it in two weeks. If it works well, I might expand this policy to the whole team.

The manager valued Tom's loyalty and constructive approach. While urgent tasks would still require overtime, the terms of engagement had shifted. This was a crucial distinction. Tom didn't break the cycle of unrealistic demands, but he established a clear Quid Pro Quo that leaned more in his favor. This could be seen as a "fixes that fail" type of solution that realistically addressed an immediate symptom (uncompensated work) but really didn't solve the long-term problem (a culture of constant urgency and the impact on his personal life). The underlying expectation to be available 24/7 remained, and the burnout risk for the team persisted.

This example highlights the nuance and complexity of altering a Loyalty Contract when you were not in a position of ultimate control. For Tom, his actions represented a significant first step. While the demand on his time continued, the banked hours allowed him to reclaim personal time helping to mend the pressure he felt from his girlfriend and restored some level of control and increased Fairness.

By making the hidden terms visible and renegotiating for a fairer exchange, Tom transformed an exploitative arrangement demonstrating that Fairness was not an all-or-nothing concept. It was a foundational element that could be woven into even the most challenging work cultures, one conversation at a time. Tom didn't just save his weekend; he saved the company the massive hidden cost of turnover, which for specialized roles can exceed an entire year's salary. By initiating this conversation, he moved from being a "flight risk" to a sustainable asset.

A Note on Cultural Implication of Fairness: Highlighting the importance of mutuality is critical because the perception of Fairness can be shaped by cultural norms. For instance, in cultures with a high-Power

Distance – meaning societies where steep hierarchies are considered normal, people accept that power is distributed unequally (Hofstede, 2011). The Korean language, with its complex system of honorifics, provides an example. Using different titles and formalities based on age and status is required, which reinforces an acceptance of hierarchical power distribution from a young age (Shin, 2021).

Ultimately, this isn't just a cultural issue. An individual manager in any society, even one that promotes equality, can unintentionally create an unfair environment by allowing the principle of mutuality to be secondary to cultural norms. Therefore, regardless of the cultural backdrop, building a fair relationship always requires intentional effort.

Clear: Everything Is on the Table

While Fairness provides the foundation, a contract can only be truly healthy if its terms are understood by everyone. This brings us to the second essential piece of a healthy Loyalty Contract: clarity. Clarity involves making all expectations, responsibilities, and definitions of success explicit and mutually agreed upon, leaving no room for ambiguity. The toxic dynamic between Sunny and Bob shows just how destructive a lack of clarity can be.

At an online education platform, Sunny led the marketing team and Bob led the sales team. While collaboration between them was critical for success, they weren't competing against market competitors. They competed with one another internally.

Sunny was an Over-Driven Loner. Her loyalty was to her own metrics, often detached from their ultimate impact on sales. To Sunny, her team's role was to generate as many marketing-qualified leads as possible. She and her team worked late and hard. When the marketing team handed the leads over to the sales team, Sunny believed their job was done. She created and led a silo of very targeted job-specific, results-oriented professionals.

Bob is a Vindictive Revenge Seeker. His primary loyalty was to his own power within the organization. When his team missed its sales target, he blamed Sunny's team for generating junk leads. He intentionally avoided defining what a good marketing lead was and refused to provide a helpful and specific definition with the marketing team. There was a reason for this: By keeping the definition ambiguous, Bob could weaponize it. He aspired to be the CEO's successor and believed this strategy of blame and control would position him as the stronger leader.

This intentionally unclear Loyalty Contract between the two managers poisoned business performance and corroded the company's culture of collaboration. It was the elephant in the room.

The Breaking Point: The company launched a new online train-the-trainer program targeting in-house learning and development professionals. The marketing budget for this launch was the largest in the company's history. True to form, Sunny didn't align with the sales team, viewing it as an inefficient distraction. She pushed her team, and they achieved a record-breaking result. However, the sales figures remained flat for the next four weeks.

The CEO was calling an emergency meeting to address the problem. As usual, Bob immediately blamed Sunny:

> *The volume of leads is high, but more than half of them are junk. My team is wasting its time.*

Sunny was blindsided and humiliated in front of the CEO and other leaders.

The CEO sighed, then addressed the room with a firm and confident tone.

> *Let me be clear. We are not missing our target because of bad marketing leads. We are not missing it because of a bad sales team. Not at all. We are missing our target because the two of you are not working collaboratively together. The reason is that you two lack a clear contract with each other. Today, we are going to build one.*

Both Sunny and Bob were surprised by the CEO's resolute attitude.

The Renegotiation Strategy: As a Self-Differentiated Leader, the CEO refused to get drawn into another emotional, finger-pointing drama. She put everything on the table and began to facilitate the negotiation of a new contract between Sunny and Bob. The CEO used The Clarity Protocol: Converting subjective complaints (junk leads) into objective criteria (Yes/No questions). Ambiguity fuels friction; clarity fuels flow. She grabbed a marker, walked to a flip chart, and turned to Bob.

> *Bob, from this moment on, you will no longer use the word "junk."*

When Bob tried to defend his choice of words, the CEO cut him off, making it clear that such language would be no longer acceptable.
She continued,

> *Give me five specific, binary (Yes/No) criteria that define a Sales Qualified Lead. For example: Does the company have a dedicated*

> *in-house L&D division? Yes/No. Is the contact at a manager's level or above? Yes/No. Was the company's previous year's revenue at least X amount? Yes/No.*

Stripped of his ability to be vague, Bob was forced to articulate his team's concrete needs for the very first time.

The CEO then turned to Sunny.

> *"Sunny, can you agree to have all five of these data points clearly filled out when passing every lead to Bob's team?" Sunny agreed. Next, the CEO looked back at Bob. "Once a lead that meets these five criteria enters the sales system, how quickly will your team make the initial follow-up call?"*

They agreed on a 24-hour maximum.

Finally, the CEO closed the loop. "Is there anything you two are not clear about?" Bob asked, "What happens if our team disqualifies a lead?" The CEO looked at Sunny. She replied,

> In that case, we would require the sales team to specify the reason by selecting from a pre-defined list – the same five criteria we just agreed on. We can create a simple dropdown menu in the system. That data will help our team refine its approach.

Bob nodded in agreement.

Toward a Clearer and Healthier Contract: Following the meeting, the new agreement was formally documented. The CEO then suggested a cross-functional meeting for both the sales and marketing teams. In that meeting, Sunny and Bob co-presented the new contract, discussing how their teams could cooperate more effectively.

Previously, the tension between the two leaders made it difficult for their team members to collaborate. Then, the dynamic shifted. The loyalty of the team members was no longer tethered to their leaders' dysfunctional archetypes. Instead, their loyalty shifted to the crystal-clear process defined in their new, shared contract. The wall that stood between Marketing and Sales was transformed into a bridge, built on the foundation of a clear and healthy contract.

This transformation was only possible because of the decisive intervention of a Self-Differentiated Leader who was willing to put everything on the table.

Functional: The How Matters

A Loyalty Contract can be both Fair and Clear on paper yet remain powerless in practice if the "how" is ignored. This brings us to the third essential point: the contract must be Functional. A Functional contract is supported by practical, well-designed processes and mechanisms that allow people to perform its tasks – such as giving feedback or challenging ideas – safely and effectively. These processes provide a structural bridge between intention and action, which is especially critical when cultural norms or power dynamics create invisible barriers, as Paul discovered when he tried to implement radical candor in a new environment.

Paul, an American executive in the food and beverage industry, was appointed as the General Manager of his company's successful subsidiary in Seoul, South Korea. While he had visited Seoul three times on business, this was his first time working there. Paul was a firm believer in "radical candor" and wanted to build a culture where the best ideas, not just the ideas of the most senior person, would win through open debate. He encouraged his Korean leadership team to challenge him, especially since he was new to the market. He expected vigorous discussion.

Instead, during the weekly 90-minute leadership meetings, members simply took turns reporting to Paul. The leadership team meeting became a series of one-on-one reports. Paul was the only one asking questions; no one challenged him or each other. There were only polite smiles and nods. A call with his European predecessor confirmed his suspicion. There was a hidden rule among the executives not to question one another, as doing so was perceived as a challenge to authority and was seen as disrespectful.

Paul ran headfirst into the high-power distance culture of the Korean workplace. The Loyalty Contract within this subsidiary was clear. Questioning a boss or colleague was perceived as a direct challenge to their authority and expertise. Directly challenging the GM's ideas was considered impolite and professionally risky.

The Breaking Point: In his quest to create an open culture, Paul decided to implement one of his company's global HR initiatives, a mandatory 360-degree feedback system. Believing the system's anonymity would provide a safe channel for feedback, he was confident that the Korean employees would feel safe to speak up. He enthusiastically presented this plan to his leadership team and key managers, asking for questions or concerns. There were none.

He launched the 360-degree assessment with the eleven leadership team members, including himself. Paul had run this assessment in other countries, but this was the first time he received perfect scores on every single item. The anonymous qualitative feedback consisted of a stream of generic praise. He checked with his HR Director and discovered that all managers had received similar positive feedback, especially from their direct reports. The HR Director secretly told him,

> *The employees who participated were very nervous. They did not trust the anonymity and worried that if they shared any negative comments, it could lead to retaliation later.*

Paul realized his critical error: he had tried to implement a tool for transparency before building the foundation of psychological safety required for it to work.

The Renegotiation Strategy: Paul met with an executive coach to discuss the matter. He needed a Functional process so that his team members could speak their minds and challenge one another without the psychological burden of fear. Together, they landed on a core principle: Change the process, not the people. With the coach's recommendation, he implemented two structured exercises.

First, for their next major project, Paul decided to create an atmosphere that was more playful, and he created a game where he encouraged people to use their imaginations to find loopholes in the plan. He officially designated three leadership team members as a "Challenge Team". He explained,

> *Your role on this project, for which you will be evaluated, is to be the enemy of the main team, including myself. Your job is to find every single weakness in our plan from the perspective of our harshest critics – angry customers, frustrated employees, and aggressive competitors. Your job is to attack our plan to spot potential failures. Moving forward, all of us will take turns being a Challenge Team.*

This new, game-like process did not automatically grant psychological safety, but it provided a structured and safer container for it to begin to develop. The key was that it reframed the nature of feedback. There was a significant difference between giving feedback to a person and giving feedback on a plan. The exercise deliberately shifted the focus to the latter. Team members were not challenging their colleagues or their boss directly; they were fulfilling an assigned role within the rules of the game. This depersonalized the act of criticism, turning a potentially disrespectful confrontation into a productive, collaborative exercise.

While this didn't immediately achieve the goal of direct, 360-degree feedback for the leader, it laid the essential groundwork. It taught the team how to disagree constructively within a safe context, building the trust and psychological muscle necessary for more direct feedback in the future.

Second, during a meeting for a new marketing initiative, he conducted a "Pre-Mortem" exercise (Klein, 2007). He addressed the group.

> *Let's imagine we've jumped forward in time one year from now. Our project has failed miserably. It's a total disaster. Now, for the next twenty minutes, I want everyone to independently do a brainwriting exercise to identify every possible reason why we failed.*

He then asked a junior member to collect the ideas and write them on a whiteboard, which sparked a robust group discussion on how to prevent potential failures.

Toward a Functional and Healthier Loyalty Contract: The impact was immediate and remarkable. By using the Challenge Team and Pre-Mortem exercises, Paul observed his team members acting differently – pointing out flawed assumptions, identifying local market risks he hadn't seen, and debating vigorously within the confines of the new rules. Paul didn't change the people or the core tenets of the organization or the Korean societal culture. He provided a functional and safe mechanism for his team to contribute and challenge constructively.

The healthier, Functional Loyalty Contract became:

> *We show our loyalty not by staying silent, but by actively participating in the structured processes designed to find the truth.*

These Functional processes transformed the team's interactions. By introducing impersonal, role-based, and process-driven methods, Paul created a new path for his team to speak up, ensuring that the best ideas, not just the boss's ideas, will finally win.

Paul's story provides a powerful example of a leader who initially exhibited the behaviors of an Oblivious Grandstander. Arriving with a know-it-all conviction in his own methods, he violated cultural boundaries by pushing his radical candor approach as a mandatory feedback tool. A classic Grandstander would likely rationalize the failure, but Paul's breaking point was a moment of self-awareness, not blame. His crucial decision to change the process rather than the people marked his journey away from the archetype and toward a more Functional, self-differentiated leadership style that successfully invites and slowly builds psychological safety.

Paul's success illustrates a critical distinction: You cannot demand Psychological Safety (trust); you must engineer it through Process Safety (structure). Paul failed when he asked for personal feedback, which carries high interpersonal risk. He succeeded when he built Process Safety – using the Challenge Team to make critique a mandatory requirement of the job, not a personal attack.

Adaptable: Knowing When to Change

The world and the people in it are constantly evolving. A Loyalty Contract that is Fair, Clear, and Functional can still fail if it cannot change along with changing times and conditions. This brings us to the fourth essential element: the contract must be Adaptable. Adaptability is the capacity for the agreement to be revised in response to new circumstances whether it's an individual's changing life needs or a smarter way of achieving business goals. Without this flexibility, a contract creates a zero-sum game between a person's health and their career, a situation powerfully explored in the story of Janice.

Janice was a reliable and high-performing management consultant who led the best team in the firm by every measure: revenue, profit, and client satisfaction. Her boss, Sarah, was a Hovering Micromanager. She took pride in upholding the firm's unwritten code: High performance is synonymous with around-the-clock availability and continual cross-checking of every detail. This culture was reinforced by Sarah's own habits: she frequently sent emails, texts, and made calls into the evening, early morning, and over weekends. This behavior created constant anxiety, making it impossible for team members to ever truly disconnect.

After working this way for 10 years, Janice experienced serious burnout and took six months leave to recover. The firm couldn't afford to lose her, so they granted the leave. Upon her return, Janice had a stark realization: While she was away, two of her high-performing team members had left the firm, citing burnout. She knew she could no longer work around the clock as she had done for the past decade. The firm's unwritten Loyalty Contract – your value is measured by your visible sacrifice – was now in direct conflict with her well-being. Its inability to adapt had pushed her, and others, to the breaking point.

***The Breaking Point*:** Two weeks after Janice's return, a massive business opportunity landed on her desk: The chance to pitch for a prestigious, global, industry-defining client. It was exactly the kind of high-stakes challenge on which Janice had built her reputation. Sarah called Janice into her office.

> *You know what I want. This is the big one, Janice. I'm still hungry. I need the old Janice back for this. I need your team on this 24/7. I'll be in touch as ideas come to me. Let's show them we own this market!*

This was Janice's moment of truth. For Sarah, this was a return to the gold standard of work. For Janice, it was a demand to walk the same path that had led to her collapse. She knew she couldn't accept the old terms, but she also couldn't refuse the opportunity. After the conversation, Janice left the office feeling cornered.

The Renegotiation Strategy: Janice sat down in a local coffee shop. On one side of a page, she wrote down her "non-negotiables": No evening work, no weekend work, and a clear communication protocol. She knew that appealing to Sarah's empathy was a guaranteed path to failure; the Hovering Micromanager would see it as an excuse. So, on the opposite page, she wrote down what mattered most to Sarah: Winning. Her strategy was to align her non-negotiables directly with Sarah's core interest.

The next day, Janice requested a meeting.

> *"You and I both want to win this, Sarah," Janice began. "And I'm sure this won't be the only win you want. We want to keep winning in this market, sustainably. For ten years, we achieved great things by working longer and harder. I've realized that is no longer a sustainable way to win. It is time for us to change."*

She laid out her plan.

> *Instead of the entire team working on everything, I will create three small, expert sub-teams to focus only on the most critical parts of the pitch. The team will work intensely from 9-to-5. No evenings, no weekends. This forces ruthless prioritization. A winning idea will come from a rested, creative team, not an exhausted one. We don't want to see more of our top talent leave due to burnout. That doesn't help us win.*

Sarah listened without expression. Leaning forward, Janice made her second proposal.

> To win this, I have another request. We need to change how we communicate to protect the team's focus. Constant pings and late-night texts fragment their attention. At the same time, I know you need to

share ideas the moment they occur to you. Let's create a shared "Project Ideas" document online, easily accessible by smartphone. If you have an insight at 10 p.m., put it there. The team will start every morning by reviewing that document. This system ensures we capture your thinking without disrupting the team's essential recovery time.

Finally, Janice sealed the deal.

Sarah, let's pilot this system for one quarter and review the results. We can define the key metrics now: Winning rate, revenue, profit, employee retention, and client satisfaction. If we see a sustainable commercial benefit after six months, I want your commitment to discussing this as our firm's new standard for high performance.

Toward an Adaptable and Healthier Contract: Sarah couldn't resist a proposal so clearly tied to the results she valued, so she agreed. The new policy with its clear evaluation measures was announced to the team. The members felt a dual sense of heightened responsibility and psychological safety, knowing their evenings were protected. Sarah also found her ideas were better received and more thoughtfully implemented by a fresh-minded team each morning. The team won the biggest pitch of the year while working smarter, shorter hours.

Janice and Sarah reviewed the results quarterly.

"We won not in spite of these boundaries," Janice asserted, *"but because of them. We replaced burnout with focused commitment."*

This was a turning point for Sarah, too. She had long assumed the only path to success was working harder and longer at great personal cost to herself. By agreeing to Janice's experiment, she realized that high performance and commitment could be redefined. Refusing to accept a brittle contract and courageously renegotiating it, Janice didn't just protect her own well-being. She proved that adaptability was not weakness, but a smarter strategy for long-term success.

Healthy Loyalty Contracts must be able to evolve. When a contract is so rigid that it cannot accommodate changes in people's lives or better ways of working, it becomes a brittle trap, destined to shatter. An Adaptable contract can bend without breaking under pressure.

Janice demonstrated that adaptability is actually a competitive advantage. By redesigning the workflow to respect human limits, she didn't just prevent burnout; she created a more resilient team capable of sprinting without injury.

Sustainable: A Shared Commitment to Growth

A contract might be Fair in its mutuality, Clear in its terms, Functional in its processes, and Adaptable to change, but if it undermines the long-term well-being of any party, it is ultimately built to fail. This brings us to the final, integrating element of a healthy Loyalty Contract; it must be Sustainable. Sustainability ensures the relationship is a platform for shared, long-term growth, not a zero-sum game of sacrifice. It transforms loyalty from a temporary arrangement into an enduring and mutually enriching partnership, a principle that Claire and Mark have to forge when a major career opportunity for one threatens the vitality of the other.

Claire, who held a Ph.D. in pharmacy, was a successful research scientist at a global pharmaceutical company. She and her husband, Mark, a rising star engineer at a global tech company, had built a strong dual-career life in Tokyo, Japan. Claire had a thriving career, leading a key research team and building a valuable professional network.

One evening, Mark came home with exhilarating news. His company had offered him a regional leadership role based in Singapore. He was thrilled and immediately began talking about their new life there, including a premium apartment and even maid service. While Claire was happy for him, she was simultaneously worried about leaving a job and a country she loved. Mark immediately started to reframe the situation.

> *"Sweetheart, do you know what this means for us? This is a huge step for us,"* he said, framing his promotion as their shared win. When she mentioned her concerns about her career, he minimized them. *"Singapore is the new hub for Asia Pacific; you can find a pharma job there. This is a regional leadership role – it's a whole different level."*

He created a false sense of urgency, claiming he needed to give an answer by the end of the week. The unspoken Loyalty Contract he was pushing was profoundly unsustainable. We would prioritize the "bigger" career opportunity, which was currently Mark's, and Claire's career must adapt. Claire's loyalty to Mark and their marriage would be measured by her willingness to sacrifice her career.

The Breaking Point: Claire felt unheard as her legitimate career concerns were dismissed as emotional resistance. During a dinner conversation, Mark's frustration boiled over.

> *"I can't understand why you're making this so difficult. Everybody I've told has been thrilled for me,"* he said with clear disappointment. *"Look, let's be realistic. My career has a higher trajectory right now.*

This is a once-in-a-lifetime opportunity. It will set us up for financial security for years to come. I thought you'd be excited for me, for us."

The words "higher trajectory" struck Claire with a painful clarity. She realized that he wasn't seeing them as a partnership of equally important careers. In his mind, his was primary and hers was secondary. If she conceded now, under what felt like manipulative terms, she would be setting an unfair precedent for all future major decisions. She knew this would be unsustainable for her and for them as an equal partnership.

The Renegotiation Strategy: Claire knew another emotional power battle would lead nowhere. Her mind went to a recent cross-functional strategic planning session she had led at her company, and she decided to apply the same framework to her marriage.

That evening, she requested a talk over the Japanese whisky Mark loved. They toasted to each other. After a sip, Claire began calmly.

Mark, I am not saying no to Singapore.

Mark listened, finishing his first shot.

What I am saying no to is making a life-altering decision for our family in one week. Imagine if I asked you to decide to move while you have a great career here, all within a week. It doesn't make sense. This deserves a collaborative, two-way conversation. Let's set aside the "move or not" discussion for a moment and instead, let's map out our next five years together. Would you be interested in doing this with me?

Mark drank his second shot and agreed.

Claire took out two sheets of paper with the headings "Mark's Career" and "Claire's Career." She asked him to map his ideal five-year progression in the Singapore role. On her own sheet, she mapped her career trajectory in Japan, including the important projects she was leading, her potential for promotion, and the value of the professional network she had built. She then taped the two sheets on the wall, visually showing both careers side-by-side.

For the first time, Mark seemed to see the true scale of what he was asking Claire to sacrifice. Until that moment, he hadn't seen it so clearly. He had been blinded by his own excitement. He thought about what it would feel like to be in Claire's shoes. With two valuable career paths made visible and tangible, it was no longer about whose opportunity was bigger.

"Claire, you're right," he said, putting down his shot glass and switching to ice water. *"This isn't just about my next opportunity. It's about our future. How can we make a shared commitment to both of our opportunities?"* Then, he asked a crucial question: *"What's important for you, Claire? What do you need?"*

"I need time," she said. *"At least six months to explore opportunities in Singapore, within my company or with others."*

While listening, Mark offered a solution.

> *What if we change the timeline, then? My new role involves managing the Asia-Pacific region, including Japan. What if I accept the promotion but propose working remotely from Tokyo for the next six months? I might have to travel to Singapore often, but that will give you protected time to activate your network and line up promising interviews there. We only make the physical move when you also have a clear and exciting career path waiting for you.*

Toward a Sustainable and Healthier Contract: Claire was relieved by Mark's proactive offer. He was promoted and began working remotely from Tokyo. Claire pursued future opportunities with focus, knowing she had a firm runway. After nine months, she accepted an excellent regional opportunity in Singapore at a competing pharma company. As soon as Claire signed her contract, Mark demonstrated his commitment to their new agreement. He moved to Singapore first to handle their family's relocation while Claire was wrapping up her work in Japan. Two months later, Claire joined him.

Through this experience, Claire and Mark built a Sustainable Loyalty Contract because it was co-created. Their redefined marital partnership was now built on a new principle: Marriage is a shared commitment to supporting each other's growth. We do not make a major life decision until we have a clear plan that supports both partners.

This story illustrates how to renegotiate with a person who is behaving like a Gaslighter. Caught in the spotlight of his own success, Mark initially minimized Claire's reality and created a sense of urgency to help rationalize his haste in making a decision. Claire's strategy succeeded by directly confronting his unconscious manipulation, making their careers visually equal which enabled him to see beyond his self-centered perspective. His crucial shift from declaring what would happen to asking, "What do you need?" marks his journey away from the unfairness embodied in this archetype toward a sustainable partnership built on genuine mutual respect and shared growth.

The stories of Tom, Sunny, Bob, Paul, Janice, and Claire are not just case studies. They are mirrors reflecting the challenges we all face. Now, it is your turn to step into the story. But where do you begin? You can use this diagnostic tool to move from intuition to data.

The Loyalty Contract Scorecard

Don't just guess whether your team's loyalty is healthy; audit it. Pick a specific relationship – with a direct report, a business partner, or even a family member, and rate your current "unspoken agreement" about how you interact based upon the five healthiness characteristics listed below.

You can use the following scale. This characteristic is...

1 = NOT part of our Loyalty Contract.
2 = Not very often a part of our Loyalty Contract.
3 = Part of our Loyalty Contract on average about 50% of the time.
4 = More often than not part of our Loyalty Contract.
5 = Consistently part of our Loyalty Contract.

1. **Fair:** There is a sense of fairness and mutuality.

   Score (1–5): ___

2. **Clear:** There are expectations that are understood and acceptable to both sides.

   Score (1–5): ___

3. **Functional:** There are established processes that make working/being together efficient, effective and/or enjoyable.

   Score (1–5): ___

4. **Adaptable:** When circumstances change, we are able to adjust with little or no conflict.

   Score (1–5): ___

5. **Sustainable:** There is a shared commitment to our long-term mutual growth.

   Score (1–5): ___

   The Diagnosis:

- Score < 15 (The Danger Zone): This contract is brittle. It relies on silence, fear, or sacrifice to survive. It carries a high risk of sudden rupture or turnover.
- Score 15 ~ 20 (The Maintenance Zone): Functional but potentially fragile. Identify your lowest score – that is your immediate friction point. Renegotiate that specific area sooner vs later. Then repeat with the next lowest score.
- Score 21 ~ 25 (The Growth Zone): A healthy, self-differentiated partnership that fuels flow.

Use your lowest score from this audit to select one relationship or situation where the Loyalty Contract feels unfair, unclear, or unsustainable. The goal is not a dramatic confrontation, but a deliberate first move.

What is the smallest possible step you can take (sending an email to schedule a coffee, writing down your non-negotiables, or practicing your opening line with a trusted friend) to begin the renegotiation process? That is where the real work of self-differentiated leadership begins. Regardless of how you scored, revisit these questions annually.

Chapter Summary

The journey from loyal soldier to self-differentiated leader is not completed by simply reading a book. The true value of this or any book lies not in the reading, but by how you apply the reading. The five DNA elements are not only concepts to be understood; they are practical blueprints for building healthier, more resilient relationships in every area of your life.

This chapter provided a way to diagnose and redesign the invisible Loyalty Contracts that shape our lives. It argues that true leadership emerges not from blindly following rules, but from consciously examining the implicit agreements we live by and rebuilding them on a healthier foundation. To achieve this, the chapter introduced the five core components of a healthy Loyalty Contract's DNA.

It argues that a healthy loyalty contract must be:

Fair,
Clear,
Functional,
Adaptable
Sustainable

These components serve as a comprehensive toolkit for building agreements that are both robust and humane.

Through a series of case studies, the chapter demonstrated these components in action. We saw how a lack of Fairness and Clarity can poison collaboration between teams and lead to individual burnout. The stories then showed how creating Functional processes for communication and ensuring contracts are Adaptable to new circumstances are essential for navigating cultural challenges and personal life changes.

Finally, the chapter illustrated that the ultimate test of any agreement is its Sustainability. Sustainability is measured by the ability to maintain stability while fostering mutual growth in a long-term partnership, whether in business or a personal relationship. By applying this five-part DNA framework, anyone can transform ambiguous, one-sided loyalties into explicit, mutually beneficial partnerships that are built to last.

There is much to learn from the incredibly poignant story of Lieutenant Hiroo Onoda being unknowingly bound for nearly 30 years by a Loyalty Contract that no longer applied. Until we are open to and trust new information, we run the risk of being stranded on a jungle-like island forever.

Key Takeaways

1 Unquestioned loyalty can trap people in outdated ways of thinking and behaving.
2 Psychological Adulthood is not about blind loyalty but about integrating loyalty with one's own individuality.
3 Healthy Loyalty Contracts have five core components: Fairness, Clarity, Functionality, Adaptability, and Sustainability.
4 Renegotiation requires intentional, skillful action, avoiding adversarial confrontation.
5 Healthy Loyalty Contracts enable shared benefit and growth, while minimizing or even eliminating personal sacrifice.

Next Level Reflections

1 Think of a recent situation where you felt pressured to agree with a group, a manager, or a family member.
- What was the invisible Loyalty Contract at play?
- What were the hidden terms?
- What would a psychological adult's response have looked like in that moment?
- What held you back from that response?

2. Identify one Loyalty Contract at work or home that feels unbalanced or unhealthy. Which of the five elements is it violating the most?
3. Consider the strategies used by the leaders in this chapter. Which specific tactic or mindset shift seems like a useful first step for addressing the unhealthy contract you identified in the previous question?
4. Richard Rohr suggests we all start as loyal soldiers. In which areas of your professional or personal life are you still operating as a loyal soldier, following old rules without question?
5. What is one small, courageous action you can take to begin the journey of renegotiating an unhealthy contract and becoming a more Self-Differentiated Leader?

Chapter 9

Uncover, Create, and Integrate (UCI)

A Step-by-Step Transformation Process

How to Self-Differentiate: The UCI Process

Throughout the previous chapters, we have acted as archaeologists of the self, carefully brushing away the dust to reveal the hidden architecture of your leadership and personal relationships. Our silent Loyalty Contracts and our archetypal patterns shape each of our reactions. But insight, no matter how profound, is not transformation. It is merely the prerequisite. Knowing why you micromanage, avoid conflict, or tend to have problematic relationships does not automatically grant you the capacity to stop.

The journey from intellectual awareness to behavioral change is often the widest chasm a leader must cross. This chapter provides the bridge. It moves us from the diagnostic to the prescriptive, offering a systematic and deeply practical roadmap – **The UCI Process** which stands for Uncover, Create, and Integrate. This is the source code of living an Integrated Life, the fourth cornerstone of effective leadership where internal values align with external actions.

To become a Self-Differentiated Leader is both deceptively simple and incredibly hard. It is not a destination you reach once; it is a continuous advancement towards Psychological Adulthood which, simply put, is growth. To navigate this journey, we have developed a three-phase roadmap called The UCI Process. There are three distinct phases with six steps in our Self-Differentiation roadmap. The three phases of this process are shown in Figure 9.1.

As you can see from Figure 9.1, each of the three phases has two action items to follow which include:

Phase One – Identify and Assess
Phase Two – Imagine and Actualize
Phase Three – Measure and Anchor

DOI: 10.4324/9781003621393-9

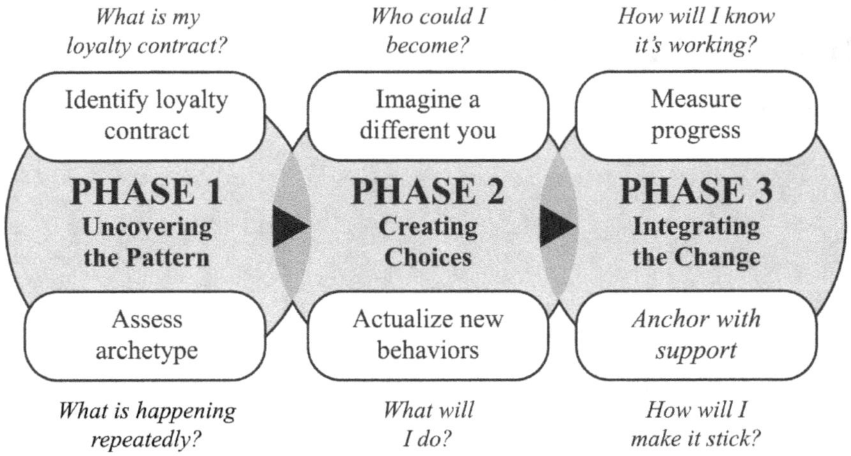

Figure 9.1 The UCI process.

Phase One – Uncovering the Pattern

A. Identify the Loyalty Contract – Chapter 1 taught us about early childhood Loyalty Contracts. We recognize these Loyalty Contracts by noticing where your emotional reactions feel disproportionate, automatic, or strangely familiar. Asking yourself questions like these will help you identify them:

- Where do I feel obligated to act a certain way?
- Whose approval am I still seeking?
- Who, if anyone, am I still trying to protect or save?
- What role did I play in my family – peacemaker, achiever, caretaker, invisible one – and do I still feel compelled (perhaps unknowingly) to play it now?
- When do I have difficulty saying no?
- What are the situations that I continue to push myself often overdoing it, just to prove myself to others?
- When do I experience chronic guilt or a keen fear of disappointing others?
- How long do I hold onto hurt feelings, and what does it take for me to let go of those feelings?
- Do I self-sacrifice to the point that it is not healthy for me?

By exploring these questions with curiosity rather than blame, you can start to see which patterns and behaviors are automatic rather than intentional. These often represent old loyalties you need to renegotiate. Armed with this knowledge, it is time to see if there is a connection with these Loyalty Contracts and the archetype characteristics in the next step of this process – Assess the Archetype at Play.

B. Assess the Archetype at Play – Here we build upon the concepts presented in Chapters 6 and 7 where you learned about the various archetypes and which one(s) might best represent some of your behaviors.

Assessing the archetype characteristics that you might exhibit requires you to connect your Loyalty Contract expectations to the various behavioral characteristics of the seven archetypes. As a reminder, we have included the list of archetypes with their general characteristics to help you with your own assessment in Phase One. Success at this phase is heavily reliant upon two basic assumptions.

You know yourself reasonably and realistically well.
and
You are being completely honest with yourself.

Are you able to make a connection between the expectations of your Loyalty Contracts to any of the behavioral characteristics listed in Table 9.1? Which descriptions (right column) capture some of your own behaviors that show up in a repeated way?

Doing this exercise with a trusted colleague, friend, family member, or coach will definitely deepen and aid the outcome. An objective third party will help contradict or confirm what you think is true about yourself. Assessing the reflection questions below requires honest candor with yourself. Mind you, there are no right or wrong responses here.

The reflection questions are:

- How much of your life has been determined by what others expect from you?
- How often does your concern about what others think stop you from doing what you want to do?
- How much of your life finds you putting other people's needs before yours?
- How much of your life is spent keeping certain parts of yourself in hiding?
- How often do you find yourself impatient with others, passing negative judgment on their inadequacies?

Table 9.1 The archetypes – Brief descriptions

The archetype	*Brief description*
Over-Driven Loner	Isolated, intense focus on personal goals/hobbies, prefers solitary activities, untrusting, emotionally guarded, self-reliant, need to prove autonomy, secretly wants (needs) approval.
Self-Sacrificing People Pleaser	Appears to be a selfless care-taker, gives to others to prove value, difficulty in delegating or receiving help, feels un(der)appreciated, holds quiet resentments, martyr, chronic self-neglect.
Hovering Micromanager	Excessive hyper-vigilance, perfectionistic standards, reluctance to delegate, constant oversight, lacks trust in the innate capacities of self or others, frequently second-guesses decisions, views their behavior as protective/helpful.
Oblivious Grandstander	Craves the spotlight, know-it-alls, constantly interrupts, violates boundaries, pushes the limits, takes credit for others' accomplishments, rationalizes or minimizes own inappropriate behaviors.
Passive-Aggressive Gaslighter	Disavows their own negative emotions, has a hidden competitive edge, projects aggression onto others while appearing concerned and/or helpful, doesn't confront directly, exhibits indirect resistance, sabotages outcomes through inaction or half-hearted effort.
Vindictive Revenge Seeker	Highly competitive, continual need for praise/validation, hypersensitive to perceived slights, values own opinions over others, threatened by success of others, externalizes blame, holds grudges, retaliates, can't apologize.
Antagonistic Nay-Sayer	Armchair critic, cautious, resistant to change, quick to explain why something won't work, challenges ideas of others, stifles innovation, rarely satisfied, seems to enjoy and takes pride in being the opposition.

- How often do you second-guess people and find the need to correct them? What do you think might be driving that need?
- How much of your daily energy is spent proving yourself to others?

By using the archetype descriptions, you will be able to raise awareness about how much of your life might be influenced more by your fears than your intentions, desires, dreams, and hopes for the future.

The goal here is to identify any behaviors that might be or are creating more friction than flow in your leadership and life. What behaviors do you want to move away FROM? You will be successful at this part of the process if you are able to fully answer one or all of these questions.

I no longer want to...."
"It doesn't help me be an effective leader when I..."
"I hurt my relationship with my friend or partner when I..."

Here again, doing this alone is an excellent exercise. Engaging someone you trust simultaneously will give you a much more accurate fix on what is actually true about you.

Now that you have identified your Loyalty Contract and what types of archetypal behaviors show up for you in some repeated or patterned way, it is time for you to change course by creating new choices.

The Trap and The Tool

The Trap – Intellectualizing: The most common defense mechanism in Phase One is treating your Loyalty Contract like a wiring diagram, something to be analyzed but not felt. You might perfectly identify that you are a "People Pleaser" yet remain completely unchanged. Why? True uncovering requires you to sit with the discomfort of why you adopted this pattern in the first place.

The Tool – Vulnerability: To break through the trap of intellectualization, you need a tool that is often avoided – vulnerability. Recognizing you are not yet fully self-differentiated means showing your true self to yourself, including the "live wires" of your uncertainties and fears. You cannot troubleshoot your internal operating system while pretending there is no voltage. Vulnerability is the willingness to feel the shock of recognition rather than just tracing the lines.

Mini Case Study: Using Vulnerability to Uncover

David, the Chief Architect at a Generative AI startup, treated the code base like his exclusive territory. He had fallen into the trap of intellectualizing, convincing himself that reviewing every line of code was simply quality control.

When a critical launch stalled because he was the single bottleneck, the CEO confronted him:

> *David, you aren't building a company; you're building a black box that only you can open. You are the single point of failure.*

David's instinct was to defend his logic. Instead, he used the Tool of Vulnerability to execute Phase One. First, he **Assessed** the pattern: his isolation and refusal to trust others marked him as a classic Over-Driven

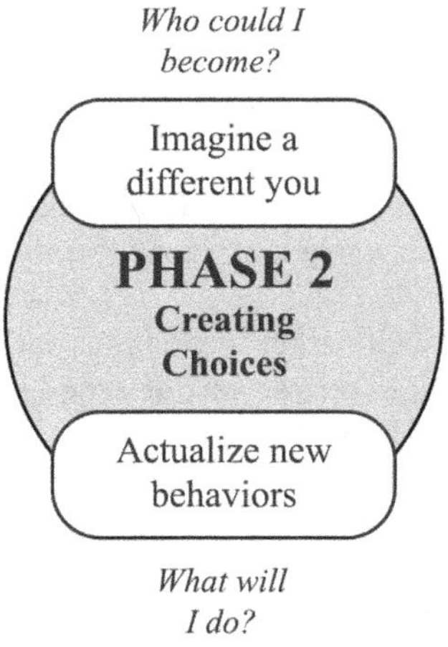

Figure 9.2 Phase Two (broken out).

Loner. Second, he dug deeper to **Identify** the source code driving that behavior: a hidden Loyalty Contract that whispered, "If I remain the only expert, I can never be rejected." By naming both the **Archetype** and the **Contract**, he stopped hoarding work and started mentoring his team.

Phase Two: Creating Choices

C. Imagine – The second phase of this process invites you to think about who you want to become (see Figure 9.2). A more effective leader? A better significant other? A more caring and compassionate friend? Based upon your reflections in Phase One, you have identified what you are trying to move away FROM. Now it's time to **Imagine** what do you want to move TOWARD? This first part of Phase Two is a creative process that asks you to put your fears aside, quiet the self-talk that cancels creativity, and let yourself imagine your own possibilities.

- What can you see as something new for your life?
- What parts of yourself have you been pushing aside?
- Who would you disappoint if you broke out of old patterns?
- What are ways that you might become more forgiving or gentle with yourself?
- What activities could you include in your routine that would add a sense of play?
- What might you begin that would add excitement, adventure, or peacefulness to your life?

After thinking about these questions and remembering what you want to move away FROM, you will be successful at this part of the process if you can answer:

What new behaviors do I choose to move TOWARD?

With a newly imagined you in mind, the next step makes it happen.

D. Actualize – The second part of Phase Two asks what can and will you do to bring about your TOWARD; your new behaviors or your new way of leading? This is where habits and past thinking that no longer serve you are replaced with more effective and healthier ones coupled with an intentional plan.

For example, you are able to Identify that you used to silence yourself, not voice your opinion too strongly out of fear of what someone might think. Now you decide to speak your mind (Actualize) because you believe it is the right way to behave regardless of what someone thinks.

Another example, you have gotten feedback that you blurt out your opinion and dominate conversations in ways that inhibit group dialogue. Now you create an intention to actively pause and take a breath before offering your opinion.

To help you find your own path from where you were (Phase 1) to where you want to be (Phase 2), here is an example of how each unhealthy archetype can be rewritten into healthy ones (see Table 9.2).

Actualizing requires you to intentionally commit to behaving differently going forward. This is where feedback is critically important so that you will know if the changes you are making are having the desired effect.

Feedback can come from:

- Asking a meeting attendee (privately) to give you feedback on how you led the meeting. Ideally, ask them *before* the meeting that you would like them to observe and provide feedback on the specific behavior you are working on.
- For larger more important meetings, do an actual evaluation of the meeting with focus on both meeting content and process (how it was led).
- Polling software like Mentimeter, Slido, Poll Everywhere, and Vevox can give you instant feedback during a meeting.
- Normal performance management reviews.
- Coaches.
- Mentors.
- Trusted friends and family members.
- Your own reflection

Table 9.2 The archetype transformation matrix

The archetype	*The old contract (Unhealthy)*	*The Loyalty Contract (Healthy)*
Over-Driven Loner	"If I do it all myself, then I never have to risk disappointment."	"If I bring my deep expertise, then I must trust the team to own the execution so we can scale."
Self-Sacrificing People Pleaser	"If I say yes to everything, then people will always like me and never reject me."	"If I am to deliver excellence on our top priorities, then I must have the determination to say 'no' to distractions."
Hovering Micromanager	"If I control every detail, then I can prevent mistakes and soothe my own anxiety and fear of shame."	"If I clearly define the 'what' (outcomes), then I must let go of the 'how' (methods) to build the team's capacity."
Oblivious Grandstander	"If I am the center of attention, then I feel valid and important."	"If I use my platform to champion the team, then I turn temporary attention into lasting professional respect."
Passive-Aggressive Gaslighter	"If I avoid direct confrontation, then I can sabotage the outcome while maintaining my power."	"If I voice my concerns openly, then I replace hidden sabotage with constructive debate and faster solutions."
Vindictive Revenge Seeker	"If I punish those who slight me, then I prove I am powerful and in control."	"If I stop keeping score against my colleagues, then I can start scoring actual wins for the organization."
Antagonistic Nay-Sayer	"If I find the flaw in every idea, then I protect myself from making mistakes and looking foolish."	"If I identify a risk or a flaw, then I am responsible for helping the team find the solution."

Feedback is the lifeblood of professional development and an integrated life.

The Trap and The Tool

The Trap – Imposter Syndrome: As you begin to Actualize your TOWARD behaviors, a voice will likely whisper, "This isn't really you." That voice is the Imposter Syndrome of growth. When you break an old pattern, the new behavior, even if it is healthy, will feel foreign, perhaps even manipulative or cold. Do not confuse unfamiliar with inauthentic. You are not faking it; you are practicing a new language of Self-Differentiation.

The Tool – Courage: To push past the feeling of being a fraud, you need **Courage.** The process of becoming self-differentiated means taking action even in the face of fear or concern. It forces you to risk disapproval and break old agreements that no longer serve you. Much like the Cowardly Lion in The Wizard of Oz, this process helps leaders realize that the courage to move into uncertain territory has been there all along.

Mini Case Study: Using Courage to Create

Marcus, a Sales Director and Oblivious Grandstander, dominated every meeting, believing his constant talking drove momentum. After uncovering that his monopolizing center stage was actually a defense mechanism, he moved to the **Create** phase. He needed to **Imagine** a version of himself who could lead without dominating. He visualized a leader who was a "miner of intelligence" rather than a "broadcaster of ideas." To **Actualize** this, he created a new choice by creating what he called: the "Three-Person Rule." He vowed not to speak until three other people had shared their ideas.

The first time he tried this, the silence in the room was excruciating. The trap of the imposter syndrome whispered that if he wasn't talking, he wasn't leading – that he was faking it. He desperately wanted to fill the void. Instead, he used the tool of **Courage** to sit in his fear. After twenty awkward seconds, a quiet junior analyst spoke up, offering a risk assessment that Marcus had missed. Having the courage to act differently before he felt confident, Marcus unlocked the team's intelligence and proved to himself that he didn't need to be the loudest voice to be the most effective leader.

Phase Three: Integrating the Change

E. Measure – The fifth part of this process requires you to Measure your progress with regard to the specific goals and behavioral changes that support your Self-Differentiation (see Figure 9.3). This might involve keeping track of how many times your self-talk slipped into old expectations, or how many times you were able to pause and demonstrate a new behavior. Quantitative measuring reflects how many times something did or didn't happen. It can also be measured by attending to feedback that others are giving you that reflect a change in your actions and behaviors.

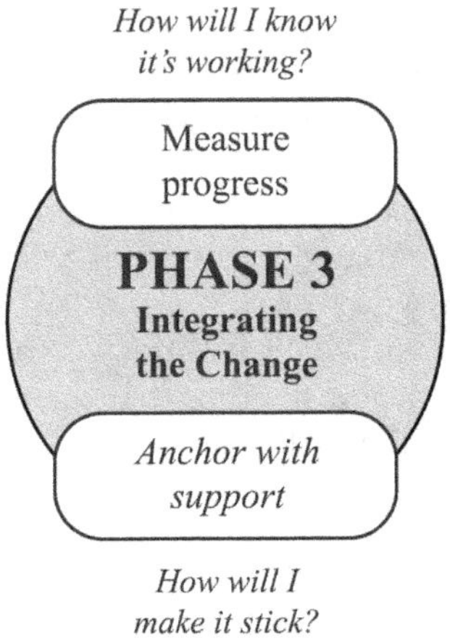

Figure 9.3 Phase Three (broken out).

Qualitative measuring would include paying attention to whether you are feeling more satisfaction, liberation, or relief, and less of a feeling of being cramped, frustrated, or unappreciated. The feedback options mentioned above are good ways to measure both your quantitative and qualitative progress.

We offer Table 9.3 as a simple way for you to keep an eye on the specific behavioral shifts that you are aiming for. You could do one sheet for your own responses and another sheet for the feedback you are hearing from others.

Of course, based upon the results you get from the measuring process, you adjust and modify along the way. The goal would be to have X's only in the "Getting Better" column and to still take actions to move further toward your goals.

F. Anchor – The sixth and last part of this process is about finding the **Support** you need to keep your new behaviors sustainable. We have mentioned several times how helpful a trusted colleague, manager, friend, family member, coach, or therapist can be in this process. Like an anchor that keeps a ship in place, you need support for your efforts, particularly when things get difficult, or the phrase "I can't do this" begins to seep into your psyche. Too often the power of this part of the process is underestimated. However, it is a necessary component in order to sustain this growth process.

Asking for an **Anchor** is essentially asking for help. We prefer asking for a partner. We also know that asking for help can sometimes feel like a

Table 9.3 Measuring the change

Phase three – Integrating the change (Measuring)				
I want to move TOWARD these Leadership skills	*Indicate which is true with an X*			*Actions I can take*
	Getting better	*Staying same*	*Getting worse*	
1 Be more inclusive of my Team.				
2 Letting go and delegating more.				
3 Realizing perfection is a myth. Excellence is the goal.				
4 Give up the spotlight. Offer it to others.				
5 Constructively confront concerns and issues.				
6 Realize that criticism is not personal.				
7 Be more open to innovation, change and others' ideas.				

weakness, where we fear that others will interpret this as a loss of confidence in our leadership. In business terms, an Anchor is an accountability partner – a way of making us smarter, not weaker. This is both developmental support and operational insurance.

Without a scheduled check-in to review your progress, the urgent will always displace the important, and your new behaviors will fade. Remember that it is rare that the journey of self-differentiation is successfully done alone.

The Potential Trap and The Tool

The Potential Trap – Emotional Tension: Peter Senge (1990) describes the gap between your vision (your TOWARD) and your reality (your FROM) as a stretched rubber band: This creates a forward energy called *Creative Tension* where there is an inherent predisposition for some kind of movement. But this stretch also generates *Emotional Tension* which usually shows up in one of two ways:

Anxiety, fear, or stress about being in the gap
or
Excitement, intrigue, or sense of possibility

Quite often, our default response is to experience this tension as anxiety. The resistance in Phase 3 is the overwhelming urge to relieve this anxiety by lowering your standards and snapping back to your old, more comfortable reality.

The Tool – Commitment: To prevent the snap-back, you need **Commitment.** This is not just a promise; it is what Senge calls the resolve to hold the creative tension. Becoming a Self-Differentiated leader requires you to be "all in" even when the emotional tension is high. A clear example of this is the laser-like stare of the gymnast just before they launch into their routine. With this kind of commitment, you maintain the tension required to propel yourself decidedly in the direction of your TOWARD, rather than allowing the rubber band to pull you backward.

Mini Case Study: Using Commitment to Integrate

Raj, a CFO known as an Antagonistic Nay-Sayer, had stifled innovation for years. He committed to a new identity: stopping the "No" and starting the "How." To ensure he wasn't fooling himself, he started measuring his "Green-Light Ratio," aiming to offer at least one viable solution for every risk he flagged.

The real test came during a budget crisis when Operations proposed a risky automation project. Raj felt the spike of emotional tension – the desperate urge to kill the idea immediately to restore safety. He knew his "Green-Light Ratio" was about to crash.

To prevent the snap-back, he used the tool of **Commitment** supported by his chosen **Anchor**: Elena, the CTO. They had agreed that if she saw him spiraling, she would signal him. As Raj opened his mouth to object, Elena deliberately placed her pen on her notebook and caught his eye. That subtle visual cue interrupted his reaction. Bolstered by that relational tether, Raj swallowed his objections and asked, "The upfront risk is high. How might we stagger the spend to make this work?" By measuring his output and anchoring himself to a trusted partner, he bridged the gap between his fear and his future.

The Ongoing Practice

As you stand at the end of this roadmap, it is crucial to recognize that the UCI Process is not a straight path to a finish line; it is a cycle of continuous evolution. You will not navigate these phases perfectly on your first attempt. There will be days when you intellectualize your feelings (Phase 1), succumb to imposter syndrome (Phase 2), or let the rubber band snap back (Phase 3). This is not failure; this is the temporary friction of growth.

The distinction between a reactive leader and a self-differentiated one is not the absence of these struggles, but the commitment to re-enter the loop. By repeatedly applying these tools of Vulnerability, Courage, and

Commitment you transform Self-Differentiation from an abstract concept into your daily operating system. You stop being a passenger in your history and become the driver of your future.

Chapter Summary

This chapter is about learning a new skill, admittedly a complex one, but one we believe is well within your reach. No gymnast gets a perfect 10 the first time at the rings exercise or the pommel horse. Similarly, no reader can absorb and then immediately execute the UCI Process perfectly on day one. We have walked you through, step-by-step, a roadmap for becoming a Self-Differentiated Leader. Because this process is still new to you, we would encourage you to let the concepts and steps percolate. Next, re-read the process a second time, and then create your implementation plan with an "anchor".

Remember the three core phases of the UCI Process are meant to flow smoothly and intentionally towards Self-Differentiation. They include:

- **Uncovering** patterns that are getting in your way by identifying your Loyalty Contract and assessing the Archetype.
- **Creating** new choices by imagining a different you and actualizing new behaviors.

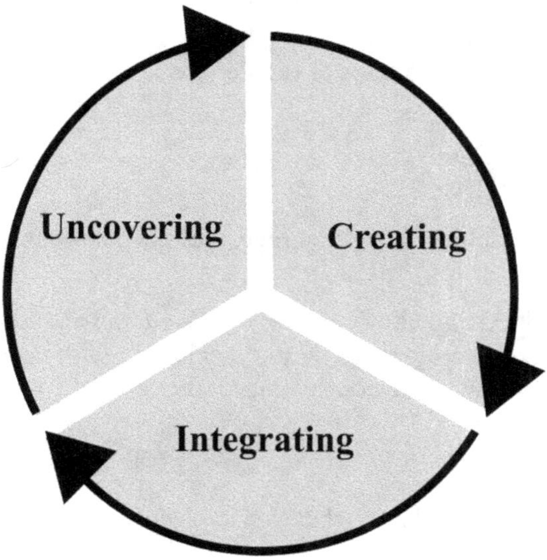

Figure 9.4 The UCI continuum.

- **Integrating** the new changes by measuring progress and anchoring it with support.

While they appear as sequential steps, they must be taken in relationship to each other, not as totally independent steps (see Figure 9.4). Each step of the UCI Loop is interconnected and inter-reliant upon each other. Mastering this loop is not about achieving a state of perfection; it is about committing to a practice of awareness.

Of all of the chapters in this book, this chapter's purpose is for you to put our words and concepts into your specific actions. This, as you know, cannot be a passive process. Our experience with coaching tells us that you will need three important tools to make this roadmap real for you.

Key Takeaways

1 The first step towards Self-Differentiation is being able to recognize the Loyalty Contracts that are at play. You cannot fix what you cannot face.
2 There is almost always some form of permission needed to break the binds of a Loyalty Contract in order to enable Self-Differentiation. This often requires allowing yourself to feel vulnerable.
3 Insights are necessary but insufficient for change. The UCI Process provides the systematic "how-to" steps to translate psychological awareness into leadership behavior.
4 You will encounter predictable traps at each phase:

- Intellectualizing (Phase 1),
- Imposter Syndrome (Phase 2), and
- Emotional Tension (Phase 3).

You need specific tools – Vulnerability, Courage, and Commitment – to break through them.

5 Feedback is the lifeblood of professional development and an integrated life. Without measuring progress and anchoring with support, the urgent will always displace the important.

Next Level Reflections

1 How clearly have you formulated what you wish to move away "FROM"?

2 What specific steps might you take to move "TOWARD" the goals or aspirations you listed in the chapter exercise?
3 In what ways can you share your roadmap for becoming a Self-Differentiated Leader for support?
4 How would you describe your own Vulnerability, Commitment, and Courage in becoming a Self-Differentiated Leader?
5 What will it take for you to take the first step?

Chapter 10

Applying the UCI Process to Self-Differentiated Conversations

How We Are Seen

A CEO client once sent an email to his coach after an executive coaching session saying:

> *Thanks for the helpful session today. Hopefully I wasn't ranting too much.*

The coach wrote back:

> *When you do rant, how can I best show up for you during that time? Simply listen? Ask challenging or clarifying questions? Are you looking for solutions? Do you want me to stop you?*
>
> *I do think that the more you rant privately with me and the less you rant at work, the better it will serve your Leadership effectiveness. Here's why; ranting rarely moves anything forward. I would suggest that you succinctly state what your concern is and then quickly thereafter, ask for what you need such as: discussion, ideas, off-loading the responsibility, accountability, systems audit, etc. Then the focus becomes the actual issue and not you.*

The coach wasn't telling the CEO to suppress his feelings. He was guiding him toward a powerful concept developed by psychologists Robert Kegan and Lisa Lahey: finding the *Commitment Behind the Complaint.* They teach that we only complain about things we care about. A rant is simply evidence of a hidden value that feels as if it's being violated. The rant is the complaint (focusing on what you don't like); the leadership move is to articulate the commitment (focusing on the value you want to protect). By shifting your language from venting to requesting, you turn a grievance into a goal (Kegan & Lahey, 2001).

DOI: 10.4324/9781003621393-10

The CEO then said:

> *Well, that is just my process of thinking out loud. As CEO, shouldn't I be able to vent?*

The coach further replied:

> *There was a line in the 2025 Netflix Danish television series called "The Asset" that stuck with me (Milsted et al., 2025).*
>
> *"They decide who you are by what you show them."*
>
> *If how you are seen and how you are experienced as a leader does matter to you, the concept of "ranting" might be worthy of taking a look at. Much of what a leader gets from an employee is decided by the emotional reality that they experience in the presence of the leader. What role do you want the ranting to play in "They decide who you are by what you show them?"*
>
> *This is not to say you should or should not rant. The point is that whatever choices you make about how you show up in any situation will impact the degree to which people will perform at a higher level – for you.*

Whether we want it to or not, how we are seen by others matters, particularly if our behaviors don't reflect the standards and values we profess to be important to us or the company's culture. As a leader or as a person in an important relationship, eyes are constantly watching you looking for consistency, approval, support, inspiration, and connection.

Some of the most effective and healthy leaders we know have "mirrors" in their lives. The term mirror refers to those trusted people who show us how we come across to people or reflect to us the effects of our actions on others. Trusted mirrors will either contradict or confirm what the leader believes to be true about their leadership.

The Self-Differentiated Leader is aware of their impact on others. This awareness is not paranoid but purposeful, not cowering but compassionate, not reactive but rational. And getting there requires having intentional conversations, particularly when there are missteps, misunderstandings, or disappointed expectations that threaten to create ruptures in relationships.

The Courage to Have a Self-Differentiated Conversation

In every meaningful relationship, there comes a time when the tension between who we are and who others expect us to be calls out for attention.

These moments often arrive quietly at first, through frustration, burnout, or the nagging sense that we are repeating the same unhelpful patterns. At other times, they surface dramatically, through conflict or emotional distance. Either way, they call for something deeper than a quick fix, a surface-level resolution, or continued avoidance. These situations are inviting us to have a self-differentiated conversation that defines who we are while staying connected to others.

A Self-differentiated conversation has no intention of blaming or defending. It is an invitation to growth, which often requires courage to speak up about what you need. It also requires you to listen intently – to yourself and the other person – from a genuine place of curiosity and a will for something different to happen. It requires you to take responsibility for your part of patterns that no longer serve you and to resist the autonomic response of emotional reactivity. Conversations like these allow us to seek and hopefully find that delicate balance between staying grounded in our own values while co-existing with and respecting the values and beliefs of others.

This chapter deepens your understanding of the three phases of becoming a Self-Differentiated Leader covered in Chapter 8 by giving detailed and real-world examples of how to have a Self-differentiated conversation. Whether it's about a tiff you had with a colleague, a needed shift with your manager relationship, or finding a different ratio of mutuality between you and an important personal relationship, being able to have self-differentiated conversations is a leadership practice of standing firmly in the realm of what is needed and what is best, all the while remaining connected and committed to building and maintaining psychologically adult relationships

Applying the UCI Process to a Conversation

In situations where expectations are disappointed or ruptures threaten relationships, we need a tool to navigate the tension. We call this the Self-Differentiated Conversation.

This isn't a new, complex technique to memorize; it is simply applying the UCI Process you learned in Chapter 8 out loud with another person.

- Phase 1: UNCOVER (Preparation): Before you speak, you must uncover the Loyalty Contract driving the friction. You ask yourself: What is really going on here?
- Phase 2: CREATE (The Conversation): During the talk, you actively create a new, fairer agreement (Quid Pro Quo) in real-time. You ask: What new choice can we make together?

- Phase 3: INTEGRATE (Follow-Up): After the talk, you measure if the new agreement is working. You ask: How do we make this stick?

Let's walk through how to apply each phase to transform friction into flow.

Phase 1: UNCOVER (The Preparation)

To prepare for this conversation, you must do the internal work first. You cannot lead a clear conversation if your own internal Loyalty Contracts are muddy.

To begin, think of a work situation where you were treated unfairly or encountered roadblocks. Reflect on these four essential questions to **Uncover** the root cause before you walk into the room.

Note: While this next section is written about the workplace, you can easily substitute the word manager with friend or family member and replace workplace with home.

- *What are the Loyalty Contracts in your life that were in place before this conversation?* This is when you identify the kinds of early Loyalty Contract expectations and behaviors that were part of you before this situation emerged. An example might be that during your early years you were told you were not smart enough to be successful. It felt as though no matter how hard you studied and learned new things, you never felt like you were seen as smart as everyone else.
  Possible answer: "I remember from an early age that when I shared my ideas with my mom and dad and even my big sister, they always seemed to discount them as childish. I remember being excited about sharing my ideas and how much it impacted me to not feel heard or appreciated for my ideas. I notice now that I have a visceral reaction when my co-workers or my manager shoots down my suggestions."
- *In what ways are those early Loyalty Contracts still showing up?* Think about what kinds of behaviors are triggered in you by your current manager that are similar to Question One above. Is your manager in some way causing you to feel you are not talented or smart or experienced enough to be good at what you do? Or perhaps your manager is expecting you to be loyal and deferential even when you disagree? Or are you asserting yourself unnecessarily because of old fears or in an attempt to be noticed and included?
  Possible answer: "As I reflect on not just my current employer but also most of the other employers I have had, there has always been an element of me working extra hard to make sure I wasn't called lazy or stupid. I could always prove myself by working harder than everyone

else, looking out for others, and doing more than what is expected. This way, I felt valued, important and liked."

- *What parts of your relationship with your manager are not healthy or lack a sense of mutuality?* Many of us work or have worked within multi-leveled hierarchy organizational structures. Inherently, the CEO makes way more money and the senior leadership team has more perks and parachutes than nearly everyone else. This is the very nature of how leadership is set up and incentivized. So, when we reference mutuality and fairness in this question, we aren't talking about pay or perks. We are talking about, regardless of your position, are you treated with respect? Is there a sense of fair play, a clear sense that the rules apply to everyone?
  Possible answer: "I work really, really hard for my manager. I come in early and I stay late. I anticipate and deliver what my manager needs. The thing is my manager rarely if ever says thank you or even acknowledges my efforts. I believe I create lots of value in my role. I just don't think my manager appreciates my effort and my expertise. My self-confidence is taking a big hit, and I fear the resentment building in me."
- *What is it that you need/want from your manager that you currently don't have?* Your response to this question needs to be realistic and reasonable. For example, what do you need to be the best employee possible? Be honest about how much of what you're asking for can or should come from your manager. Also, remember the age-old saying, "Asking ain't getting." Just because you ask for a different kind of Loyalty Contract with your manager, doesn't mean they are willing or capable of being part of creating one. Remember, your manager has early Loyalty Contracts too that were made long before you arrived and yet you are the recipient of how they manifest at work.
  Possible answer: "I want to be appreciated for the value that I bring to the workplace every day. Not being valued for my work to me is disrespectful. Maybe if I received regularly scheduled feedback from my manager, I would have a clearer, more accurate sense of my value as an employee. Perhaps my manager really does value me but just doesn't articulate it. And if my manager doesn't value my work or respect me as an employee, is this really where I want to work?"

Once you have **Uncovered** these truths, you are ready to move toward Creation. The first step of creating a new reality is inviting the other person into it.

Checklist. Before you initiate the conversation, pause and audit your mindset. How would you answer these three questions?

1 The Trigger: What old story (Loyalty Contract) is this person triggering in me?
2 The Truth: What is my legitimate business need versus my emotional want?
3 The Goal: Am I walking in to win the argument, or to align the relationship?

Bridging to Phase 2: The Invitation

Creating any invitation can be rather tricky. In our head we know what the invitation is supposed to say but oftentimes putting the invitation into words can be challenging. There is a need to find the words that the other person needs to hear to believe the invitation is worth the time and is safe to have. Doing the invitation in a personalized way addresses both.

Emails and texts fail miserably at conveying the business imperative or the emotional need of having this conversation. However, we recognize that email is the default for many, if not most of today's workplace communication. We suggest that you have the invitation conversation in person or by telephone if it is at all possible.

Whether in person or via email, you need to create a welcoming invitation expressing how you believe both of you would benefit from having a conversation with the hope of:

- Being a more effective leader
- Becoming a more efficient employee
- Having a more respectful relationship
- Having a stronger voice in the team
- Creating a happier life
- Being more aligned as manager and employee
- Having clearer performance expectations
- Being clearer about what support you need
- Having a greater sense of safety
- Creating more collaboration between us

Invitation Script (Many people find that it is a good practice to write out the invitation first as a "rehearsal." Then, it becomes easier to articulate the request in person or on the phone. For example:

- Subject: Touching base on (Project X)
- Hi Elizabeth, I've been reflecting on our workflow regarding (Project X). I think we have an opportunity to align our expectations so we can both move faster. Do you have 30 minutes on Thursday to discuss how we can support each other better?

These are some of the entry points of how you can articulate why you would like to meet. Having an agenda and inviting input to that agenda is very important.

Timing is everything. Part of the invitation is agreeing to a date, time, and location that meets each other's needs and feels safe. People often underestimate the impact that timing and location have on a conversation. The space in which you have the conversation can help or hinder the outcome you are looking for. For most people, this space should optimally be relatively quiet, where there is privacy even if it might be in a public setting and is relatively convenient to get to. Allot enough time without squeezing it in between other important meetings. The more relaxed, the more private, the safer the space, the better the outcome.

Believing you deserve to be heard is key. Whatever emotion comes up for you about having this conversation, harness that emotion into a permission-giving belief that you <u>can</u> do this. We believe everyone has the ability to push through anxiety rather than retreat into avoidance.

Remember, on the other side of fear is always a wiser and more courageous you.

Phase 2: CREATE (The Conversation)

Now we enter the conversation itself. This is where you use specific tools to create a new understanding. We have identified specific Conversation Tools that help you stay in the loop.

Tools for a Self-differentiated Conversation

To help you feel prepared for having the Self-Differentiation conversation, we offer here some specific behavioral tools that you should have at your side ready to use (see Figure 10.1). Notice there are three types for you to use.

- Tools that are effective at connecting with the other person.
- Tools that are helpful in clarifying what is being said, heard, and understood.
- Tools that are helpful as you bring the conversation to a close.

Let's look at how Peter, a manager at a non-profit, used these tools with his boss, Lucille. Even though Peter had done his **Uncover** work (Phase 1), he was still nervous.

1 **Connecting and Setting Context**
   - **Welcome and Express Gratitude:** First impressions set the tone.

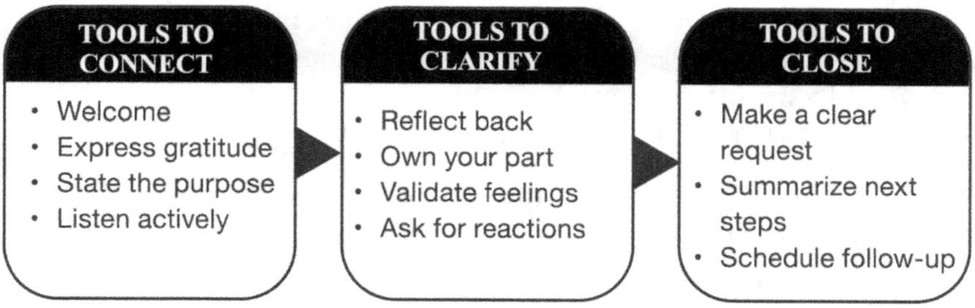

Figure 10.1 The conversation behavior tools.

    - Peter: "Lucille, thank you for taking time to meet with me today. I know you have a busy week."
  - **State the Purpose:** Peter restates the purpose from his invitation.
    - Peter: "I have been feeling like I am on the outside looking in... I was not included in the Strategy Session last week... Is there a reason I was not part of this effort?"
  - **Listen Actively:** Peter listens to Lucille's intention, not just her words.
    - Lucille: "I knew that you were having a challenging time with Project Advance... I intentionally left you alone not wanting to over-stretch you."

2 Clarifying and Reacting Wisely
  - **Reflect Back:** Peter summarizes what he heard to ensure accuracy.
    - Peter: "So, what I heard you say is that you were concerned about my workload... Do I have this right?"
    - Lucille: "Yes... This was a business decision... so that the Senior Team knows we are using our resources wisely."
  - **Own Your Part:** Peter acknowledges his own feelings without blaming Lucille.
  - Peter: "I wasn't aware that Senior Management was keeping close tabs on it... I thought you trusted me and relied on my expertise. Both of these took a hit by being excluded."
  - **Validate Feelings:** Peter recognizes the pressure Lucille is under.
    - Peter: "Thank you for really hearing my concerns... I have a much better understanding for the kind of pressure you are under."
  - **Ask For Reactions:** Lucille is curious about how Peter heard what she has just said.
    - Lucille: "So what is your reaction to what I just said?"

3 Close the New Agreement
  - **Make a Clear Request:** Peter makes a clear request for the future. This is the moment a new Loyalty Contract is created.

- Peter: "May I ask that once Project Advance is over, would you be willing to include me in your Strategy Sessions going forward? This is really important to me."
- **Summarize Next Steps:** They agree on specific actions and some kind of a timeline.
  - Lucille: "My next steps are to check in with you regularly about Project Advance... and I will also send you the Strategy Session document for your general feedback."
  - Peter: "Can we agree on what we understand 'check in with you regularly' means?"
- **Schedule Follow up:** Quite often, even with summarizing and clarifying what is next, people can leave the Self-Differentiation conversation with different assumptions. Also, there is an emotional dynamic that occurs during the aftermath of having an important conversation like this.
  - Peter: "Lucille, I know you have been busy. When we last met, we agreed to check in regularly so I thought I would drop you a note to follow-up on our conversation regarding Project Advance. Is there a time next week we can meet to reconfirm our understandings as well as share feedback?"

By using these behavior tools, Peter transformed a moment of friction (feeling excluded) into flow (clarified expectations). He **Created** a new agreement where he gets to participate in strategy, but with clear boundaries around his time.

A Master Class in Creating Safety: The Heckler

While Peter's example shows how to use these behavioral tools in a private meeting, you might be wondering if these steps really work when emotions are high and the pressure is public?

We see a profound answer in a viral moment from former U.S. President Barack Obama's 2013 speech on immigration. In the middle of his address, a student activist began shouting, interrupting the President to demand an immediate halt to deportations. The "System" (the crowd and security) reacted with anxiety, trying to boo the man and remove him.

Notice the sequence Obama used. It is the exact opposite of our instinct. Instinct says: Silence the threat. Leadership says: Validate the emotion, then hold the boundary. Instead of fighting or freezing, Obama used the very "Create" tools we just outlined to transform the friction.

- **Listen Actively (Connect):** First, he stopped the security team, saying, "No, no, no… let him go." He quieted the crowd to create a space for the conversation.
- **Validate Feelings (Clarify):** He validated the emotion behind the disruption without agreeing with the tactic. He looked at the heckler and said, "I respect the passion of these young people because they feel deeply about the concerns for their families..."
- **Make a Clear Request (Close):** Once the person felt heard, Obama held his boundary clearly: "...But we're also a nation of laws."

By **Validating Feelings** to address the emotion and **Making a Clear Request** to address the reality, he metabolized the anxiety of the entire room. He proved that you don't need to destroy the opposition to lead them; you simply need to use the tools of connection to make them feel heard (The White House, 2013).

Phase 3: INTEGRATE (The Follow-Up)

Now that Peter and Lucille have successfully had their initial conversation, their shared responsibility is to check back with each other as agreed.

This stage is where many efforts to self-differentiate fail. Following up, providing feedback, making tweaks and adjustments, and staying true to the commitments made are all essential for this process to work. After having the conversation, people often get swept away by their many other priorities and the follow-up slips far down on the priority scale.

The follow-up process begins at a brief check-in meeting to discuss four questions.

1. What questions have come up since we met?
2. In what ways did our conversation create more flow and lessen friction?
3. To what degree have our concerns been sufficiently addressed?
4. What, if anything, do we need to do going forward?

Adjust as Needed

As a result of the follow-up sessions and at any other time along the way, allow yourselves the ability to change course if and when needed. There needs to be an agreed upon fluidity to how things will progress. Keep to the changes you agreed to; alter them when it is beneficial to do so.

While the follow-up conversation will most likely be a shorter one, you can still use each of the tools suggested in this chapter. For every effective leader, these tools need to be readily available for every conversation.

Initially expect some awkwardness. At first it might feel a bit artificial. Practicing a new skill always feels a bit artificial at first. Please note that it is anything but artificial because you are doing it with intention and with a specific goal.

Signs of Success

So, having had the self-differentiated conversation, how will you know if you were successful (see Figure 10.2)?

The answer is that you notice differences in:

- *How you behave* – A solid sense of who you are and your own self-worth will begin to emerge because you are no longer defined by the old, internalized dialogue that weighed you down. No longer are you automatically bound by what others have expected from you.
- *How you feel* – You will feel lighter emotionally. That harsh, self-blaming, or disappointed internal voice inside you will be lessened if not, silenced. Your past pain points looking outside of yourself for validation of who you are will be gone or at least, greatly reduced. Disagreements are no longer frightening because you have built the emotional capacity for a sturdy sense of self.

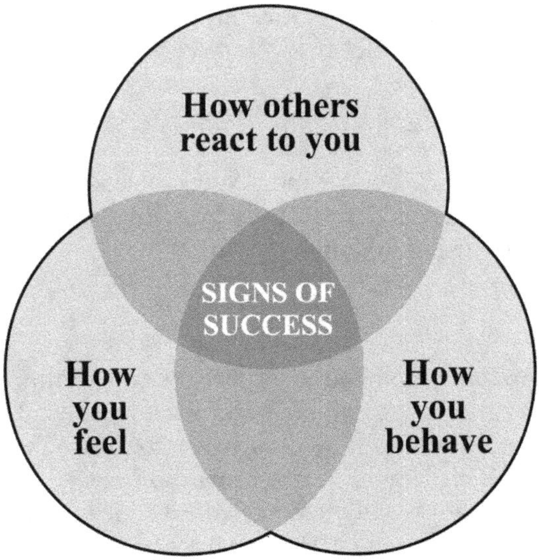

Figure 10.2 Signs of a successful self-differentiated conversation.

- *How others react to you* – You will notice that people will react differently to you because you have essentially changed the rules of engagement towards a more mutuality-based, more respectful relationship. Those that used your vulnerability, your loyalty, your over-accommodation, might appear surprised that you are requesting new and different boundaries.
  Or those who had given you feedback where your comments or efforts were overbearing will welcome your newly found ability to pause, change your tone, ask for help, which will result in a more productive and meaningful connection with co-workers and loved ones.

Chapter Summary

Self-Differentiation is a life-long journey with no specific or tangible destination. And that journey does not mean shifting from self-sacrifice to self-absorption. It means holding the benevolent tension between staying true to oneself while simultaneously creating a fair and healthier environment for others.

When you master the UCI Process you have a reliable process to navigate this tension. You can uncover the hidden contracts, create new choices in the moment, and integrate those choices into a sustainable future.

When it comes to living a self-differentiated life, no one gets a perfect ten out of ten score. Each of us has to allow for the natural and occasional "violation" of one or more of these critical skill sets. This is called being human. When we have done the hard work to acquire the knowledge and build the mental and emotional muscles to use these skills, Self-Differentiation becomes the steady, centered voice that is now your constant companion.

Key Takeaways

1 A Self-Differentiated Conversation is not a script to memorize; it is the UCI Loop applied in real-time with another person.
2 Uncover: You cannot lead a clear conversation if your own internal Loyalty Contracts are muddy. The most critical step is identifying your own triggers *before* you enter the room.
3 Create: To shift from friction to flow, use specific tools to Connect (e.g. Listen Actively) and to Clarify (e.g. Validate Feelings).
4 Integrate: The conversation does not end when you leave the room. Feedback is the lifeblood of integration; without an agreed-upon follow-up, old habits will return.

5 Signs of Success: You know the conversation worked when you see a shift in three areas:
   - How you behave (less reactive),
   - How you feel (lighter and less burdened), and
   - How others react to you (more respect).

Next Level Reflections

1 When you think about the specific phases of the UCI Process which one is most natural for you?
2 Which phase might be the most challenging, and why?
3 Which relationships in your life might benefit from a self-differentiated conversation?
4 What do you need to take that first step to have a self-differentiated conversation?
5 Who will you invite to check in with you to see if your new conversation has actually shifted the relationship?

Chapter 11

Applying UCI Process to Coaching

Real World Failures, Mixed Results, and Successes

While this chapter is geared for professional coaches, we recognize that psychological adults who are **not** professional coaches intentionally use the art of coaching at work and in their personal lives. So, even though we use the term "coach" throughout this chapter, we encourage each reader to pick up and use the tools we include here.

No book on leadership can provide insights and learnings that will work every time for every situation. Sometimes in spite of trying everything we know how to do, we still fail to realize the desired outcomes. It takes a while to accept the fact that failure happens, and it plays an important part in success. We suggest using any failure to your advantage.

This chapter is designed for the professional coach, the mentor or the leader acting as a guide. In the previous chapters, we introduced the UCI Process as the master framework for Self-Differentiation.

- In Chapter 9, we applied the process to Leading the Self.
- In Chapter 10, we applied the process to Having a Self-differentiated Conversation.
- In Chapter 11, we apply the process to the Art of Coaching Others.

You do not need to memorize a complex new methodology to help your clients. Your role is simply to act as the "navigator" for the journey of Self-Differentiation they are already learning to navigate.

- **Phase 1 (Uncover)**: They cannot see their own blind spots or Archetypes. Your job is to be the mirror. You help them **Identify** the hidden Loyalty Contracts running their lives, and you **Assess** which specific Archetype is driving their friction.
- **Phase 2 (Create)**: They see the problem but feel trapped by their history. Your job is to help them imagine a new choice. You encourage

DOI: 10.4324/9781003621393-11

them to **Imagine** a self-differentiated version of themselves and support them as they **Actualize** that vision into real-world behavior.
- **Phase 3 (Integrate)**: They make a change but slide back into old habits when pressure mounts. Your job is to be the anchor. You help them **Measure** the impact of their new choices and establish the support needed to **Anchor** the change against the pull of the past.

Part of inviting our clients into engaging in a process of becoming more self-differentiated requires that we recognize that people who come to us present with varying degrees of defensiveness and limitation. In presenting the descriptors for the seven archetypes in Chapters 6 and 7 our hope is to give coaches a clear means of assessing the degree of limitation, as well as strategies to either move toward Self-Differentiation or contain disruptive behavior in the workplace.

This chapter provides real-life coaching examples that offer a range of challenges to help present a picture of the continuum of:

Failure
Mixed Results
Success

Most conventional coaching often focuses on modifying behaviors by addressing symptoms that are frequently measured by one-on-one conversations, assessments, and 360-degree feedback tools (Boyatzis et al., 2019; Hull, 2017). While helpful, these approaches sometimes feel like trimming the weeds without pulling the root. In our experience we have found that lasting and integrated change comes from going deeper and uncovering the invisible Loyalty Contracts that are feeding the weeds.

In Chapter 9 we presented the UCI Cyclical Process (Uncover, Create, Integrate) that created a roadmap to becoming more self-differentiated. This chapter will expand upon the explanation of how to apply the steps of this process by connecting them to three case scenarios used in various coaching situations.

Figure 11.1 reviews the three-phase process.

Phase One – Uncovering the Patterns of Behavior(s)

Phase Two – Creating Choices

Phase Three – Integrating the Change(s)

By way of review this three-phase process assists coaches in helping their clients connect outward behaviors to their internal operating system.

An Important Word About Coachability

Here, as a coach, you need to ask yourself whether your client is "coachable" or not. "Coachability" can be defined as the willingness and ability to

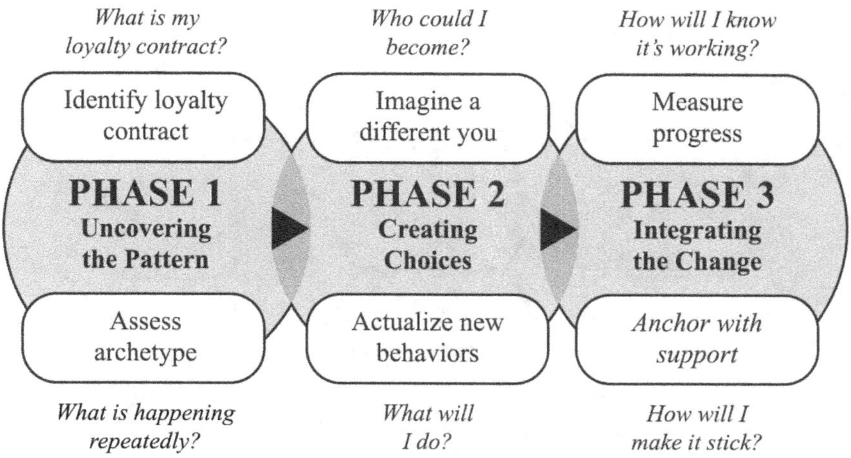

Figure 11.1 Three phases of the UCI process.

seek, receive, and act upon constructive coaching conversations to foster growth (Haden, 2013; MacGabhann et al., 2025).

After a systematic literature review spanning five decades, MacGabhann et al. (2025) identified six components of coachability. For practical application, we have adapted their academic terminology and framed each component as 6 diagnostic questions to help coaches assess a client's coachability (see Figure 11.2).

1 **Attentiveness** – How well do they take in new information?
2 **Resilience** – How steady and perseverant are they when faced new challenges?
3 **Receptivity** – What is their reaction when receiving feedback?
4 **Motivation** – How motivated are they to use feedback and new learning?
5 **Initiative** – How often do they ask for feedback at work or at home?
6 **Curiosity** – How curious are they to seek new learning?

We recommend considering this as a dynamic and situational status check-in for yourselves rather than using this assessment as a foregone conclusion about a personality or trait. Before taking a coaching conversation to the topic of a Loyalty Contract, check the client's status by asking:

> *Are you interested in having a coaching conversation that includes exploring a possible connection between your current behavior and underlying events or beliefs from your past that might be coloring the situation?*

Figure 11.2 Components of coachability.

The response to this question is critically important. You will get one of three responses.

1 "Absolutely yes! I really want to have that conversation because I believe there is a connection between my behavior and some underlying cause."
  This is a "Go" for the coaching relationship.
2 "I am not sure. This seems a little fuzzy or confusing to me. How can what happened to me so many years ago be causing my behavior today?"
  This would imply more time, and dialogue is needed for the coachee to fully understand what will be involved in the coaching process.
3 "Oh, please. This is a bunch of nonsense. I don't believe that what happened to me in the past has anything to do with how I behave today.

That was then and this is now. I am a grown adult, and I make my own choices irrespective of the past. Besides, I am not looking for therapy."

First of all, make sure the client clearly understands that talking about your past is not therapy. Explain that we are looking for data points and patterns that drive your current leadership decisions, not trying to resolve what happened in the past. Connecting the past to the present where appropriate is a form of fact finding.

If you continue to get the above response, it would suggest a "No Go" or at least you would need to take a pause for a period of time for the potential client to reflect on the conversation. This could then be followed by an additional meeting to see if curiosity or a deeper understanding of the process emerges.

Note: We have had clients that waited for a year or more before the proverbial light went on, where the coachee was willing to enter into a coaching process. If, during this process, a client reveals deep trauma, clinical depression, or an inability to function in daily life, this moves beyond "uncovering patterns" and into psychological risk assessment. In these instances, the ethical boundary is clear. The coach must pause the engagement and refer the client to a mental health professional.

Three Case Studies

The case studies provided in this section will walk you through the UCI Process. These case examples include one failure, one that had mixed results, and one that was a success.

Failure: Andrew – CFO of a Global Manufacturing Company

Phase 1: Uncovering the Pattern

Assess and Identify: Reporting to the President, Andrew had a long history of lashing out at co-workers particularly those who disagreed with him, holding grudges and keeping a score card of past perceived grievances. Over the course of his 25-year tenure, Human Resources had to become involved when Andrew was accused of retaliation against people adhering to the company policies that Andrew didn't support. He was known for having very thin skin that often came with loud and sometimes table-pounding defensiveness. Being in a meeting with him was laden with fear, as you never knew if you would be the recipient of his publicly demeaning criticism. When Andrew was given feedback about his caustic behaviors, he was quick to deflect and object. He often said,

"People just don't get me."

or

"People that have worked with me for a long time don't have any issues with my leadership."

Andrew's current state of bluster, bullying, and non-accountability for his behavior needed to shift to a different state of being, one that was more approachable, non-blaming, and more in line with the company's core values.

Showing clear characteristics of the Vindictive Revenge Seeker Archetype, Andrew's coach was unsure of how to address what appeared to be his impenetrability. Nothing seemed to get through to Andrew when it came to feedback or suggestions for improving his leadership effectiveness. Andrew's coach wondered why he was so hypersensitive and blaming. This wondering became clearer when the coach asked Andrew,

Andrew, why are you so angry so much of the time?

In a millisecond Andrew slammed his fist on the table, sternly looked into his coach's eyes and said,

You'd be mad too if you had the son-of-a-bitch father that I had!

Stunned, the coach sat silent for a few minutes as Andrew recognized his outburst with a hint of embarrassment. Not able to apologize for his behavior, he said, "Let's move on!" The coach saw this as an opportunity to invite Andrew to be curious about what just happened. The ensuing conversation revealed that Andrew learned early on in his life that you must always be on your guard and to not trust people. He then told the coach that he was fine and didn't want to discuss this any further.

Being extremely careful not to cross the line into therapy, the coach didn't dig deeper into the trauma of Andrew's childhood. Instead, the coach validated the origin of the behavior but immediately pivoted to the impact of that behavior on his current team. The coach asked him,

So, Andrew, what do you think caused you to respond so strongly just now?

While he was unable to verbalize it, it was clear that Andrew was embarrassed by his outburst. When the coach asked Andrew what he would like to be different about his leadership, the best he could state was that he wanted his team to be more productive. He felt that he had to learn how to hold people more accountable. Even with the coach's suggestions, Andrew was unable to identify any specific leadership behaviors of his own that needed to change. Every suggestion that Andrew made centered on how other people needed to behave differently. He continued to insist he had done nothing wrong.

Andrew's lack of self-awareness created a challenge for the coach to find a way for him to fully understand the impact of his leadership style. The coach was beginning to notice Andrew might be missing some of the six key coachability factors in Figure 11.2.

After several coaching sessions, many of which were argumentative and rejecting of suggested behavior changes, Andrew reluctantly agreed to an anonymous 360 Feedback process where his manager, his peers, and his direct reports would each provide feedback with a set of quantitative and qualitative questions. Andrew was convinced that this data would show how much people respected and valued his leadership. The data was gathered, and a report was provided to him and his manager, the company President. Andrew's coach reviewed the data with him and with the President separately.

As the coach expected, the candid but constructive data indicated many behaviors in need of improvement. An enraged Andrew said he was suspicious of the process and implied that the good comments were not included. What the coach didn't anticipate was Andrew's insistence on knowing the names that went with each comment.

Andrew had convinced himself that knowing who said what, he could go to each person and "set the record straight." Andrew was visibly shaken and upset by the candor and consistency of the comments towards the negative and he was livid that the coach would not reveal the names.

Andrew spent many hours dissecting the feedback with graphs and charts attempting to see consistency in terminology and references in an effort to find out who said what. Andrew pressed the President to force the coach to identify who said what. To his credit, the President told the coach to stand firm in keeping the feedback anonymous which was the original agreement.

Andrew personified the archetype, Vindictive Revenge Seeker by his:

- Vehement denial of the feedback he received,
- His hypersensitivity of what was in reality, constructive feedback,
- Display of anger and volatility and
- His need to find out who gave him feedback that he didn't like.

The coach knew Andrew was going to be a challenging client.

Phase 2: Creating the Choice

Imagine and Actualize: This is where the process broke down even further. Andrew's impenetrability and unwillingness to own any part of the negative feedback was quite severe. After two more coaching sessions, encouraging Andrew to think about his own accountability for the negative feedback, it was clear that this part of the process – Imagine – was not possible given his intractability. This process only works if each of these steps can be accomplished. Since Andrew was not able to Imagine anything different for himself (only for others) there was nothing to Actualize. Simply put, Andrew was stuck. Put more accurately, Andrew chose to remain stuck by not considering anything but his own viewpoint.

Phase 3: Integrating the Change

Measure: Since there was no *Imagine Phase* possible, there was nothing to measure other than how often Andrew expressed his disappointment in his coach. Andrew terminated the coaching process as a result. Ironically, the coach was about to terminate the coaching relationship at about the same time as it was clear to the coach that Andrew was not coachable. In retrospect, the coach might have terminated sooner, yet the coach wanted to extend every possibility for Andrew to accept some accountability and to agree to the kind of coaching that he seriously needed.

Anchor: Sadly, there was nothing to anchor for Andrew. He never made it this far in the three-phase process. The coach never saw any signs that Andrew allowed new viewpoints other than his own. If Andrew had read the feedback and was able to see that the data showed a clear pattern over time, maybe there would have been some hope for change. Andrew was so thoroughly controlled by his need to cover up his sense of inadequacy, so frequently puffing himself up by tearing others down, that he continually remained on guard, thus never being able to expand beyond his limited leadership capacity.

The President of the company did see the patterns and the limitations, however. Not long after this intervention, Andrew was encouraged to retire. His termination was the beginning of a new and welcomed culture change at the company. The coach was told there was a huge sigh of relief by most of the employees as news of Andrew's retirement spread.

This coaching engagement failed not so much because of what the coach did or didn't do but more because of Andrew's recalcitrance and impenetrability. Robertson Davies (1951) wrote in his book *Tempest-Tost*:

> *The eye sees only what the mind is prepared to comprehend.*

Choosing not to prepare himself to comprehend his own realities, Andrew remained serving his self-imposed lifelong prison sentence. The coach's only mistake might have been waiting too long to terminate. In leadership, recognizing an uncoachable employee early is a success, not a failure. It allows you to redirect resources to higher potentials.

Success: Annika – The Transformation of a High-Tech Division Manager

Phase 1: Uncovering the Pattern

Assess and Identify: Annika was a female division manager for 8 years in a thriving high-tech company. She had earned respect and credibility from senior management and the team she led through her intellect, technical prowess, her willingness to try new things, and a relentless drive for results. Ever since Annika could remember, the feedback she received about her leadership style often centered on a kind of insensitivity, impatience, and self-centered autonomous decision-making. Team members described her as brilliant, yet distant and frequently dismissive. These less than favorable characteristics caused morale to suffer within her division, leading to stalled innovation and high staff turnover. Annika's manager realized there might be deeper issues and a need for urgent change.

To her credit, Annika admitted that she could be overly ambitious and that sometimes there was unintended collateral damage in relationships and the perception of her leadership. In conversation with her coach, this observable pattern was identified as the manifestation of her dominant non-differentiated archetype: The Over-Driven Loner.

Once the coach and Annika identified the archetype, then, they *assessed* the "root cause" by uncovering the Loyalty Contract (see Figure 11.3). Her drive for excellence stemmed from having parents who made it clear that failing at anything was just not acceptable and you must always do better. Layered on top of this were the words that still ring in Annika's head today, "Don't be a baby!" As far back as she could remember, showing emotions was met with a stern look and a firm, often yelled, "Stop complaining!" Early on, Annika had to adopt a Loyalty Contract of "Suck it up and don't you dare fail and we (her parents) will be nice to you."

Adding to this her years of working in highly competitive, male-dominated environment, Annika had also conditioned herself to prioritize results over relationships.

Phase 2: Creating the Choice

Imagine: Despite her aloof and somewhat disconnected exterior, Annika privately longed for a more harmonious and productive team, one with

Figure 11.3 Annika's Loyalty Contract Quid Pro Quo.

whom she could share the heavy responsibilities of making the division a star within the company. She wanted to be respected not only for results but also as a leader who could inspire loyalty and creativity. She wished to break the cycle of feeling alone coupled with staff departures that were embarrassing. She wanted to be recognized as a holistic leader, one who could balance performance with empathy. Above all, she wanted to feel less isolated and more connected to her colleagues.

The coach invited Annika to visualize a "different you," free from her constraints of her old, unfair Loyalty Contract. The coach began by focusing on a prevalent belief Annika held, pointing out that perhaps Annika had difficulty connecting with her team because she often viewed emotional concerns as distractions and deficiencies rather than opportunities for insight and growth.

The coach worked with Annika to imagine a leader who was respected not just for results but for being open to hearing employee concerns as well as inviting creative ideas to flow during staff meetings. In this phase of the coaching process, Annika could envision how she no longer needed to be an isolated loner but a connected, holistic leader who could balance performance with encouragement and empathy. This self-differentiated version of herself looked collaborative, sounded encouraging, and felt connected.

Actualize: The turning point came during a coaching session. At first Annika said,

Well, I lead this way because that is how I was taught to lead by my previous managers and what I learned in school.

But when her Coach asked her, if she was taught to be disconnected and so over-driven that she ended up feeling alone, tears welled in Annika's eyes. Sensing an emotional nerve had been touched, the coach gave her a moment to reflect and collect herself. Annika then said,

There is so much noise in my head telling me that I cannot fail. I am not allowed to complain. I cannot ask for help or be vulnerable. Maybe that has also shaped how I am leading?

This was the point at which Annika demonstrated her coachability and readiness to change. The coach empathically showed a slight smile and simply let Annika sit with her question. It was then that Annika and her coach discussed the connection between the noise in her head from long ago and how she, unaware, let that guide how she approached leadership. It was at that moment that Annika decided that the old rules of the past would no longer determine the kind of leader she wanted to be.

This revelation along with a comprehensive 360° feedback process catapulted Annika to a much clearer and deeper understanding of her leadership. Annika's prompt became,

The self-differentiated version of me will practice active listening skills, pause before reacting, and seek understanding before offering solutions. She also found role-playing actual workplace scenarios to be both informative and skill building.

Phase 3: Integrating the Change

Measure: By setting high expectations with compassion and open communication, Annika created specific methods to measure her leadership success such as:

- Soliciting specific and measurable departmental goals from her team.
- Regularly soliciting qualitative and quantitative feedback from each team member, which served as powerful reality checks.
- Becoming more mindful of the power of positive feedback and recognition of her individual team members.
- Instituting a yearly departmental retreat.
- Continuing her 360° Feedback process annually.
- Deploying an annual team survey to capture evidence of the department's performance.

By the end of the fiscal year, creativity and a spirit of shared purpose became the norm for Annika's department, *and* her leadership was trending positively. That fiscal year, staff turnover decreased significantly, and Annika's division outperformed previous quarters. At the organizational level, her division became a model of engagement and innovation, attracting new talent and high-level recognition within the company.

Note that Annika didn't just become nicer. Her psychological shift directly impacted the bottom line. Innovation increased because safety increased. Turnover costs dropped because connection deepened. She proved that for a Self-Differentiated Leader, empathy is a revenue driver.

Anchor: Through coaching, Annika was able to identify the noise in her head that was getting in the way of her becoming more of a psychological adult and effective leader. She learned that, when handled mindfully and effectively, vulnerability can be a strength and that empathy, patience, and deeper self-awareness of her own Loyalty Contracts are as vital as high-performance standards and technical mastery.

The process taught her that diverse perspectives and inclusive environments enhance not threaten her success. Annika still checks in with her coach at least once a year and has left the door open to reach out whenever she needs an independent mirror for her leadership.

Annika's journey provides convincing evidence that by changing her Loyalty Contract from the past, it had the power to unleash the fully effective leader that was always inside of her. By bravely addressing her blind spots, quieting her Monkey Mind, and embracing continuous self-improvement, Annika was transformed. And her newly found leadership confidence has never left her. By building a system of self-monitoring and team monitoring, along with external support, Annika's new, self-differentiated behaviors became more integrated and less of a conscious effort. Annika was now free.

Mixed: Mika, Breaking the Cycle by a Japanese American CEO

Phase 1: Uncovering the Pattern

Assess and Identify: Mika, the 44-year-old CEO of the Akebono-Kentucky Distillery, ("Akebono" meaning "dawn" in Japanese), led a respected mid-sized independent distillery in the heart of the Kentucky Bourbon Trail. Her father, Osamu, a second-generation Japanese American, was a legend who built the company by perfectly fusing Japanese precision with Kentucky tradition.

Being a woman in the male-dominated world of bourbon, Mika had always felt a dual pressure: to live up to her father's legacy and to constantly prove her own capability in a business deeply rooted in its local identity. The distillery was respected but seen as stagnant. They were losing ground to more innovative craft distilleries. Mika, who inherited the CEO role, enforced her father's methods, creating a culture that was highly disciplined but creatively stifled. She initiated coaching to "improve leadership to increase their stalled market share," not yet seeing that her own risk-averse leadership was the core problem.

The coaching began by assessing the symptom. Mika described a workplace with "more friction than flow." Her talented team was passive, waiting for her direction on every minor decision leading to a lack of innovation.

> *"It feels like I'm pushing a boulder uphill every day," she confessed. "No one takes initiative. I'm working so hard for everyone, why isn't anyone stepping up to help?"*

Without realizing it, Mika had never created the space for them to do so.

The coach introduced the archetypes of non-differentiated leadership. "Mika," the coach said gently, "it sounds like you're putting everyone else's needs – your father's, the legacy's even your team's perceived need for stability – ahead of your own vision, to the point of exhaustion. What is your reaction to the archetype of the Self-Sacrificing People Pleaser?"

As Mika slowly removed her reading glasses and took a visibly deep breath, it was clear that the question landed with profound weight. Mika was silent for a long time before speaking about her childhood, the immense pride and pressure she felt, and her life-long search for her father's approval, especially as a daughter in a world of sons. Together, she and the coach uncovered the powerful, unspoken Loyalty Contract she had operated under for more than 40 years. They articulated its "Quid Pro Quo" as follows (see Figure 11.4):

> *I will put your (my dad's) feelings and the security of your legacy entirely before my own needs or ideas. I will achieve this by never causing conflict, taking on the full burden of responsibility to prevent any mistakes, and sacrificing my own vision to maintain the harmony you built. In return, I will feel safe from your disapproval and the anxiety of conflict. Your continued approval will validate my worth, confirming that I am a "good daughter" and that I belong here. I will be shielded from the terrifying feeling of letting you down.*

Figure 11.4 Mika's Loyalty Contract Quid Pro Quo.

Mika saw the direct link between her childhood Loyalty Contract (the need to be the "good daughter") and her present-day Self-Sacrificing People Pleaser Archetype. The passivity of her team was a direct reflection of her own conflict-avoidant leadership. She was perpetually seeking approval. This new awareness, while unsettling, made her coachable. When the coach checked her readiness for the next step by asking "Would you be interested in exploring a possible connection between your archetype behavior and an underlying cause from your past?" Mika was ready and answered with a firm "Yes."

Phase 2: Creating the Choice

Imagine: This phase began not with actions, but with identity. The coach guided Mika through a visualization exercise:

Let's put the tactics aside for a moment, Mika. I want you to imagine yourself in the state of self-differentiation. For now, let go of the Self-Sacrificing People Pleaser. What does this "different you", the one free from the constraints of that old contract, look like? What does "different Mika" sound like? What does "different Mika" feel like? What is possible for this "different Mika" that was not possible before?

This coaching conversation happened virtually over Zoom. Mika asked the coach if she could turn off the Zoom video for a moment. The coach said yes. Mika looked out the window and closed her eyes to imagine a different self. The self-differentiated Mika stood taller. She wasn't looking for approval from her dad. She was meeting her team's gaze with calm confidence.

"She's not just a steward," Mika said over Zoom, her video still off. "She's a visionary. Her voice... it is quieter, but more resonant. She asks powerful questions instead of giving anxious orders. She feels... grounded. Centered. She feels like the CEO, not just the founder's daughter."

Then, she turned on the video. The coach asked, "Did you realize your voice was different?" Mika said, "It was?" The coach let her know her voice tone over Zoom had sounded stronger and more firm than the coach had ever heard from her.

Actualize: This powerful vision of a different Mika created a new choice. The next step was to actualize the new behavior from this self-differentiated version of herself.

The coach offered a prompt: "The self-differentiated version of me will do and say _______."

Mika completed the sentence with newfound resolve.

The self-differentiated version of me will honor our heritage my father built by adding a new chapter to it, one that I will lead. The new me will trust my own instincts. She will launch an experimental cask program.

Her facial expression showed an intriguing combination of pleasant surprise, joy, and a newly found confidence. This was not just a wish; it was a declaration of will. This led directly to the "Mizunara Cask Project," a confidential initiative where she sourced rare Japanese oak barrels – a nod to her own heritage – to finish a small batch of their mature bourbon.

Phase 3: Integrating the Change

Measure: The Mizunara Cask bourbon winning "Whiskey of the Year" was not only a commercial success, but it was also a massive external validation of the different Mika. It was also the catalyst that forced Mika's hidden internal conflict into the open. Not everyone liked the different Mika. The Master Distiller, Mr. Tanaka said the award was not a victory but a betrayal. He confronted Mika by saying,

> *This award means nothing." His voice strained. "You've turned your back on the soul of what your father and I built. This is not Akebono-Kentucky bourbon. I cannot be the Master Distiller for a product I don't believe in. You must choose Mika. It's this new fad, or it's me.*

The ultimatum like a magnet, attached itself to Mika's Self-Sacrificing People Pleaser archetype. Her every instinct screamed at her to capitulate, apologize, and restore the harmony. After a sleepless night and an emergency call with her coach, Mika made the hardest decision of her life. She chose her new vision and accepted Mr. Tanaka's resignation.

Her father was shocked and angered by the news. His voice trembling with anger, he roared:

> *You pushed out Tanaka-san? A man who is like family to me. How dare you? After all he has done for us. For what? A fancy bottle and a gold sticker? This is not how I raised you and not what I expected from you as my successor! You are throwing away our soul!*

The non-differentiated Mika would have been shattered. But now, grounded by her coaching and her own difficult choices, she was different. Even during that brief moment, she imagined a different Mika with self-differentiated leadership. She took a breath, letting her anger wash past her without letting it drown her.

> *"Father,"* she said, her voice quiet and clear. *"I respect Mr. Tanaka and the perfect bourbon you created more than I can say. He was the perfect man for the company you built. But I am not you, and my role is not just to be your daughter who protects the past. It is to be the CEO who builds the future. I have a responsibility to build the right team for the company we need to become. This responsibility is now mine."*

There was a moment of cold, heavy silence on the line before Osamu spoke again, his voice flat.

> *The daughter I knew wouldn't have done this. If this is the leader you have chosen to be, then, there is nothing more for us to talk about.*

He hung up. Mika held the phone for a long moment, a profound wave of grief washing over her for the relationship that now felt gone. This was followed by the quiet, steely calm of knowing she had made the only choice she could.

Anchor: In the wake of this profound personal loss, she leaned heavily on her daily decision point and journaling practices. They were her frequent proof that her different self was real and resilient. To anchor her support, she immediately promoted her lead distiller, a talented young woman she had been mentoring, to Master Distiller. This woman became more than an employee; she became Mika's key accountability partner and the foundation of her new professional family – the one she was building, not the one she had inherited.

Mika achieved resounding professional success. She transformed a stalling company, shattered a glass ceiling in her industry, and established a new, healthy culture of innovation. Mika's struggle is a classic business case of transitioning from a family operation to a professional enterprise. To save the company from stagnation, she had to fire the "founder's mindset" (represented by the rigid loyalty to her father's era). While this evolution was the necessary price of the company's survival, the result was truly mixed. The victory came at the ultimate personal price: the complete rupture of her relationship with her father.

Her story serves as a sober, powerful lesson that becoming a Self-Differentiated Leader is not without sacrifice. Sometimes breaking an unfair Loyalty Contract means breaking a cherished, yet unhealthy, personal connection, and finding the strength to anchor oneself in the new reality you have built. One can only hope that with time, Mika and her father can reconcile. However, the grief over the current rupture must be acknowledged with the hope that repair will happen in the future.

As the journeys of Andrew, Annika, and Mika demonstrate, the path to Self-Differentiation is as varied, unpredictable, and as complex as we are. Some might refuse the journey. Some will begin the journey only to stop when it gets difficult. And yet, others will transform completely. The Self-Differentiation framework provides a map, but the courage to look inward, to choose a new way of being, and to accept the mixed results of an integrated life, it is essential for your clients and maybe even for yourself as a coach. As coaches know, before any single step our coaching clients take in this journey, the traveler must possess the will to make a new choice for the future they were meant to have.

Chapter Summary

The Self-Differentiated Coaching process is a navigation system for going beyond treating a symptom by going to the root source of the behavior which usually provides identity-level change. By using the **UCI Process,** you move beyond "trimming the weeds" (managing symptoms) to "pulling the root" (uncovering the Loyalty Contracts driving the behavior).

As we saw in the varied journeys of Andrew, Annika, and Mika, this path is rarely a straight line.

- **Failure** is possible when a client (like Andrew) refuses to **Uncover** their own role and is convinced he is the only person that really knows what is going on. A fatal flaw in leadership.
- **Success** is unlocked when a client (like Annika) has the courage to let go of old rules that no longer served her. She **Created** an entirely new landscape for her leadership to expand in productive and healthy ways.
- **Mixed Results** are a reality (like Mika), proving that **Integrating** a new self often requires the painful sacrifice of old relationships. That sacrifice allowed the company to catapult to an entirely new level now well poised for a more sustainable future.

Whether you are a professional executive coach, a manager developing talent, or a parent guiding a child, your role is not to fix the person. Your role is to be the mirror that helps them see the pattern, the guide that helps them Imagine a new choice, and the Anchor that keeps them steady as they integrate their new self into the world.

Key Takeaways

1. Never start the UCI Process without checking the fuel gauge. Use the Six Components of Coachability (Figure 11.2) to determine if a client is ready. As seen with Andrew, a client who blames others and lacks curiosity is not yet ready for this deep work.
2. Conventional coaching often traps itself in fixing surface behaviors. Sustainable change only happens when you identify the Loyalty Contract and archetype fueling those behaviors.

3 The bridge between a trapped past and a free future is the Create Phase. A client must be able to visualize and articulate a "self-differentiated version" of themselves before they can act on it.
4 As Mika's story illustrates, Self-Differentiation is not cost-free. Breaking a Loyalty Contract often disrupts the system, and the coach must prepare the client to withstand the pushback from others.
5 The most precarious phase is Integration, where old habits try to return. The coach's primary value here is not teaching a new concept but providing the measurement and accountability needed to make the new behavior permanent.

Next Level Reflections

1 What are your criteria for determining "coachability"?
2 How would you describe the coaching model that you use for creating self-differentiated leadership?
3 In what ways might you use some of the elements of the UCI Process to enhance your own coaching process?
4 As a coach, to what degree do you get to the root cause of a client's ineffective leadership style?
5 In the three case studies in this chapter, what would you have done differently and why?

Chapter 12

A Blueprint for Organizational Turnarounds

Three Case Studies

The dynamics of non-self-differentiation covertly and quietly shapes an organization's culture, influences decision-making, and can hinder both individual development and organizational growth. Its visit doesn't require an invitation, nor does it announce itself and yet, we know when it's in the room. Its impact is felt deeply in awkward discomfort, resistance to change, struggle for control, taking credit, avoidance of conflict, or destructive reactivity. Its unacknowledged presence creates a pressure to conform at the expense of effective and autonomous leadership. No matter the setting, whether it's a successful corporation, a church leadership team, or a third-generation family business this visitor will become obvious at some point bogging down the system, curtailing creativity, fueling friction, and compromising flow, leaving only two questions. When and how will it show up?

In our final chapter, we take a grounded look at three real-world case studies that reveal the challenges, techniques, and transformations that occur when individuals, teams, and entire organizations rise to the difficult but liberating work of self-differentiated leadership strategies. The case studies we provide in this chapter are not theoretical examples. They come from real-world cases and our direct experiences of coaching and organizational work around the globe.

The three case examples are:

From Adversary to Ally – A company in crisis
When Opposing Archetypes Clash – A religious institution
A Legacy Built with Asphalt – A family business

Each case study presents the unique expression of several of our archetypes beneath which we examine the unspoken Loyalty Contracts and how to address them. Our purpose is to immerse readers into a more detailed dive into diverse organizational challenges, illustrating how to create a catalyst for sustainable development thereby bolstering organizational success and sustainability.

DOI: 10.4324/9781003621393-12

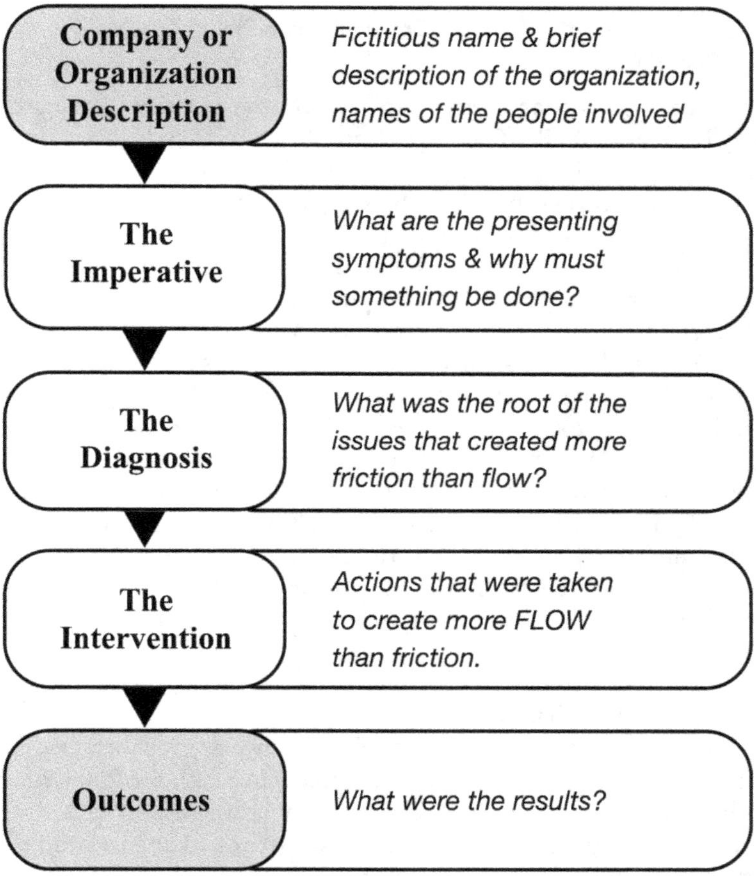

Figure 12.1 Case study review process.

Figure 12.1 illustrates our process for delving into these case studies. What unites them is the powerful shift that occurred when individuals began to identify and then address the often-unconscious dynamics usually rooted in unspoken or unknown Loyalty Contracts and some level of lack of Self-Differentiation.

In each of these case studies, extraordinary effort was made to name the root causes for what caused the problem and then create intervention strategies that would afford opportunities for leaders to make intentional, more holistic-based choices.

From Adversary to Ally: A Corporation in Crisis Mode

The field of crisis management is, in essence, the practice of repairing a severely breached Loyalty Contract. A corporate crisis, whether a product recall, an environmental disaster, or a public scandal, is rarely just a financial or operational problem. It is a profound violation of the trust that underpins the psychological contract (Kim et al., 2015) between the company and its stakeholders. The public outcry, plummeting sales, and tanking stock prices that follow are symptoms of this broken contract. Effective crisis management, therefore, is not merely about issuing press releases or controlling a narrative. It is about diagnosing the specific terms of the Loyalty Contract that have been violated and taking transparent and decisive action to restore the healthy Loyalty Contract.

In 2009, this concept was put to a dramatic test when Timberland, a company celebrated for its corporate social responsibility (CSR), was severely challenged by Greenpeace, one of the world's most formidable environmental activist groups. The crisis, detailed by then-CEO Jeff Swartz in his Harvard Business Review article (Swartz, 2010) serves as a masterclass in diagnosing a broken Loyalty Contract and deliberately intervening to forge a healthier one.

Brief Introduction of Timberland

Timberland was started in 1952 by Nathan Swartz, a shoemaker from Ukraine by acquiring Abington Shoe Company in South Boston. Renamed The Timberland Company in 1973, the company grew from a humble bootmaker into a global lifestyle outdoor footwear and apparel brand. Jeff Swartz, grandson of the founder, became CEO in 1998 and worked until he sold the company to VF Corporation in 2011.

Timberland was a prominent advocate for CSR and they considered commercial interests and social justice as two sides of the same coin. The company engaged in extensive community service and published detailed CSR reports long before it was fashionable and actively worked to reduce its environmental footprint. For its customers and employees, the Loyalty Contract was clear: When you buy from or work for Timberland, you are supporting a business that genuinely tries to do well by doing the right thing.

The Imperative

The crisis began abruptly. In 2009, Greenpeace launched an aggressive, high-profile campaign directly targeting Timberland. The impact of this severe organizational crisis was immediate.

- The Public Accusation: Greenpeace alleged that Timberland was complicit in the deforestation of the Amazon rainforest. They claimed that leather used in Timberland's products originated from cattle ranches operating on illegally cleared rainforest land. This accusation struck at the very heart of Timberland's brand identity.
- The Digital Attack: Greenpeace mobilized its supporters, flooding the CEO Swartz with over 65,000 emails. They created a parody website that mimicked Timberland's official site but featured damaging information and calls to action against the company.
- The Existential Threat: For Timberland, it was an identity-defining threat. The Loyalty Contract it held with its stakeholders was predicated on environmental stewardship. The Greenpeace campaign directly challenged this core premise, creating a profound disappointment among customers and employees. The very people who bought Timberland boots as a statement of their values were now being told they were contributing to environmental destruction.

The Diagnosis

The demand by Greenpeace was absolute: boycott Brazilian leather to prove loyalty to the cause of ending deforestation. The conventional crisis management approach, adopted by many on Swartz's own team, suggested capitulating to these terms. Their recommendation to announce a boycott was a logical, risk-averse reaction aimed at ending the public relations crisis quickly.

However, Swartz diagnosed this proposed contract as fundamentally flawed. His challenge revealed the true root of the friction:

- Irresponsible: It would be irresponsible to punish the entire Brazilian leather industry, including the suppliers who were operating responsibly, without solving the underlying issue.
- Ineffective: It wouldn't actually stop deforestation. The demand for leather would simply shift to other, perhaps less scrupulous, buyers.
- Inauthentic: It ran counter to Timberland's core value of engagement and justice. Cutting and running was the easy way out, not the right way forward.

Swartz reframed the problem. He pushed his team away from asking "How do we make Greenpeace go away?" and toward asking

> *How do we actually help solve the problem of deforestation in the Amazon?*

The Intervention

The pivotal challenge forced the team to move beyond reactive public relations and develop a more engaging, collaborative and ultimately more effective solution. They proposed a healthier Loyalty Contract.

- Step 1. Timberland did not issue a blanket apology, nor did it attack Greenpeace. They contacted Greenpeace and clearly stated their position: Timberland agreed with
  Greenpeace's goal, but it won't simply boycott the Brazilian leather. This masterstroke reframed the entire dynamic. It validated Greenpeace's mission while simultaneously asserting Timberland's right to forge its own path toward a shared objective: Protecting the environment.
- Step 2. Swartz sent his team to meet with Greenpeace leaders in Amsterdam. This direct, face-to-face engagement moved the relationship from a public war to a private negotiation. The goal was to transform the dynamic to potential partnership united by a common cause even if they disagreed on the tactics.
- Step 3. Timberland committed to tackling the root cause diagnosed earlier: which was supply chain transparency. Swartz announced that Timberland would take the lead in building a system to trace leather back to its source.
- Step 4. Having engaged Greenpeace and presented a more viable strategy, Timberland then turned to the vehicle they had helped create years earlier: the Leather Working Group (LWG). They mobilized their industry partners, transforming their mission to include upstream traceability. This action was now backed by the knowledge that Greenpeace saw it as a legitimate and powerful solution. This prevented Greenpeace from continuing its public attacks and allowed Timberland to focus on the collaborative systematic change.

The Outcome

The results of Timberland's intervention were transformative, not just for the company but for the entire industry.

- From Adversary to Ally: After Timberland demonstrated its serious commitment by leading the systematic improvement, Greenpeace publicly acknowledged the company's efforts. Instead of continuing the attack, Greenpeace praised Timberland's leadership, citing it as a constructive and positive example for other corporations to follow. This public endorsement from the attacker was the ultimate validation of Swartz's strategy. It was a healthy Loyalty Contract based on mutual respect (Butler, 2009; Swartz, 2010).

- Systematic Industry Change: The Leather Working Group became a powerful force for change. It established traceability protocols and environmental standards that are now industry benchmarks, forcing a level of transparency that had been absent. It contributes directly to a reduction in the leather industry's impact on deforestation.
- Reinforced Brand Identity: The crisis and Timberland's handling of it ultimately strengthened the brand's reputation for authenticity. By facing the problem head-on and investing in a real solution, they proved their "belief" was more than a marketing slogan. They had honed their Loyalty Contract with their customers by demonstrating a genuine commitment to the values they espoused.

Ultimately, the Timberland case exemplifies a healthy Loyalty Contract in action during the intensive crisis. By establishing a **Fair** sense of mutuality around a shared goal and being **Clear** about its own vulnerabilities, Jeff Swartz's team created a new foundation for trust. They proved the "how" is critical, choosing a **Functional**, systematic solution over a reactive boycott or passive responses. This **Adaptable** strategy replaced conflict with a **Sustainable**, shared commitment to industry-wide growth, proving that the most resilient Loyalty Contracts are not demanded through force, but deliberately and authentically built.

Timberland demonstrated how to turn an existential threat into a catalyst for industry-wide environmental progress.

The Business Translation. Timberland didn't just do good; they protected their supply chain from existential risk. In today's market, your brand promise is a Loyalty Contract with the public. If your supply chain violates that contract, no amount of PR will fix it. You must fix the system.

When Opposing Archetypes Clash: A Struggling Religious Organization

Religious institutions are meant to be places of refuge and spiritual comfort. People who join these communities hope to find a spiritual family, where members share common values, beliefs, and spiritual practices. But imagine the impact when one's spiritual community becomes a toxic environment, filled with back biting, betrayal, or competitive cliques that threaten the very foundation of the community.

Unfortunately, this is an all-too-common experience because human beings bring their unfinished baggage wherever they go, even to church. The difference between religious institutions and secular organizations, however, is that the core beliefs that join people together in religious institutions include forgiveness, tolerance, and grace. Unlike the corporate world, it is difficult to use the nuclear option of firing people when they misbehave. This creates a unique challenge when working within religious institutions.

Brief Introduction

A Protestant church in small city in the southeastern part of the US recently elected a female pastor after their beloved minister of 30 years retired. Soon after her appointment, Pastor Jane became the target of a small, dissatisfied group of parishioners. Toni, their ringleader, a long-time member and favorite of the former pastor, felt slighted because Pastor Jane hadn't given her the attention she was awarded by the former minister. The tipping point occurred when Toni ran for Chairperson of the Executive Council and lost the vote. Toni believed that Pastor Jane secretly worked behind the scenes to make sure she lost the election. Toni experienced this loss as a blow to her ego, and because she exhibited many of the characteristics of a "Vindictive Revenge Seeker", Toni was determined to get even.

The new minister, Pastor Jane, A Self-Sacrificing People Pleaser, came to Grace Church as her first appointment as senior pastor. Now in her new role, she hoped that she could use her gifts to serve people who would appreciate her. She began her ministry with a bang, which included welcoming homeless individuals to worship services on Sundays, and she also began flying the rainbow flag in support of LGBTQ+ community.

The Imperative

As part of Jane's Self-Sacrificing People Pleasing archetype, her enthusiasm to be inclusive was driven in part to prove herself to the congregation. However, she failed to weigh the potential consequences of moving too quickly without the support of key leaders in the congregation. Not surprisingly, she left herself open to become a target of criticism and suspicion, when several members of the congregation began to voice their concerns about her "left wing liberal moves."

It was at this point that Toni saw her opportunity to get even. She gathered other disgruntled members together and began to hold secret meetings where they discussed their concerns, such as claiming that Pastor Jane was giving homeless people money out of the church coffers to pay for their drug habits or declaring that Pastor Jane wasn't "spiritual enough." Toni further escalated her efforts to undermine Pastor Jane by making public accusations at meetings, taking personal calls on her cell phone during church services, and not responding to Pastor Jane when she asked to meet with her privately in an attempt to reconcile their differences.

Diagnosis

It had become clear that there was a very distinct clash in ideology and direction within the church. The growing tension was beginning to take a toll, as an increasing number of the congregation complained that Grace Church no longer felt like a safe place of worship. Clearly, Pastor Jane's leadership was not up to the task of calming the unrest on her own. Furthermore, many church members were longing for "the good old days" when the pews were full, and the parish functioned more like a country club than a mission-driven parish.

At this point consultants were called in to help resolve the escalating tension. After speaking with clergy, members of the lay leadership group, and key leaders of the disgruntled parishioner's group, the consultants highlighted several specific factors that contributed to the current unrest.

A After the 30-year tenure of their former minister, there had been no intentional on-boarding process to work with lay leadership in an effort to set new goals and a new beginning for Grace Church.

B Toni was able to successfully turn Pastor Jane into a scapegoat due to the fact that Jane had introduced new initiatives too quickly without gaining the buy-in from parishioners and lay leadership.

C There seemed to be an unrealistic fantasy among many parishioners that Grace Church could be brought back to "the good old days" which helped fuel a delusion that things could go back to how they used to be if only they had the right minister in place.

D The rise in the homeless population that camped outside the church property was a situation that had not been successfully managed by the city. Therefore, parishioners who felt uncomfortable with this situation were easily manipulated by Toni into believing that Pastor Jane was to blame for a situation that was a city-wide problem.

E Pastor Jane, who was new in her clergy position, had not been given proper guidance or coaching at this critical transition point for the church, leaving her unprotected and unprepared.

F As a Self-sacrificing People Pleaser, Jane was quick to try to please and equally quick to avoid conflict, leaving a leadership gap in terms of her being able to effectively contain the rumor mill and Toni's antagonistic revenge-seeking behavior.

The Intervention

As an initial step, the coaches interviewed clergy, support staff, lay leadership, Toni, and several other disgruntled parishioners. They also conducted listening sessions with the entire parish to assess the degree of their concerns and their hopes for Grace Church moving forward. Listening sessions and survey data confirmed that the majority of parishioners seemed to be happy with Pastor Jane's leadership. Data also revealed that people were tired of Toni's divisiveness and the ongoing tension.

Based on this data, the consultants held a retreat with clergy and lay leadership with the goal of building consensus as a leadership body. The first order of business was to get agreement from all lay leaders that they needed to present as a strong and visible presence, in support of church unity and in support of Pastor Jane during this time of transition. This included:

- Offering training to this group of well-meaning but conflict avoidant lay leaders who needed guidance in terms of how to challenge disrespectful behavior,
- Making themselves more available to parishioners with the aim of listening to and reassuring parishioners in hopes of quieting the rumor mill and dismantling the power of Toni's divisive efforts.

A final aspect of the leadership retreat was to charge the group with creating a set of guiding principles that the leadership group would follow, including how they would hold each other accountable to maintain agreed upon standards. Once this work was completed, they would then read these principles aloud at a parish-wide meeting, each signing this code of conduct, with the congregation as witnesses.

After the retreat, the leadership group was now prepared to meet with Toni. They offered her another opportunity to speak to the leadership body and Pastor Jane in hopes of repairing grievances so they could move forward together. Toni declined this invitation, stating that Pastor Jane hadn't heard the last from her and her group.

The lay leaders and Pastor Jane together gave Toni notice in writing, stating that her divisive email communications needed to cease, and any further communication needed to be conducted in person. Toni continued to defy the ground rules. Clearly, the limit-setting on behalf of the group only further fueled her need for vindictive retaliation. In a final defiant act Toni broke into the church offices late at night, hacked into the website and wrote disparaging words about Grace Church and Pastor Jane. The website was shut down, but Toni managed to break into the website three more times before the police went to her home to press charges.

Outcomes

Grace Church survived this unfortunate drama and in fact, is now a much more unified parish. However, this is an all too frequent example of what happens when a Vindictive Revenge Seeker is not contained in a timely fashion. When this archetype is allowed power and influence, and their bad behavior remains unchecked, it is difficult to reverse course to salvage the relationship. In this instance when the leadership group did set firm, consistent limits, Toni chose a path of further escalation, even if it meant direct defiance of the law.

This example also illustrates how difficult it is for any one individual to contain a Vindictive Revenge Seeker. It takes a strong, unified group of people to exert enough influence to reestablish a sense of safety and well-being for the entire community. Vindictive Revenge Seekers are not interested in compromise. They are driven by winning at any cost. In the case of Grace Church, Toni was unwilling to repair the situation because the only repair in her mind was to punish Pastor Jane for causing her a loss of perceived status.

Church groups who live by rules of forgiveness, kindness, and reconciliation have a difficult time understanding that these solutions do not work with more extreme cases of the archetype of the Vindictive Revenge Seeker.

The Business Translation. In a business, someone like Toni is often the high-revenue salesperson or the brilliant engineer who holds the culture hostage. The lesson here is stark: You cannot appease a Vindictive Revenge Seeker. Leadership must unify to set appropriate and adequate boundaries, even if it means losing that individual to save the collective.

Legacy Built with Asphalt: A Family-owned Business Case Study

A Brief Introduction of Roadway Construction

Roadway Construction began in 1925 with a humble mission: smooth parking spaces for neighbors in a dust-ridden midwestern town in the United States. Frank Stanton, a practical man with a deep love for his community, had no formal education beyond high school, but he had a strong back, sharp eyes, and a keen sense of opportunity. With a wheelbarrow, a few hand tools, and a rented roller, he laid the first smooth slab on Birch Street.

Within a decade, Frank's reputation reached neighboring towns. What began as driveways evolved into parking lots and then municipal roads. After World War II Roadway Construction, with little competition, was laying blacktop faster and cheaper than anyone else. When Frank's son, Harold, returned from the war, he joined the business and expanded it even further, paving county roads and regional highways throughout the heartland.

Today, Roadway Construction is a major contractor across three states employing over 450 people, managing multimillion-dollar projects, and maintaining one of the most respected reputations in the Midwest. But behind the glowing client testimonials and contracts lie decades of buried family tensions.

With Frank and Harold both gone, the company now legally belongs to the fourth grandchildren, Daniel, Miles, Caroline, and Emily. Only two of them actually run the company, Daniel and Miles.

The two sisters, Caroline and Emily, both chose successful lives outside the company one as a high school teacher and the other a nurse in a large city hospital with having little say in the business. Because of their emotional loyalty to their brothers, they are mostly silent during board meetings, reluctant to choose sides fearing they might enflame the already volatile brother relationship.

The Imperative

Daniel Stanton, 51, is the CEO. He's meticulous, pragmatic, and loyal to the past. Because he genuinely cares about the employees, he can't help himself from getting very involved in the operation. He has been told many times that he is a micro-manager. While his brother Miles talks of expansion, Daniel worries about quality, safety, and keeping the smaller more local contracts. He's well-liked by the long-tenured field crews, especially the older workers who see his brother Miles' pace of innovation as reckless.

Miles Stanton, 48, is the company's COO. A born operations-guy, he is engaging, has big ideas, and a relentless drive for efficiency. He believes Roadway Construction should evolve with the times embracing AI-enabled machinery, sustainable asphalt technologies, and digital procurement systems. Miles is the reason Roadway Construction has stayed competitive in an increasingly competitive and regulated market.

As children, they were close. But when their father (Harold's only son, Luther) died unexpectedly in 1997, a fissure opened. Daniel, then just 20, was forced to step up and help their grandfather Frank during his final years. Miles, meanwhile, left the Midwest and pursued a degree in engineering returning five years later expecting a leadership role. Instead, he found his older brother entrenched and unwilling to share the reins.

Over the next five years, the conflict intensified. Daniel accused Miles of "bulldozing" new projects without including him in the decision-making process. Miles accused Daniel of "dragging his feet" and sabotaging the changes needed for Roadway to be sustainable. At one board meeting, Miles floated a buyout of the siblings' shares to consolidate control. Miles walked out.

At another meeting, Miles attempted to install an external CFO to "protect the legacy" and to save the company from what he called "poor leadership." The family voted 3 to 1 to install the new CFO. This set off a cascade of triangulation which made the brother relationship dynamics even worse.

That the two brothers can barely stand each other had created huge dysfunction throughout the company and, needless to say, not good role models for the company's core values. The two brothers' conflict was not merely operational or philosophical; it was deeply personal.

The Diagnosis

As the tensions escalated all of the family members realized they were facing a leadership crisis that threatened the future of the family business. Their engagement of a family business consultant to help diagnose what was going on, dramatically and positively changed the conversations being had at all levels of leadership. This was a classic case of **complicated loyalties**, misaligned and undefined roles and an absence of formal governance, all of which amounted to a severely diminished level of trust between the brothers and, consequently, the employees. The consultant also pointed out to the brothers the unspoken unresolved grief of losing their father at such an early age.

The Intervention

The consultant began conducting interviews, one-on-one sessions with each sibling, key managers, key long-term clients, and even retired employees. The goal was not just to understand the business operational gaps but identify the impact of the emotional undercurrents born from complex family loyalties going back decades. What emerged was a pattern of unspoken resentments stemming from lack of clarity and lack of safety. At the base of this pattern was the life-long antagonism between the brothers made worse by the triangulation that was happening with the newly installed CFO.

Daniel felt Miles turned his back on the family by going away to college. He resented the fact that Miles never acknowledged Daniel's early sacrifices and his unflinching loyalty to Grandpa Frank and dad. Miles felt Daniel had micro-managed the company for his own ego and has never acknowledged Miles' commitment to the business.

Caroline and Emily, meanwhile, felt torn. On one hand, they believed the company should belong to family. On the other, they feared that selling the company would betray their grandfather's legacy. They also resented that their legal co-ownership afforded them no say or influence upon the business.

The intervention strategy included three focus areas:

a **Family Governance Restructuring**
The siblings were guided to create a Family Council and an Operating Board which were separate but collaborative. The Family Council would represent the needs and desires of the family and its values. The Operating Board would manage business decisions and longer-term business strategies. Caroline and Emily were given clear roles in the Family Council, allowing them to engage and be heard but without operational entanglement.

b **Role Clarification and Leadership Coaching**
Daniel and Miles underwent individual and facilitated joint coaching sessions. These sessions helped them map the kind of friction and flow that existed between them. The use of various assessments as well as 360 feedback allowed the brothers to engage with data. This was a game changer because it shifted the conversation from opinions to facts. Unexpectedly, during a coaching session Daniel brought up their father's death which clearly reopened old grief for them both. The consultant, keeping vigilant not to cross the line between coaching and therapy, put out the question,

How much of your own grief might be causing each of you to over-react and misinterpret each other's leadership?

Both brothers sat silently with this question as tears became visible in their eyes. Miles chose to seek professional therapy while Daniel, as far as we know, chose not to learn more about the connection between his grief and his leadership behaviors.

c **Ownership and Exit Planning**
The brothers then went through a series of structured discussions about shared ownership, dividends, and succession planning. Rather than forcing a buyout, split, or outright sale, the family created a phased buy-in/buy-out mechanism, allowing the siblings to either divest or reinvest on agreed upon terms. This gave Caroline and Emily a pathway to exit with dignity, or to remain as legacy stewards.

The Outcomes

During this two-year process there were setbacks. When Daniel tried to push decisions before gaining consensus, Miles refused to attend meetings, yelling matches ensued, table pounding, and even throwing things against the wall. Slowly, clarity began to emerge but the tension never disappeared.

The most significant outcomes were:

- **Rebalanced Leadership**
  - The new structure designated Daniel as CEO and the visionary leader but gave Miles formal authority over operations with veto power on logistical decisions. While they still disagreed often, they began to respect the lanes they each occupied. The brothers recognized how the CFO, with good intentions, was inadvertently pitting the brothers against each other. The brothers decided to no longer let this happen.
- **Shareholder Equity Redistribution**
  - Caroline opted to sell her shares back to the company under the new buyout structure. Emily kept hers and chose to remain a passive shareholder. The redistribution allowed for clearer communication lines and reduced ambiguity.
- **Legacy Preservation**
  - The Family Council initiated a Legacy Project that digitized old blueprints, recorded interviews with former employees, and commissioned a short documentary on Frank Stanton's founding of Roadway Construction. This project gave the family a shared source of pride beyond profit. The siblings felt like they could maintain their sense of family loyalty.
- **Cultural Shift**
  - Internally, nearly all of the employees noticed the change. Field managers reported improved morale, especially after Daniel began holding quarterly "boots on the ground" meetings; an idea Miles had pushed for years. Meanwhile, Daniel, with his ever-present reticence to like his brother's ideas, began supporting pilot programs for new technology starting with Miles' AI-driven asphalt grading initiative, which reduced project overruns by 12% in its first year.
- **Personal Shift**
  - At one particularly heated quarterly strategy meeting, Miles snapped at Daniel over a delayed contract. Daniel, instead of escalating, said simply, "We're not doing this again." For the first time, they both stopped, took a breath, as Miles said, "You're right." That moment marked a turning point.

In 2025, Roadway Construction celebrated its 100th anniversary with a ceremony on the original parking slab Frank Stanton laid next to that white house on Birch Street. Daniel gave a speech about "building roads not just across states, but across generations." Miles stood beside him, arms crossed, but smiling slightly.

For all its progress, Roadway's future remains uncertain. Family businesses rarely make it to the fourth generation intact. But thanks to this challenging but honest intervention, the Stanton family no longer avoids the hard conversations. They face them, like they pave roads, by focusing on the road ahead.

The Business Translation. While this was a family business, the friction here is common in scaling organizations where roles rely more on history rather than clarity. When interpersonal dynamics are too tangled to resolve through conversation alone, you need Structural Differentiation. The brothers couldn't fix their relationship, so they fixed the organizational chart – creating clear, separate lanes (CEO vs. COO) with formal governance. When emotional maturity lags, structural clarity can bridge but not remove the gap.

The Space

Long before modern self-help authors popularized the idea of choosing our response in moments of rupture, Galloway (1917) described The Space or a "third region ... between stimulus and response ... where our real personal values lie. This is where we grow most" (p. 55) (see Figure 12.2). Decades later, psychologist Rollo May (1994) crystallized this concept, writing that,

> *Human freedom involves our capacity to pause between stimulus and response and, in that pause, to choose the one response toward which we wish to throw our weight.*
>
> (p. 100)

This early articulation preceded similar words often attributed – incorrectly – to Viktor Frankl and later echoed by Stephen R. Covey, emphasizing that personal growth and freedom emerge in The Space between stimulus and response (Viktor Frankl Institute, n.d.).

In each of the case studies we just shared with you, this concept definitely applied. Something happened, and each example found alternatives to an auto-response or typical way of dealing with the scenario.

- In The Space, Timberland affected impact of a global manufacturing supply chain and in so doing, doubled down on their core values.
- In The Space, beloved Pastor Jane no longer felt alone and with her strengthened Vestry, faced and overcame belligerence and divisiveness.
- In The Space, Daniel and Miles, while not able to vanquish their lifelong sibling tension, realize a clarity and a new focus allowing the company to move forward.

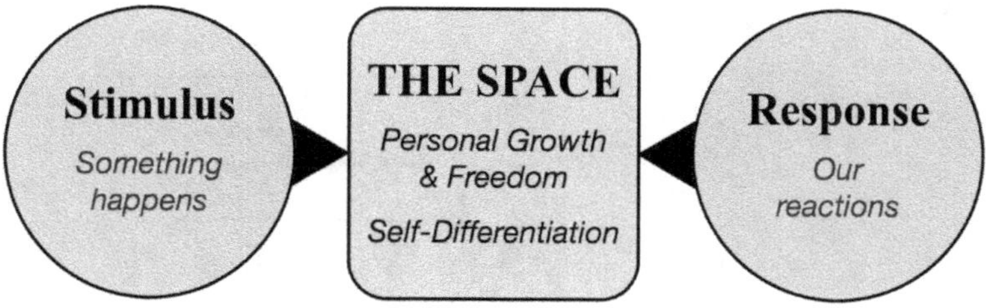

Figure 12.2 The Space.

But let's be honest, The Space between stimulus and response that we refer to, when obscured by economic threats, frustrating policies or archetypal leadership, can be hidden, fleeting, or elusive. As Self-Differentiated Leaders, we must trust that The Space is always there for us to find it and grow from it

The metaphor of an Operating System might be helpful here as well; not the one in your computer but the one in your head. Our own operating system is continuously running in the background dictating our relationship assumptions, leadership behaviors, emotional triggers, and our autonomic responses. As the world changes and what it means to be an effective leader changes, we are wise to consider updating our own operating system when the friction exceeds the flow. Such was true for Jeffrey Swartz, the Stanton Family and Pastor Jane. In each example they updated their Operating System, creating The Space, by using these leadership strategic behaviors (see Figure 12.3):

1 Pause – This is when you are mindful to take a moment, weigh all of your options, recalibrate, and then more wisely react.
2 Reaffirm – Reminding yourself what is most important.
3 Examine – Taking the time that it takes to identify what is really getting in the way of what is most important.
4 Inquire – Being genuinely curious about the opportunities that come with contradiction and paradox.
5 Listen – Reaping the benefits of hearing other perspectives to broaden and deepen your own.
6 Recognize – Coming to terms with the possible Loyalty Contracts that are at play and are no longer healthy.
7 Create – Creating new choices, you are able to chart a different course which breaks a friction-laced pattern to more flow-based outcomes.

Implementing this kind of operating system update gives us an additional layer and quality of the kind of space that scholars highlight as

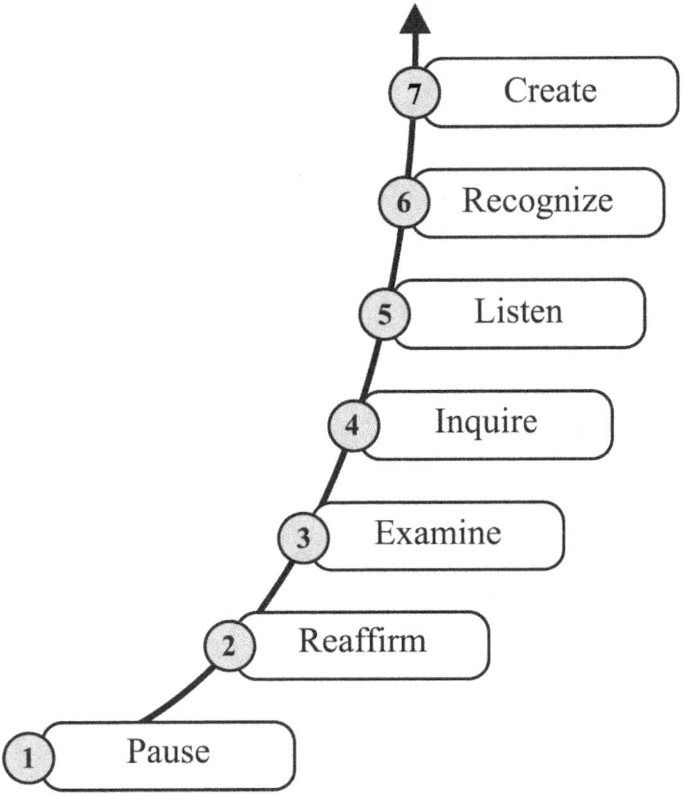

Figure 12.3 Updating your operating system.

necessary in the ever-evolving world in which we are now called to lead. At the end of this seven-step process is of course, learning – learning how to be more self-differentiated.

The Intervention Playbook: Naming, Pausing, and Reframing

While Loyalty Contracts define the problem, Self-Differentiation presents a solution. It's the capacity to remain grounded in one's principles in the face of emotional pressure. As the cases show, this capacity can be required of a single leader, an entire team, or the organizational system itself.

- Jeff Swartz personified the Differentiated Leader. He single-handedly resisted the anxious, reactive pull from his team to capitulate and from

Greenpeace to retaliate. By staying calm and holding to his principles, he was able to think systematically, an act of individual leadership that scaled to the entire organization's successful response.

- At Grace Church, where the primary leader initially struggled with differentiation, the solution came from the Differentiated Team. The lay leadership, with coaching, learned to function as a unified, principled body. They collectively defined their values, held a firm line against toxic behavior and absorbed the community's anxiety. Their story proves that when a single leader is vulnerable, a strong leadership team can provide the necessary backbone.
- The Stanton family was so emotionally enmeshed that individual differentiation was not possible. The solution was to build differentiation into the System itself. By creating separate structures for family and business matters, they built the boundaries the brothers could not maintain on their own. This demonstrates a crucial lesson: when interpersonal dynamics are too tangled, a well-designed system can provide the clarity and stability needed to move forward.

Across all three interventions, a clear pattern emerged for moving from friction to flow. This three-step playbook is central to updating any leader's "Operating System" in a conflict or a crisis (see Figure 12.4).

First was the courage to **Name the Real Problem**, moving past the surface-level issues. For Timberland, the problem wasn't Greenpeace; it was the shared challenge of deforestation. For Grace Church, the problem wasn't just a difficult parishioner; it was a culture of conflict avoidance. For the Stanton family, there was a clear inability for the brothers to self-differentiate.

Second, each leader or group had to create a **Pause**, deliberately find The Space between stimulus and response. Swartz refused the immediate

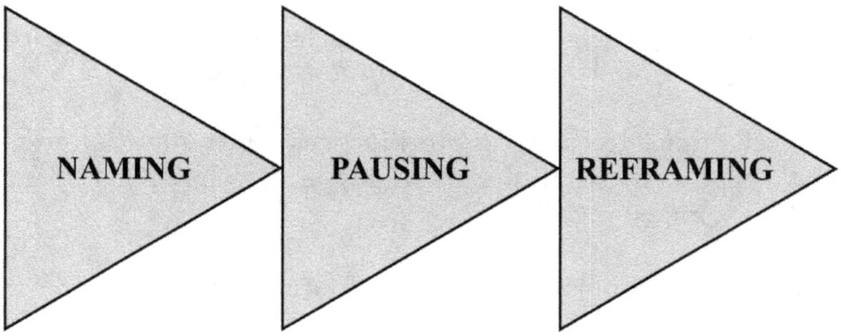

Figure 12.4 Intervention playbook.

demand for a boycott; the church consultants initiated a retreat for leadership to learn skills that enabled them to deal more effectively with conflict; and the family business consultant used data to slow down emotional arguments.

Finally, this pause allowed them to **Reframe the Challenge** from one of adversarial attacks to creating systematic alliances. The objective shifted, in varied degrees, and evolved to create a more functional and sustainable future for all stakeholders, turning a moment of crisis into a catalyst for profound and lasting growth.

Chapter Summary

This final chapter moves from theory to grounded practice, demonstrating how the covert dynamics of non-self-differentiation shape organizations and how to intervene effectively. We examined three real-world case studies, each revealing how unexamined, unhealthy Loyalty Contracts create systemic friction that hinders growth and compromises flow. The cases – a corporation in crisis (Timberland), a religious institution in conflict (Grace Church), and a multi-generational family business (Roadway Construction) – illustrate that solutions must be scaled and customized to the problem. We see this through three levels of Self-Differentiation.

- First, the Differentiated Leader: Timberland CEO Jeff Swartz personally absorbed immense pressure and resisted a reactive response, single-handedly reframing a public adversary (Greenpeace) into a systemic partner.
- Second, the Differentiated Team: At Grace Church, where the leader struggled with differentiation, the lay leadership was coached to become a unified body, strong enough to set boundaries and contain a toxic "Vindictive Revenge Seeker."
- Third, the Differentiated System: In the enmeshed family business, individual differentiation was insufficient. The solution required building new governance structures (a Family Council and Operating Board) to create the clarity and boundaries the brothers could not.

These interventions are united by a practical, three-step "Intervention Playbook" that serves as an update to any leader's internal "Operating System." This process involves:

- Naming the real problem beneath the surface symptoms (e.g., deforestation, not Greenpeace; conflict avoidance, not just a difficult person);
- Creating a Pause to deliberately find what is called the "space between stimulus and response"; and

- Reframing the goal from winning a fight to creating a functional, sustainable future.

These cases prove that by making the unconscious conscious, leaders can intentionally choose a response that leads to profound organizational growth and personal freedom.

Key Takeaways

1. Loyalty Contracts based on an honest intention of mutuality are the foundation of sustainable business growth and its reputation.
2. By establishing a fair sense of mutuality around a shared goal and being clear about its own vulnerabilities, an organization, a team or a couple can create a new foundation for trust.
3. It takes a strong, unified group of people to exert enough influence to reestablish a sense of safety and well-being for the entire community.
4. Sometimes our own grief might be causing our over-reaction and misinterpretation of someone's leadership.
5. We must trust that The Space is always there for us to find it and grow from it.

Next Level Reflections

1. As you read about the three examples, what leadership behaviors did you notice that impacted the overall outcome?
2. What was your reaction to the processes used in each of the three scenarios?
3. What techniques resonated with you and why?
4. Based upon your experience and expertise, what techniques that were not used might have been helpful?
5. As you read about each of these scenarios, how do you think your own level of Self-Differentiation would have performed?

Afterword

Change no longer arrives in cycles; but more as waves eroding the stabilizing once terra firma beneath our feet. Where we once found stability in well-understood roles and predictable environments, we now face a landscape where our longed-for sense of certainty is fleeting and paradox and complexity promise to be ever-present neighbors going forward. This reality only amplifies the importance and value of the concepts we have shared with you. Our hope is that you treat them less as aspirations and more as practical daily disciplines for effective leadership and greater happiness at home.

As we stated in the introduction, technology, especially artificial intelligence, has intensified both the promise and peril of 21st century leadership. Of course, technology will continue to offer the world extraordinary advantages like greater insights, efficiencies, and production capabilities.

And yet it could tempt us to desensitize our intuition, bifurcate our attention, and outsource our judgment. For all leaders, one of the major challenges will be to maintain our own organizational and personal agency, using technology as a tool, not a surrogate for discernment. This growing demand for balance will define the next generation of effective self-differentiated leadership.

At the same time, the erosion of community and the rise of digital connection without true connectedness have reshaped our loyalties. Loyalty Contracts, implicit or explicit, have always bound teams, organizations, nations, and leaders to shared purpose. But today those bonds strain under the pressures of transient work, remote interactions, political divide, and increased isolation. Reexamining and renewing Loyalty Contracts is not an exercise in pragmatic advancement. Leaders must create spaces where mutual expectations are clear, trust is intentionally built, and belonging is not an accident but an outcome of psychologically adult intention.

Ultimately, an integrated life remains a leader's most powerful anchor. Integration does not mean perfect balance or calm circumstances; it means

DOI: 10.4324/9781003621393-13

alignment between who we are, how we lead, and what we value, even as the world reshapes itself around us. But the work of integration, of choosing congruence over fragmentation, will always remain a choice within our control.

AI must not replace our own human capacities; but perhaps it can free us to do the work that only humans can do. It is calling us to redefine *smart* not as a measure of what we know but as a measure of how we interact at work and at home. The future of leadership will be defined by a different kind of intelligence: **relationship-smartness.**

As AI commoditizes data analysis and technical execution, *smart* is no longer a differentiator; it is a commodity. The only competitive advantage remaining for human leaders is the ability to do what algorithms cannot:

build trust,
navigate ambiguity, and
repair ruptures.

This will be the major competitive advantage of the future.

In the 21st century, Relational Intelligence (RQ) is not a soft skill; it is the currency of leadership. This is the core competency of the 21st century, and it is the quiet urgent work of this book. We can only hope that leadership in the 21st century, one that understands the importance of relational connection as foundational to human progress and evolution, will act as the moral compass that guides the rolling out of AI.

The Two Tales of "Relationship-Smartness"

"Relationship-smartness" has two distinct but deeply interconnected geographies: the external landscape of our connections with others and the internal landscape of our connection with ourselves.
The external landscape is the more visible of the two. It is our ability to:

- build trust,
- navigate conflict with grace,
- foster psychological safety, and
- inspire collaborative energy.

These are not *soft skills*. As we alluded to in the introduction, they are the essential capabilities, value-creating activities in a world where AI can handle the technical brief. An AI can draft a project plan, but it cannot sit with a team member whose motivation is flagging, listen with genuine empathy and help them reconnect with their purpose. An AI can map a complex project timeline, but it cannot sit with a team member who is quietly disengaging and help them find their way back to purpose. An AI can highlight performance gaps, but it lacks the intuition to spot the elephant in the room – delicate, unspoken friction – and facilitate the difficult conversation required to repair the rupture.

But this external work is impossible to sustain without a solid foundation of our own internal landscape. This brings us to the profound insight offered by thinkers like Peter Senge (2025) who describes "personal mastery" as founded upon the "relationship of self with self." This is the epicenter of self-differentiated leadership. It is the journey toward becoming a psychological adult – a person who can hold their own center, regulate their own emotional state, and engage with the world from a place of clarity and intention, rather than from a place of reactivity and fear.

Psychological maturity is not a destination but a practice. It is measured in the moments of rupture and disappointment that are inevitable in work and in life. When a project fails, when a difficult conversation looms, when we receive critical feedback, these are the moments that reveal our level of personal mastery. The psychologically immature self is hijacked by emotion, seeking to blame, defend, or withdraw. But as Senge (2025) reminds us, what truly matters is "how we show up."

The Self-Differentiated Leader shows up with curiosity. They can feel the sting of disappointment without being consumed by it. They can take responsibility without shame. They can see the conflict as a data point, an opportunity for learning and repair, rather than a personal threat or a deadly defeat.

The Danger of Yesterday's Logic

As mentioned in the Introduction of this book, Peter Drucker (1980) offered us a stark warning with regard to using yesterday's logic in our rapidly changing world. As we have illustrated in the chapters of this book, the danger of clinging to old business models or outdated strategies isn't the only way we are at risk for failure. This book illustrates that one of the keys to breaking free of yesterday's logic is changing what has been etched into our nervous systems. Early Loyalty Contracts are the relational experiences that have been hard-wired into our nervous systems early in life, and often remain unquestioned or under-examined.

Our early Loyalty Contracts were initially brilliant, adaptive strategies for navigating the power dynamics of our early families. They taught us how to secure love, maintain connection, and ensure our survival in our first "organization." We learned to be the high achiever, the peacemaker, the invisible one, or the rebel. These roles and their corresponding rules became our internal operating system. The potential danger is that we carry this outdated programming into our adult lives and our leadership roles, long after its original rationale has disappeared.

In the software industry, the term "Technical Debt" refers to the cost of choosing an easy, short-term solution that causes operating glitches later. Unexamined Loyalty Contracts are "Cultural Debt." Every time you avoid a difficult conversation or act from a childhood script, you pay interest on that debt. Eventually, the interest steadily mounts and then it comes due. That's when the culture defaults and potentially goes bankrupt.

This is not just ineffective. In our interconnected and fast-paced world, it is a profound liability. It wastes money, creates toxic environments, stifles innovation, and breaks trust. The work of becoming a Self-Differentiated Leader is the work of identifying this outdated logic. It is about having the courage to look at the Loyalty Contracts that once kept us safe and asks, with compassion and clarity, if they still serve us. Systems thinker Peter Senge teaches us to let go of the mental models that no longer serve us. It is the messy but courageous work of discernment and setting boundaries, of disappointing people vs sacrificing our own integrity. It is willingness to choose the discomfort of growth over the familiar comfort of compliance.

From Mechanic to Gardener: The Wisdom of Living Systems

For decades, "Yesterday's Logic" taught us to treat our organizations like machines. Much of our leadership thinking had been if we pulled the right levers, issued the right commands, and tightened the right screws, we could control the outcome. We viewed our people as parts to be optimized and our relationships as transactions to be managed.

Enter the revolutionary book *The Fifth Discipline* where Senge challenged this kind of mechanistic approach to leadership.

> *Organizations are living realities; they exist and grow through the actions and commitments of people.*
>
> (1990, p. 289)

More recently, Margaret Wheatley (2006) reminds us that organizations are not machines; they are living systems. As she writes,

> *Power in organizations is the capacity generated by relationships. It is an energy that comes into existence through relationships.*
>
> (p. 39)

A machine operates through control. A living system thrives on connection, communication, and a recognition of the need for interdependency. A leader trapped in yesterday's logic treats their organization like a machine. They pull levers, issue commands, and try to control outcomes, only to be frustrated when the complex, human "parts" don't behave as predicted. They are focused on functions, roles, and positions. They are focused on the organizational chart, not the organizational heart – it's people.

Self-Differentiated Leaders, however, understand that their primary role, not unlike a gardener's, is to lead as a cultivator of a healthy living system. They focus on the quality of relationships to manufacture, create, build, innovate, engineer, reimagine, produce, and yes, to make money. They know that if the connections are strong, if information flows freely, and if trust is the nutrient in the cultural soil, then resilience, creativity, and extraordinary results will emerge. Perhaps, they are not the master mechanic but the master gardener. As any master gardener will tell you, "You cannot control a garden; you can only create the conditions for it to flourish."

This is the ultimate expression of a Self-Differentiated Leader. They have done the internal work to loosen their firm grasp of control and in doing so unleash the full, collective potential of the system they lead. They create clarity of purpose and then trust their people to find the way. They host conversations rather than dictating solutions. They nurture emergence rather than enforcing restrictive conformity.

A Final Note to You, Our Readers

This book is about practice not perfection. As you finish reading this final chapter, there is one more to go. The one you write. There will be moments when you revert to the old Loyalty Contracts and react from fear or old habits rather than the skills acquired from the self-differentiated leadership required for the 21st century. It is a normal part of the growth process to expect bumps in the road.

The key is not to become discouraged by these lapses. Come to expect them and willingly accept the wisdom they offer. Treat them as data points for insight generation and the rightsizing of your own powerful leadership.

Embrace the sometimes-uncomfortable journey to becoming a Self-Differentiated Leader. We are often led to believe that a successful life is a kind of package tour – we follow a map drawn by others to a destination they have chosen for us. But the path to Self-Differentiation is the freedom of taking the wheel and trusting that the journey is in fact worthy of your trust. It demands not that we follow a map, but that we make the map.

Every time you choose to flex your newly acquired Self-Differentiation muscles, remember that you are not just changing your own life. You are breaking a generational cycle and giving rise to a healthier path for others to follow and in doing so, you create systems that give others permission to realize their own full potential.

Our hope is that you will use the keys we promised you in the introduction to not necessarily change the course of human events on your own. Simply play the part you are able to play in making a difference in your own sphere of influence at work and at home. The world does not need another leader driving on autopilot. It needs you behind the wheel. That's where all change begins.

And that's the echo we hope you hear when you close this book.

References

Adair-Toteff, C. (2005). Max Weber's charisma. *Journal of Classical Sociology*, *5*(2), 189–204. https://doi.org/10.1177/1468795X05053491

Bass, B. M. (1990). *Bass & Stogdill's handbook of leadership*. Free Press.

Beebe, B., Jaffe, J., Markese, S., Buck, K., Chen, H., Cohen, P., Barrack, L., Andrews, H., & Feldstein, S. (2010). The origins of 12-month attachment: A microanalysis of 4-month mother–infant interaction. *Attachment & Human Development*, *12*(1–2), 3–141. https://doi.org/10.1080/14616730903338985

Beebe, B., Knoblauch, S., Rustin, J., & Sorter, D. (2005). *Forms of intersubjectivity in infant research and adult treatment*. Other Press.

Beebe, B., & Lachmann, F. M. (1988). The contribution of mother-infant mutual influence to the origins of self-and object representations. In N. J. Skolnick & S. C. Warshaw (Eds.), *Relational perspectives in psychoanalysis* (pp. 83–117). Routledge.

Beebe, B., & Lachmann, F. M. (2005). *Infant research and adult treatment: Co-constructing interactions*. Routledge.

Benjamin, J. (2018). *Beyond doer and done to: Recognition theory, intersubjectivity and the third*. Routledge.

Bhushan, B. (2013). *Introduction to tribology* (2nd ed.). Wiley.

Bowden, F. P., & Tabor, D. (2001). *The friction and lubrication of solids*. Oxford University Press. (Original work published 1950)

Bowen, M. (1978). *Family therapy in clinical practice*. Jason Aronson.

Bowlby, J. (1951). *Maternal care and mental health* (Vol. 2). World Health Organization.

Bowlby, J. (1958). The nature of the child's tie to his mother. *International Journal of Psycho-Analysis*, *39*, 1–23.

Bowlby, J. (1983). *Attachment and loss: Vol. 1. Attachment* (2nd ed.). Basic Books.

Bowlby, J. (1988). *A secure base: Parent-child attachment and healthy human development*. Basic Books.

Bowlby, J. (1990). *A secure base: Parent-child attachment and healthy human development (Routledge Classics)*. Routledge.

Boyatzis, R. E., Smith, M. L., & Van Oosten, E. (2019). *Helping people change: Coaching with compassion for lifelong learning and growth*. Harvard Business Review Press.

Bretherton, I. (1992). The origins of attachment theory: John Bowlby and Mary Ainsworth. *Developmental Psychology, 28*(5), 759–775.

Burns, J. M. (2004). *Transforming leadership*. Grove Press.

Bushe, G. R. (2001a). *Clear leadership: How outstanding leaders make themselves understood, cut through the mush, and help everyone get real at work*. Davies-Black.

Bushe, G. R. (2001b). Self-differentiation: The missing ingredient in leadership. *OD Practitioner, 33*(2), 25–30.

Buswell, R. E., Jr., & Lopez, D. S., Jr. (2013). *The Princeton dictionary of Buddhism*. Princeton University Press.

Butler, R. A. (2009, July 29). *Timberland announces policy to avoid using leather produced by Amazon destruction*. Mongabay. https://news.mongabay.com/2009/07/timberland-announces-policy-to-avoid-using-leather-produced-by-amazon-destruction/

Cavico, F. J., & Mujtaba, B. G. (2016). Volkswagen emissions scandal: A global case study of legal, ethical, and practical consequences and recommendations for sustainable management. *Global Journal of Research in Business & Management*, *4*(2), 303–311.

Chokshi, N., Ember, S., & Nerkar, S. (2024, March 28). 'Shortcuts everywhere': How Boeing favored speed over quality. *The New York Times*. www.nytimes.com/2024/03/28/business/boeing-quality-problems-speed.html#:~:text=%E2%80%9CThe%20theme%20is%20shortcuts%20everywhere,safety%20experts%20and%20more%20than (Accessed on 14th of June, 2026).

Chua, A. (2011). *Battle hymn of the tiger mother*. Penguin Press.

Coleman, F. (2020). *A human algorithm: How Artificial Intelligence is redefining who we are*. Catapult.

Colvin, G. (2014, March 20). *The world's 50 greatest leaders*. Fortune. https://fortune.com/2014/03/20/worlds-50-greatest-leaders/

Cooke, R. A., & Lafferty, J. C. (1982). *Organizational culture inventory*. Human Synergistics International.

The Culture Factor Group. (n.d.-a). *Country comparison tool*. Retrieved June 1, 2025, from www.theculturefactor.com/country-comparison-tool

The Culture Factor Group. (n.d.-b). *Country comparison tool (legacy)*. Retrieved November 30, 2025, from www.theculturefactor.com/country-comparison-legacy

Danielian, J., & Gianotti, P. (2012). *Listening with purpose: Entry points into shame and narcissistic vulnerability*. Jason Aronson.

Davies, R. (1951). *Tempest-tost*. Clarke, Irwin & Company.

Ding, D., Zhao, Q., Guo, Q., Liang, X., Luo, J., Yu, L., Zheng, L., & Hong, Z. (2015). Prevalence of mild cognitive impairment in an urban community in China: A cross-sectional analysis of the Shanghai Aging Study. *Alzheimer's & Dementia*, *11*(3), 300–309. https://doi.org/10.1016/j.jalz.2014.01.005

Doidge, N. (2007). *The brain that changes itself*. Viking.

Drucker, P. F. (1980). *Managing in turbulent times*. Harper & Row.

Edmondson, A. C. (1999). Psychological safety and learning behavior in work teams. *Administrative Science Quarterly*, *44*(2), 350–383.

Edmondson, A. C. (2003). Speaking up in the operating room: How team leaders promote learning in interdisciplinary action teams. *Journal of Management Studies*, *40*(6), 1419–1452.

Edmondson, A. C. (2018). *The fearless organization: Creating psychological safety in the workplace for learning, innovation, and growth*. Wiley. (See specifically Chapter 2: "The Avoidable Failure at Volkswagen").

Ewing, J. (2017, March 16). Engineering a deception: What led to Volkswagen's diesel scandal. *The New York Times*. www.nytimes.com/interactive/2017/business/volkswagen-diesel-emissions-scandal.html (Accessed 14th of June, 2026).

Felitti, V. J. (2002). The relation between adverse childhood experiences and adult health: Turning gold into lead. *The Permanente Journal*, *6*(1), 44–47.

Follett, M. P. (1942). Power. In H. C. Metcalf & L. Urwick (Eds.), *Dynamic administration: The collected papers of Mary Parker Follett* (pp. 95–115). Harper & Brothers.

Forrester, J. W. (1961). *Industrial dynamics*. Pegasus Communications.

Forrester, J. W. (1969). *Urban dynamics*. MIT Press.

Forrester, J. W. (1971). *World dynamics*. Wright-Allen Press.

Friedman, E. H. (1985). *Generation to generation: Family process in church and synagogue*. Guilford Press.

Friedman, E. H. (2007). *A failure of nerve: Leadership in the age of the quick fix*. Church Publishing, Inc.

Fritz, R. (1989). *The path of least resistance: Learning to become the creative force in your own life*. Fawcett Columbine.

Fuchs, E., & Flügge, G. (2014). Adult neuroplasticity: More than 40 years of research. *Neural Plasticity*, *2014*, Article 541870. https://doi.org/10.1155/2014/541870

Galloway, T. W. (1917). *The use of motives in teaching morals and religion*. The Pilgrim Press.

Gelb, D. (Creator), & Hall, B. (Director). (2022). Franco Pepe (Season 1, Episode 4) [TV series episode]. In D. Gelb (Exec. Producer), *Chef's table: Pizza*. Boardwalk Pictures; Supper Club.

Gelb, D. (Creator), & McGinn, Z. (Director). (2022). Ann Kim (Season 1, Episode 3) [TV series episode]. In D. Gelb (Exec. Producer), *Chef's table: Pizza*. Boardwalk Pictures; Supper Club.

Gelb, D. (Creator), & Shiraki, A. (Director). (2022). Yoshihiro Imai (Season 1, Episode 6) [TV series episode]. In D. Gelb (Exec. Producer), *Chef's table: Pizza*. Boardwalk Pictures; Supper Club.

Gelb, D. (Creator), & Weaver, C. (Director). (2022). Chris Bianco (Season 1, Episode 1) [TV series episode]. In D. Gelb (Exec. Producer), *Chef's table: Pizza*. Boardwalk Pictures; Supper Club.

Gelfand, M. J., & Jackson, J. C. (2016). From tight to loose: A cultural theory of behavior. *Current Opinion in Psychology*, *8*, 78–83.

George, B. (2007). *True north: Discover your authentic leadership*. Jossey-Bass.

Gianotti, P. (2022). *Embracing therapeutic complexity: A guidebook to integrating the essentials of psychodynamic principles across therapeutic disciplines*. Routledge.

Ginott, H. G. (1969). *Between parent and teenager*. Macmillan.

Gladwell, M. (2008). *Outliers: The story of success*. Little, Brown and Company.

Global Indian. (2022, January). *Chanel No 1: An inside take on the life and career of HR pundit Leena Nair, who became the CEO of a global luxury brand*. Global Indian. www.globalindian.com/story/cover-story/chanel-no-1-an-inside-take-on-the-life-and-career-of-hr-pundit-leena-nair-who-became-the-ceo-of-a-global-luxury-brand/

Godlewski, M. (2024, June 1). *Boeing workers reluctant to speak up, FAA panel tells Senate*. Flying. www.flyingmag.com/boeing-workers-reluctant-to-speak-up-faa-panel-tells-senate/

Greenleaf, R. K. (1970). *The servant as leader*. The Robert K. Greenleaf Center for Servant Leadership.

Greenleaf, R. K. (1977). *Servant leadership: A journey into the nature of legitimate power and greatness*. Paulist Press.

Haden, S. (2013). *It's not about the coach: Getting the most from coaching in business, sport and life*. John Hunt Publishing.

Hamilton, P. (1938). *Gas light*. Constable & Co.

Harter, J. (2022, September 6). *Is quiet quitting real?* Gallup. www.gallup.com/workplace/398306/quiet-quitting-real.aspx

Helliwell, J. F., Layard, R., Sachs, J. D., De Neve, J.-E., Aknin, L. B., & Wang, S. (Eds.). (2024). *World happiness report 2024*. University of Oxford: Wellbeing Research Centre.

Hoffman, B. G. (2012). *American icon: Alan Mulally and the fight to save Ford Motor Company*. Crown Business.

Hofstede, G. (2011). Dimensionalizing cultures: The Hofstede model in context. *Online Readings in Psychology and Culture*, 2(1), 1–26. https://doi.org/10.9707/2307-0919.1014

Hogan, R. (1997). *Hogan development survey*. Hogan Assessment Systems.

Honneth, A. (2014). *The I in we: Studies in the theory of recognition*. Polity Press.

Honneth, A. (2019). *Axel Honneth and the critical theory of recognition*. Palgrave Macmillan.

Horney, K. (1945). *Our inner conflicts: A constructive theory of neurosis*. W.W. Norton & Company.

Horney, K. (1950). *Neurosis and human growth: The struggle toward self-realization*. W.W. Norton & Company.

Hull, J. (2017, September 25). *From alpha to beta and back: Coaching the post-heroic leader*. Institute of Coaching. https://instituteofcoaching.org/resources/alpha-beta-and-back-coaching-post-heroic-leader

Institute for Economics & Peace. (2025). *Global Peace Index 2025: Measuring peace in a complex world*. www.visionofhumanity.org/resources/

Isidore, C. (2024, January 30). *Boeing was once known for safety and engineering. But critics say an emphasis on profits changed that*. CNN. https://edition.cnn.com/2024/01/30/business/boeing-history-of-problems

Joosse, P. (2014). Becoming a god: Max Weber and the social construction of charisma. *Journal of Classical Sociology*, 14(3), 266–283. https://doi.org/10.1177/1468795X14536652

Joy, M. (2019). *Powerarchy: Understanding the psychology of oppression for social transformation.* Berrett-Koehler Publishers.

Jung, C. G. (1981). *The archetypes and the collective unconscious.* Princeton University Press.

Kegan, R., & Lahey, L. L. (2001). *How the way we talk can change the way we work: Seven languages for transformation.* Jossey-Bass.

Kennedy, R. (Director). (2022). *Downfall: The case against Boeing* [Film]. Netflix.

Kenrick, D. T., Cohen, A. B., Neuberg, S. L., & Cialdini, R. B. (2018). The science of anti-scientific thinking. *Scientific American, 319*(1), 36–41.

Kets de Vries, M. F. R. (2006). *The leader on the couch: A clinical approach to changing people and organizations.* Jossey-Bass.

Kets de Vries, M. F. R. (2013, December 18). The eight archetypes of leadership. *Harvard Business Review, 18,* 1–3

Kim, H. (2022). Improving crisis communication: When good advice becomes impractical. In W. T. Coombs, S. J. Holladay, & J. Wiley (Eds.), *The Handbook of Crisis Communication* (pp. 525–544).

Kim, H., & Lee, S. (2023, November 29). *Speaking of Microsoft's 'Contribution Leadership'.* Folin. www.folin.co/article/5066

Kim, H., Park, J., Cha, M., & Jeong, J. (2015). The effect of bad news and CEO apology of corporate on user responses in social media. *PLoS One, 10(5),* e0126358.

Kirk, D. (2002, March 26). New standards mean Korean Air is coming off many 'shun' lists. *The New York Times.* www.nytimes.com/2002/03/26/business/new-standards-mean-korean-air-is-coming-off-many-shun-lists.html

Klein, G. (2007). Performing a project premortem. *Harvard Business Review, 85*(9), 18–19.

Kluckhohn, C. (2017). *Mirror for man: The relation of anthropology to modern life.* Routledge.

Lee, H.-J. (2017). Thinking style across cultures: An interview with Richard Nisbett. *Cross Cultural & Strategic Management,* 24(1), 99–104. https://doi.org/10.1108/CCSM-10-2016-0181

Lipman-Blumen, J. (2005). *The allure of toxic leaders: Why we follow destructive bosses and corrupt politicians--And how we can survive them.* Oxford University Press.

Lovallo, D., & Sibony, O. (2010). The case for behavioral strategy. *McKinsey Quarterly,* 2, 30–43.

Lucado, M. (1993). *He still moves stones.* Word Publishing.

MacGabhann, S., Newman, P., Witchalls, J., Dowse, R., Waddington, G., & Cobley, S. (2025). Why do some respond and develop more from coaching than others? A systematic review of coachability and its constituent components. *Sports Medicine, 55,* 2147–2189. https://doi.org/10.1007/s40279-025-02267-6

Maier, S. F., & Seligman, M. E. (1976). Learned helplessness: Theory and evidence. *Journal of Experimental Psychology: General, 105*(1), 3–46.

May, R. (1994). *The courage to create.* W.W. Norton & Company.

McCurry, J. (2024, February 28). South Korea's fertility rate sinks to record low despite $270bn in incentives. *The Guardian.* www.theguardian.com/world/2024/feb/28/south-korea-fertility-rate-2023-fall-record-low-incentives (Accessed on 14th of June, 2026).

Merriam-Webster. (n.d.). Quid pro quo. In *Merriam-Webster.com dictionary*. Retrieved December 23, 2025, from www.merriam-webster.com/dictionary/quid%20pro%20quo

Milsted, D., Jarek, J., & Mleczek, M. (Executive Producers). (2025). *The asset* [TV series]. Profile Pictures; Netflix.

Minkov, M., Dutt, P., Schachner, M., Morales, O., Sanchez, C., Jandosova, J., Khassenbekov, Y., & Mudd, B. (2017). A revision of Hofstede's individualism-collectivism dimension: A new national index from a 56-country study. *Cross Cultural & Strategic Management*, *24*(3), 386–404.

Nickerson, R. S. (1998). Confirmation bias: A ubiquitous phenomenon in many guises. *Review of General Psychology*, *2*(2), 175–220. https://doi.org/10.1037/1089-2680.2.2.175

Ohlheiser, A. (2013). Malcolm Gladwell's cockpit culture theory and the Asiana crash. *The Atlantic*.

Onoda, H. (1974). *No surrender: My thirty-year war*. Kodansha International.

Ordóñez, L. D., & Welsh, D. T. (2015). Immoral goals: How goal setting may lead to unethical behavior. *Current Opinion in Psychology*, *6*, 93–96. https://doi.org/10.1016/j.copsyc.2015.06.001

Pearson, C. S., & Mark, M. (2001). *The hero and the outlaw: Building extraordinary brands through the power of archetypes*. McGraw-Hill.

Peckham, H. (2023). Introducing the Neuroplastic Narrative: A non-pathologizing biological foundation for trauma-informed and adverse childhood experience aware approaches. *Frontiers in Psychiatry*, *14*, 1103718. https://doi.org/10.3389/fpsyt.2023.1103718

Perez, A. M., Spence, J. S., Kiel, L. D., Venza, E. E., & Chapman, S. B. (2018). Influential cognitive processes on framing biases in aging. *Frontiers in Psychology*, *9*, 661. https://doi.org/10.3389/fpsyg.2018.00661

Picchi, A. (2024, June 18). Boeing CEO David Calhoun grilled by lawmakers as new whistleblower claims emerge. *CBS News*. www.cbsnews.com/news/boeing-ceo-david-calhoun-senate-hearing-testimony-whistleblower/ (Accessed 14th of June, 2026).

Rhodes, C. (2016). Democratic business ethics: Volkswagen's emissions scandal and the disruption of corporate sovereignty. *Organization Studies*, *37*(10), 1437–1454. https://doi.org/10.1177/0170840616641984

Rohr, R. (2011). *Falling upward: A spirituality for the two halves of life*. Jossey-Bass.

Rousseau, D. (1995). *Psychological contracts in organizations: Understanding written and unwritten agreements*. Sage Publications.

Scharmer, O. (2016). *Theory U: Leading from the future as it emerges*. Berrett-Koehler.

Schein, E. H. (2010). *Organizational culture and leadership* (4th ed.). Jossey-Bass.

Schore, A. N. (2012). *The science of the art of psychotherapy*. W.W. Norton & Company.

Schore, A. N. (2016). *Affect regulation and the origin of the self: The neurobiology of emotional development*. Routledge.

Schore, A. N. (2019). *Right brain psychotherapy*. W.W. Norton & Company.

Semuels, A. (2024, February 21). Chanel CEO Leena Nair is testing a world run by women. *TIME*. https://time.com/collections/women-of-the-year/6691525/leena-nair-2/ (Accessed on 14th of June, 2026).

Senge, P. (2025, September 26–28). *Personal mastery – Collective practices* [Keynote address]. Global SoL Conference, Hanoi, Vietnam.
Senge, P. M. (1990). *The fifth discipline: The art and practice of the learning organization*. Doubleday.
Shin, J. (2021). *Eoneo-ui nopi ttwigi [A leap in language]*. Influential.
Siegel, D. J. (2003). An interpersonal neurobiology of psychotherapy: The developing mind and the resolution of trauma. In M. F. Solomon & D. J. Siegel (Eds.), *Healing trauma: Attachment, mind, body and brain* (pp. 1–56). W.W. Norton & Company.
Siegel, D. J. (2007). *The mindful brain: Reflection and attunement in the cultivation of well-being*. W.W. Norton & Company.
Siegel, D. J. (2020). *The developing mind: How relationships and the brain interact to shape who we are* (3rd ed.). The Guilford Press.
Siegel, D. J. (2022). *IntraConnected: MWe (Me + We) as the integration of self, identity, and belonging*. W.W. Norton & Company.
Siegel, D. J., & Solomon, M. F. (Eds.). (2003). *Healing trauma: Attachment, mind, body and brain (Norton series on interpersonal neurobiology)*. W.W. Norton & Company.
Solomon, M. F., & Siegel, D. J. (2017). *How people change: Relationships and neuroplasticity in psychotherapy*. W.W. Norton & Company.
Stern, D. N. (1985). *The interpersonal world of the infant: A view from psychoanalysis and developmental psychology*. Basic Books.
Stern, D. N. (1989). The representation of relational patterns: Some developmental considerations. In A. J. Sameroff & R. N. Emde (Eds.), *Relationship disturbances in early childhood: A developmental approach* (pp. 52–69). Basic Books.
Stern, D. N. (2007). *The first relationship: Infant and mother* (2nd ed.). Harvard University Press.
Swartz, J. (2010, November 2). Can profit and sustainability go together? *The Guardian*. www.theguardian.com/sustainable-business/blog/jeff-swartz-timberl and-sustainability-profit (Accessed on 14th of June, 2026).
Swartz, J. (2010). Timberland's CEO on standing up to 65,000 angry activists. *Harvard Business Review*, *88*(9), 39–127.
Takahara, K. (2024, February 27). Number of babies born in Japan falls to record low. *The Japan Times*. www.japantimes.co.jp/news/2024/02/27/japan/society/2023-births-record-low/
Taluja, I. (Host). (2024, April 23). Leena Nair on leading with empathy and compassion [Audio podcast episode]. In *View from the top*. Stanford Graduate School of Business. www.gsb.stanford.edu/insights/leena-nair-leading-empathy-compassion
Triandis, H. C., & Gelfand, M. J. (2012). A theory of individualism and collectivism. In P. A. Van Lange, E. T. Higgins, & A. W. Kruglanski (Eds.), *Handbook of theories of social psychology* (pp. 498–520). Sage.
Tronick, E. Z. (1989). Emotions and emotional communication in infants. *American Psychologist*, *44*(2), 112–119. https://doi.org/10.1037/0003-066X.44.2.112
Tronick, E. (2007). *The neurobehavioral and social-emotional development of infants and children*. W.W. Norton & Company.

Tronick, E., Als, H., Adamson, L., Wise, S., & Brazelton, T. B. (1978). The infant's response to entrapment between contradictory messages in face-to-face interaction. *Journal of the American Academy of Child Psychiatry, 17*(1), 1–13. https://doi.org/10.1016/S0002-7138(09)62273-1

Tronick, E., & Gold, C. M. (2020). *The power of discord: Why the ups and downs of relationships are the secret to building intimacy, resilience, and trust.* Little, Brown Spark.

Viktor Frankl Institute. (n.d.). *Alleged quote.* www.viktorfrankl.org/quote_stimulus.html

Weber, M. (1947). *The theory of social and economic organization.* Free Press.

Wheatley, M. J. (2006). *Leadership and the new science: Discovering order in a chaotic world* (3rd ed.). Berrett-Koehler.

The White House. (2013, November 25). *Remarks by the President on immigration reform – San Francisco, CA* [Transcript]. The White House Office of the Press Secretary. https://obamawhitehouse.archives.gov/the-press-office/2013/11/25/remarks-president-immigration-reform-san-francisco-ca

World Health Organization. (2021). *Suicide worldwide in 2019: Global health estimates.* www.who.int/publications/i/item/9789240026643

World Health Organization. (2023). *Depressive disorder (fact sheet).* www.who.int/news-room/fact-sheets/detail/depression

Index

Note: Figures are indicated by *italics*. Tables are indicated by **bold**.

For Product Safety Concerns and Information please contact our EU
representative GPSR@taylorandfrancis.com
Taylor & Francis Verlag GmbH, Kaufingerstraße 24, 80331 München, Germany

www.ingramcontent.com/pod-product-compliance
Lightning Source LLC
LaVergne TN
LVHW011451121026
849885LV00033B/340
* 9 7 8 1 0 4 1 0 2 9 0 9 0 *

"This is a work of deep experience with leaders made practical and accessible. Yet, it needs to be named that these insights and practices were born from the authors' steadfast and loving search for clarity. It is their passionate engagement and devotion to understand leadership that shines through every detailed explanation."

Margaret Wheatley, Ph.D., *Organizational Behavior, Harvard University Consultant, Teacher, Trainer and Author of many books from* Leadership and the New Science *(1992) to* Restoring Sanity *(2024)*

"In *The Fifth Discipline*, Peter Senge introduced us to system archetypes that enabled us to see the underlying structures that were producing undesirable system behavior and provided guidance for taking high leverage actions. *Becoming a Self-Differentiated Leader* offers us with an equally insightful set of leader archetypes that offers us a powerful set of lenses to see, understand, and act on the invisible underlying structures that are the drivers of many relationship dysfunctions. Their clear, simple, and yet powerful frameworks and practices provide anyone who wants to become a better leader, whether in professional or personal settings, with the means to transcend their present self and realize their fullest potential as a fully integrated self-differentiated leader. This is essential reading for all who have aspirations to be that kind of leader."

Daniel H. Kim, Ph.D., *Former Research Director, MIT Center for Organizational Learning, founding trustee, the Society for Organizational Learning*

"The conflicts and crises described in this welcome book occur in every venue where humans interact. With tremendous and generous compassion both for leaders, as well as for those who make healthy leadership so difficult, the authors of this guide provide insights that are every bit as much spiritual as they are emotional, psychological, and organizational. Whether you're in the midst of a crisis of leadership and you're desperate for some new insight to help navigate it (and who is not?) or whether the heat of the catastrophe is past and you simply hope to learn about "what just happened, and how can I do better next time" (and there *will* be a next time!) this is a concise, supremely organized, and clear road map to inner change that can free and empower. The insight about *The Space* is really all about the care of the soul of a leader. This is a must read for anyone engaged in leading communities through the quagmires that can so easily cause us to unnecessarily forfeit our best selves, to no one's benefit."

The Rt. Rev. A. Robert Hirschfeld, D.D., *Episcopal Bishop of New Hampshire*

"*Becoming a Self-Differentiated Leader*" is a rare leadership book that goes beneath behaviors and tools to the human patterns that truly shape results. By integrating attachment theory, neuroscience, and real-world leadership practice, the authors offer a powerful framework for understanding loyalty, motivation, and relational dynamics at work and in life. Clear, courageous, and deeply practical, this book equips leaders, coaches, and change-makers to navigate conflict, build trust, and lead with steadiness in an increasingly complex world. It is both a wake-up call and a roadmap for modern leadership."

Jeffrey Hull, Ph.D., BCC, *Executive Director, Institute of Coaching, Harvard Medical School Affiliate, Co-author of Thinkers50 award winning book,* The Science of Leadership.

"At a time when yesterday's logic is not only failing us but deepening our most urgent crises, *Becoming a Self-Differentiated Leader* offers a powerful beacon of possibility. The authors go beyond refining strategies—they invite us to transform the inner place from which we lead, freeing ourselves from the unconscious patterns that keep us reacting instead of creating.

With clarity and courage, they present strategies that root leadership in what the world needs most: intention, presence, and a renewed understanding that our shared future depends on how we listen, relate, and work together. Each chapter introduces concepts that challenge old assumptions and open new pathways for leadership in action.

This book is a rare and timely gift. It is a practical roadmap filled with coaching prompts, case studies, and key takeaways for emerging and more seasoned leaders to not only to navigate change but to shape the future we are being called to create."

Patricia A. Findley, Dr.PH., MSW, LCSW, *Dean, School of Social Work, Loyola University Chicago*

"This exceptional book is a true soul portrait - allowing the reader to look at themselves: past, present, and future. It is a mirror to the soul. This is a book about hope—it is about changing the traditional movie of rules, frameworks, and assessments to bringing in a rich, values-based authentic leader who contributes humanity in interpersonal communication, conflict, and collaboration.

This book is about Tikkun Olam—Hebrew for 'repairing the world'—taking personal responsibility for the chaos and the trouble and finding ways to rebuild a kinder, more compassionate world. By using the skills, tools, attitudes, and behaviors found in this book—authentic leaders will create a better universe. These leaders will change one human at a time!!

From Coaching to Organizational Behavior, I see this wonderful book by these 3 esteemed authors as a future survival kit. If the reader applies even 10% of the wisdom in this collection—we will see leaders as better versions of themselves. We will see transformation. And most of all—we will have the opportunity to be stewards and guardians of an emerging world which sets the stage for the human communication interface revolution."

Mark Alan Rittenberg, Ed.D., *Fullbright Scholar, Founder and Chief Creative Officer Berkeley Executive Coaching Institute; Senior Lecturer and Leadership Communications Professor Haas School of Business, University of California - Berkeley*

"In a world of continuous, convulsive change, *Becoming a Self-Differentiated Leader* offers a beacon of clarity for moving beyond divisiveness and conflict. A former Chairman of the U.S. Federal Reserve once observed that America faced three deficits: fiscal, trade, and leadership—and that the greatest of these was the leadership deficit. If that was true in 2005, how much more so is it today?

Gianotti, Gianotti, and Kim remind us that in an AI-infused, information-overloaded, and politically polarized world, friction is unavoidable—but conflict is not. They argue persuasively that most conflict stems from either a lack of clarity or a lack of safety. Whether in families, communities, organizations, or governments, leadership failure almost always arises from confusion about the real problem at hand or from an inability to make people feel safe enough to follow. The authors underscore a vital truth: meaningful change is inherently uncomfortable, and those who prioritize comfort rarely achieve growth. Breakthroughs often emerge from the catharsis of individual or institutional breakdown.

This brilliant book does more than draw on a wide range of the best leadership scholarship; it brings those ideas to life through highly relevant examples of both leadership failure and success. As a former CEO and current executive coach, I found the insights immediately relatable and the lessons eminently practical—especially in navigating problematic leadership. Whether you are seeking to strengthen personal relationships, lead (or follow) more effectively at work or in your community or are a frustrated citizen hoping for leaders who can move us beyond division and decline, *Becoming a Self-Differentiated Leader* is a must-read."

Paul Laudicina, *Chairman Emeritus of Kearney and Korn Ferry CEO Coach, has been a leadership columnist for* Forbes *and a well-known global business strategist and author. He writes and speaks regularly on leadership, strategy, and global geo-strategic trends.*